1972

Community Problem Solving

Irving A. Spergel

# Community Problem Solving
## The Delinquency Example

The University of Chicago Press          Chicago and London

For W. Paul Simon and Lloyd E. Ohlin

The University of Chicago Press, Chicago 60637
*The University of Chicago Press, Ltd., London*

© 1969 by The University of Chicago. All rights reserved
Published 1969. Second Impression 1971. Printed in the
United States of America

International Standard Book Number: 0–226–76930–5
Library of Congress Catalog Card Number: 69–17000

*This work was developed under
Grant No. 66213 from the Office of
Juvenile Delinquency and
Youth Development.*

# Contents

# Preface

This book is an organizational approach to the problems of people living in the slums and inner areas of our large cities. It is concerned mainly with youth and delinquency; but the ideas, principles, and techniques for community action discussed in it are relevant to other social problems which afflict those trapped in the ghettoes.

The point of view of the book is social work; at the same time a wide variety of perspectives of community problem solving is examined. New structures, strategies, and tactics have evolved from the anti-poverty programs, civil rights movement, black power struggles, new types of grass-roots organizing, and large scale social planning, but have not been fully explored for their possible use in social work practice.

The present work does not pretend to prescribe an appropriate social work methodology to community work. But it is possible that a broad analysis may afford a more effective base for the development of social work objectives and procedures. While urban problems are interrelated and interdependent, for the sake of relative simplicity in analysis, attention is focused on one social problem—delinquency.

Nevertheless, a general framework for community organizing or problem solving is formulated. The volume, furthermore, is an attempt at fusion of old and new ideas to explain the varieties of intervention which community workers, including social workers, perform today. The analysis of community problem solving presented here is concerned less with the scientific explanation of the organization of the community and the interrelationship of its parts than it is with the *why* and, especially, the *how* of the worker as he influences community interest and concern in particular directions.

While I have fashioned the content of the book primarily for the social work student preparing for a professional career as a community worker and for community-oriented personnel engaged in delinquency control and prevention, the volume may be of value to others, including researchers and laymen. The distinction between these categories of workers and concerned persons, however, is somewhat artificial during a period of extraordinary community crisis and change, since so little is known (and even less done) to modify the enormous social difficulties which confront us.

I have also assumed that a problem solving orientation underlies community organization efforts. It states that men can know and do something about organizational and community behavior. I believe that the worker, be he professional or nonprofessional, can contribute significantly to the modification and prevention of serious social problems, but he must increasingly use a conscious and systematic rather than an intuitive or ad hoc approach.

This inquiry focuses on organizational strategies and tactics, and especially on the roles of the worker, in the conduct of the complex community-work job. The data for the study were gathered in the course of field visits to a great many organizations and groups concerned with the community problem of delinquency. Dozens of agency executives, professionals, nonprofessionals, board members, citizens, as well as delinquents or problematic youth were interviewed or observed as they engaged in the various intervention approaches to be described. The data were collected mainly during the spring, summer, and fall of 1966. Agencies and groups in the following cities were among those providing material:

> *Chicago*—Chicago Commission on Youth Welfare; Chicago Youth Centers; Chicago Youth Development Project; Illinois Youth Commission; JOIN Community Union; South-

ern Christian Leadership Conference; West Side Organization; Young Men's Christian Association; Youth Action.

*Columbus, Ohio*—East Central Citizens' Organization; Family Court; Youth Civic Center.

*Los Angeles*—California Center for Community Development; Catholic Youth Organization; Commission on Human Relations; Crenshaw Youth Studies Center; Department of Community Services; Economic and Youth Opportunities Agency of Greater Los Angeles; Los Angeles Region Welfare Planning Council; Special Service for Groups; Temporary Alliance of Local Organizations; University of Southern California Youth Studies Center; Westminster Neighborhood Association.

*New York City*—Harlem Youth Unlimited; Mobilization for Youth; New York City Youth Board; United Block Association of Harlem.

*Paterson, New Jersey*—Community Action Program.

*Philadelphia*—Community Action Council; Crime Prevention Association; Department of Public Welfare; District Attorney's Office; Friends Neighborhood Guild; Human Relations Commission; Philadelphia Police Department; University Settlement; Young Great Society.

*San Francisco*—Bay Area Social Planning Council; Hunterspoint–Bay View Youth Opportunity Center; "Mission Rebels in Action"; San Francisco Police Department; Youth Participation in Community Action of the State of California, Department of Youth Authority; Youth for Service.

*Washington, D. C.*—Commissioner's Youth Council of Washington, D. C.; "Rebels with a Cause," Howard University Center for Youth and Community Studies; Police Department of Washington, D. C.; Recreation Department; and the United Planning Organization.

The content of the volume is arranged as follows: An introductory chapter focuses on the basic *problem solving process, organizational context* and the nature of the *problem*. Chapter 2 describes different types of community *worker role* in relation to problem solving. Chapter 3 commences a series of chapters on method, dealing first at a general level with the *influence* process underlying all community intervention efforts. Chapters 4 and 5 delineate sets of *organizing* tactics or techniques. Chapters 6, 7, and 8 discuss various forms and techniques of *interorganizing*. Chapter 9 deals with *intraorganizing* or certain administrative practices and problems related to use of clients as staff members. The difficulties of *evaluation* of community action efforts are explored in Chapter 10. The concluding Chapter 11 recommends *policies* at the national level for modification of the delinquency problem in the urban community.

## Acknowledgments

The Office of Juvenile Delinquency and Youth Development provided support (Grant No. 66213) for this work. A very large number of agency and organizational representatives and individual persons provided invaluable aid in the conduct of this study. Many of them and their affiliations have already been mentioned. The critical comments of Darrel Vorwaller, Morris Janowitz, and David Street are gratefully acknowledged. I am indebted to Robert Weagant, Frances Polson, Margaret Baker, and Joan Barrie for efficient administrative and clerical labors in connection with the project. Finally, to my wife Bertha, my sons, Barry, Mark, and Danny, I continue to owe special obligations for patience, understanding and precious time not spent with them.

I. A. S.

Community Problem Solving

# 1

# Introduction

Community problem solving may be described as purposeful intervention by people within an organizational context in relation to a specific community problem. The general components of intervention, organization, and community problem are interrelated and interactive, and each represents a complex system of alternate values, perceptions, behaviors, and structured relationships. They comprise the theoretical grounding for our conceptions of differential worker roles and methods. "Community organization" is the term used to describe efforts to bring about adjustment, development, or change among groups and organizations in regard to community problems or social needs. (Community organization, as one of the three major methods of social work—the other two are casework and group work—was conceptualized in the early 1930's and professionally legitimized only in the 1940's.) In the present analysis, however, the term "community work" or "community problem solving" is preferred for several reasons. Community organization in social work has in the past suggested a process of coordination of established social agencies in the community, and has implied a primary objective of achieving a balance of human needs and existing organizational resources through consensus seeking, often involving only elite leadership in the neighborhood

3

and larger community. Community organization, as it is developing today, however, suggests a practice which has more varied objectives, methodologies, and constituent populations. Community work is thus potentially broader than practice with established organizations, and it may seek to disarrange, rearrange, and change organizational patterns as well as to stabilize and augment them. Further, the client or service population may become a critical decision-making body in this process.

Community work, then, suggests a more inclusive practice, encompassing certain efforts of direct service agencies as well as of strictly community groups. In other words, the efforts of agencies directed to winning and maintaining external support for their programs, relating their work to other agencies, and influencing other organizational programs are subsumed under the notion of community work.[1] Then, too, the term would seem more naturally cognate with "casework" and "group work." (In the present study, the words "community organization" and "community action" will occasionally be used because they appear in the literature and are still used by many practitioners, but when they are, they will suggest the broader meaning of "community work.")

The idea of "community" itself [2] is indicated by any of three forms of population confronting social problems, and any one of these represents the direct or indirect beneficiary of intervention. Two are organized collectivities, and the third is an aggregate of people. First, community may refer to people living and interacting in a particular territorial area; this is a geographic community. In the second type, often referred to as a functional community, a population is dispersed, usually over a wide geographic area, and shares specific interests and characteristics. It may be represented by an ethnic or religious group, an association of the blind or deaf, or a council of social agencies. A third type of community is a population aggregate having certain assigned characteristics in common, such as delinquency, poverty, mental illness, slum housing. This third kind of community is relevant in most social

1. Violet M. Sieder, *The Rehabilitation Agency and Community Work: A Source Book of Professional Training,* p. 2.
2. See Irving Spergel, Darrel Vorwaller, and Elaine Switzer, "Community Organization from a Perspective of Social Work," February, 1968 (unpublished paper).

planning efforts. All three perceptions of community may, in fact, be overlapping, but the distinctions are significant in the determination of the kind of community work which gets practiced.

It may also be appropriate to note that the problem-solving energies of the practitioner are seldom directed at the total community as such, but rather to its relevant subparts, such as individuals, groups, committees, and organizations—the manageable sections of the community to which the practitioner relates. The consequences of practitioner intervention with these subunits must, however, in some important way affect the social welfare of the larger community.

## Purposeful Intervention

Community problem solving is becoming a disciplined and conscious work process carried out within an evolving framework derived from democratic tradition, social science, social work, other experience, and especially the demands of the rapidly changing world. Problem solving also has strong roots in the relatively short history of the theory of community organization.

### Historical Perspectives

The pioneers of the theory of community work in the period after World War I—for example, Walter Pettit, Jesse Steiner, Eduard Lindeman—believed that social welfare should have a broad, all-inclusive base and that the initiation and sustenance of a democratic process at the grass-roots level were of paramount importance. According to these men, clearly committed to social reform, community organization should be a process of pervasive social interaction rather than simply a method of limited organizing and interorganizing.[3]

During the 1940's, Arthur Dunham, Kenneth Pray, Wilbur Newstetter, and others formulated the balance or adjustmental theory of community organization, which emphasized intergroup and interpersonal relations within a narrowly defined field of social welfare practice and gave scant attention to important organiza-

3. The material in this section is adapted from Meyer Schwartz, "Community Organization."

tional or interorganizational factors. The notion of basic community problem solving was largely ignored. The primary purpose of community organization for social work was described as "the art or process of bringing about and maintaining a progressively more effective adjustment between social welfare services and social welfare needs," or the "facilitation of the process of social adjustment of individual people, through the development and constructive use of social relationships," or the "achievement of mutually satisfactory relations between groups." [4]

Emphasis on problem solving appeared in the mid 1940's when Arlien Johnson said, "The community organization worker becomes a professional worker . . . when he helps people in a community to discover their common social problems that may interfere with the desirable norms of living, and to do something about these problems." [5] McMillen saw the primary objective of community organization practice as helping people "find ways to give expression to these inherent desires to improve the environment in which they and their fellows must carry on their lives." [6] Murphy clearly repudiated the interpersonal and intergroup emphasis in community-organization theory. He said that the "focus of practice was the solving of a community problem rather than meeting the inner needs of the individuals or groups involved." [7]

One of the outstanding theoretical contributions to community-organization practice has been the work of Murray Ross, who was perhaps the first to delineate various types of worker strategies. He focused on the method and the principles rather than simply on the general objectives and activities of community organization, and he also broadened the scope of practice. Community organization was not to be restricted to the field of social welfare, but had potential use in a wide variety of settings with any number of problems—for instance, in agriculture, education, and community development. [8]

For Ross, the primary objective of community organization was "community integration"—the exercise of cooperative and collaborative attitudes and practices which lead to identification with the community. [9] Implied was the notion of community stability or

4. *Ibid.*, p. 179.    5. *Ibid.*    6. *Ibid.*, p. 180.
7. *Ibid.*, pp. 182–83.    8. *Ibid.*, p. 183.
9. Murray G. Ross, *Community Organization: Theory and Principles*, p. 52.

equilibrium as the satisfactory state of community affairs to be achieved as readily as possible through a strategy of consensus. Ross believed there were three primary orientations of practice: the "specific content objective or reform orientation"; the "general content objective or planning objective"; and the "process objective or process orientation." He postulated that the last-mentioned orientation contained "the heart of community organization process—the achievement of self-determination, cooperative and collaborative work among various groups, and the capacity to solve community problems." [10]

Ross, however, either ignored or deemphasized the value of direct confrontation, conflict, or the use of power. He did not see their relevance as depending on organizational structure, the community problem, and the solution desired. He did not basically see problem solving as a preferred orientation of community organization practice. Ross formulated various principles of practice: "Discontent with existing conditions in the community must initiate and/or nourish the development of the association"; "Discontent must be focused and channeled into organization, planning, and action in respect to specific problems"; "The discontent which initiates or sustains community organization must be widely shared in the community." [11] But these principles are limited or conditioned by other principles: "The association must involve leaders (both formal and informal) identified with, and accepted by major subgroups in the community"; "The association must have goals and methods of procedure of high acceptability." [12] Ross stated, further, that social action is outside the social work process. In essence, therefore, the discontent mobilized must be relatively nonthreatening and acceptable to the established groups in power in the community. The objective of a process approach would appear to be primarily that of social adjustment rather than of social problem solving.

In recent years, however, problem solving as the general orientation to community organization has found increasing recognition. Sieder describes practice as a direct problem-solving service, engaging human beings in the content of interaction of groups and

10. *Ibid.*, pp. 18–24.     11. *Ibid.*, pp. 158–68.
12. *Ibid.*, pp. 168–75.

individuals, and involving organizational patterns of group life.[13] Carter states that it is task- or goal-centered and is focused on the solution of a community problem or on the development of means to solve the problem rather than therapeutically on individual needs.[14] Attention, nevertheless, must be directed in practice to the expressive or solidarity needs of people, if community problem solving on task functions are to be achieved. The emphasis given to these needs appears to vary with organizational strategy. For our purposes, however, the relevance and validity of any activity for community work is whether it serves to achieve the solution to, prevent or control the occurrence of, a community problem.

### Values

Community problem solving is, in addition, more than a set of strategies and techniques guided by systematic knowledge for achieving certain objectives and goals. It is also guided by a set of ethical principles for intervening or influencing people. The principles are functions of professional and organizational value orientations. In other words, problem solving does not signify a neutral set of steps or phases of action. Preferences about the ends or goals of action are basically infused into each procedure and step. Values and action are perhaps separable analytically but never in practice.

The value infusion in community problem solving derives from the American democratic experience—social justice, equality, and self-determination. The human relations professions—including social work—have generally adapted and made operational only part of this tradition, that part concerned primarily with individual, rather than group or corporate, interests. For example, Friedlander says:

> The feelings, attitudes, orientations, and practices of social workers in the American Culture are inspired by the following democratic values:
>     1. Conviction of the inherent worth, the integrity, and the dignity of the individual.

13. Violet M. Sieder, "The Tasks of the Community Organization Worker."
14. Genevieve W. Carter, "Social Work Community Organization Methods and Processes."

2. The individual . . . has the right to determine himself what his needs are and how they should be met.

3. . . . equal opportunities for all, limited only by the individual's innate capacities.

4. Man's individual rights to self respect, dignity, self-determination, and equal opportunities are connected with his social responsibilities toward himself, his family, and his society.[15]

The process approach particularly stresses the individualist ethic. The "articles of faith" of the community worker, according to Ross, include:

The essential dignity and ethical worth of the individual, the possession by each individual of potentialities and resources for managing his own life, the importance of freedom to express one's individuality, the great capacity for growth within all social beings, the right of the individual to those basic physical necessities (food, shelter, and clothing) without which fulfillment of life is often blocked. The need for the individual to struggle and strive to improve his own life and environment, the right of the individual to help in time of need and crisis, the importance of a social organization for which the individual feels responsible and which is responsive to individual feeling. . . .[16]

We have here examples of a highly particularistic view of man and his rights and potentialities in a democratic society. It is the responsibility of the individual directly to create the social conditions which are desired and deemed good. The idea of the environment as basically structuring the welfare of the individuals through its institutions and organizations is only touched upon. In the final analysis, action and change are somehow to result from intrapersonal or interpersonal processes. Change is to be created by the individual's perception "of a gap between his present condition within the framework of his society and the position he feels he

15. Walter A. Friedlander, *Introduction to Social Welfare* (2d ed.), pp. 2–7.

16. Ross, *Community Organization: Theory and Principles*, pp. 78–79; see also Muriel W. Pumphrey, "The Teaching of Values and Ethics," pp. 43–44.

might attain through his own efforts." [17] The institutional structure of the society and the community is implied as given and generally not subject to change. Change is mainly personal. Whatever pressure or discontent motivates the individual drives him to seek a new personal situation within the existing framework; it does not mainly drive him to see change in some aspect of the framework itself.

An alternate view of the values requisite for community work, one based in political theory, is that in a democratic system certain group or corporate, as well as individual, interests must be created and protected. Optimal conditions for group and corporate function are sought. Change may be desired not only in the individual and his relationship to other individuals but in the relation of groups and organizations to one another. The desire for corporate or political change suggests there may be something wrong with, and something which requires changing in, the institutions or framework of society itself.

Some of the corporate or political values, and the means for implementing them, emanating from our democratic experience and relevant for community problem solving are:

> The largest possible part of the population should seek to influence major decisions of community and political organizations.
>
> Equal opportunity for achievement of all should be structured into the institutions of society.
>
> Democracy should not only, or even primarily, be a means through which different groups can attain their ends or seek the good society—it is the good society itself, in operation.
>
> Democracy requires organizations which support conflict and disagreement as well as those which sustain legitimacy and consensus.
>
> A high level of citizen participation in the democratic society should be required to facilitate social change.

Individual and corporate values are not necessarily opposed to one another—they are often complementary or reciprocal. For example, it is hard to think of a condition in which each individual is regarded as an object of infinite worth or fully develops his

17. Kenneth E. Boulding, "Social Justice in Social Dynamics," pp. 81–82.

potentials without the availability of equal opportunity for achievement by all. On the other hand, if every aspect of a human being, including his ideas and the power he controls, is regarded as an object of infinite worth, we may run into corporate difficulties. For example, if we respect an individual, this may extend to acceptance of his biases and negative influences on a community. Similarly, an organization committed to militancy and conflict may seek to impose its will on an opposing group and compel it to acquiesce in a point of view or path of action not conducive to the best interests of that group.

The emphasis given to corporate or individualistic aspects of the democratic ethic may be in part a function of the ability of a society at a given time to meet the basic needs of its people. It has been suggested that in a rapidly changing society in which most individuals can, with a little effort, easily participate in the general affluence, value orientations will be personalized and express themselves in efforts on the part of individuals to advance their position within the existing social framework. A society, on the other hand, which is stagnant or not changing rapidly enough will be more likely to generate cultural discontent and emphasis on corporate change. The individual who attempts to solve his problems by purely personal means in this kind of society will have little success.[18]

## The Process of Community Problem Solving

Community problem solving may be delineated as a series of rational actions—a set of progressive and usually nondiscrete behaviors—conducive to an end. It is less a single easily definable system of principles and exact procedures than a loose constellation of interrelated method elements leading to a problem resolution. It consists of interpersonal procedures for working with individuals and groups as well as techniques of education, public relations, coordination, supervision, social action, and administration. These elements of practice may be grouped as three major methods of community work: organizing, interorganizing, and intraorganizing. Community problem solving is thus both a sequence of steps and a series of methods—all interconnected.[19]

18. *Ibid.,* pp. 85–86.
19. See also Ronald Lippitt, Jeanne Watson, and Bruce Westley, *The Dynamics of Planned Change.*

The process is characterized by the following sequences of activity: problem identification, study, analysis, goal development, planning of intervention, intervention, and evaluation and feedback.

### Problem Identification

The community, the worker's organization, and the worker must be aware of the existence of a problem. Is it a *felt* problem? How deeply concerned is the community or organization by it? This notion of the presence of a perceived problem may arise from organizational purpose, intensity of agency commitment, on-going agency program, verbalized concern about a problem by various segments of the community, independent research, and so on. Indeed, there may be different degrees of awareness and reaction to the problem within both the community and the organization sponsoring the worker.

Perception, a key—and complex—aspect of problem identification, is the process by which individuals as members of groups and organizations come to be aware of their environment. It must be recognized, however, that "perception is not identical to reality." [20] There are different degrees and variations of "reality." Erroneous percepts may develop—indeed, they may create the reality they had implied. What people believe they perceive and expect to be "true" comes to be defined as fact—we tend to find what we look for. This gives rise to the so-called self-fulfilling prophecy. Thus, the delinquent may or may not be hostile, aggressive, untrustworthy, ruthless, hopeless, and a menace to the community; but if he is so defined, he himself may come to believe the definition in due time. The perception of a problem is extremely complicated, particularly since reality may not be the same at a given time for observers belonging to different groups.

At this early stage, the worker needs to determine on what basis a particular matter is a problem. What are and whence derive the criteria which dispose the worker to decide, for example, that delinquency is a problem or that some pattern of delinquency control services is a problem? Professional values, agency purposes, and community group pressures may be the sources which

20. Ross Stagner, "The Psychology of Human Conflict," pp. 46–47.

suggest the criteria for problem determination. The rise in delinquency rates, the increased severity of youth crime, the school dropout rate, conflicting agency programs—all may be defined as problems only as they are selectively perceived and noted by the value-prepared worker, the predisposed agency, and community groups which may be affected by these "realities."

### Study

All the possible aspects of a problem are not—and, indeed, cannot—be examined fully. The limits of the study phase include the time, energy, and skills available to the worker, agency purpose, the nature of community concern, and the availability of present and potential resources. Focus at this stage is on the collection of data which bear on impact, structure and history, organizational commitment, locus of power, and citizen role in relation to the problem.

The most obvious, but certainly not the simplest, dimension of study is the nature of the problem as it affects individual persons and families. What is the scope of delinquency in a specific community—that is, its prevalence and rate of incidence? What do these statistics represent in terms of social, and psychological as well as economic, costs for the victim, the delinquent, his family, and the community? It may well be that although delinquency rates are on the rise, only certain types of offenses are actually increasing—for example, curfew violations, runaways, waywardness, thefts. For certain types of offenses there may be a greater cost to the delinquent and his family than to the rest of the community—indeed, the delinquent may be the major victim himself. For other types of offenses—for example, gang fighting—the people in the immediate neighborhood, rather than the community at large, bear the major costs. Further, the qualitative as well as the quantitative components of a problem need to be estimated. Cold statistics may be insufficient for arousing a community or its organizational parts to action.

The structure and history of the problem in the particular community need to be investigated. What are the significant ecological, economic, cultural, social, and political conditions and processes which have caused, contributed to, and maintained the problem of delinquency in the community? What, for example, are the physical conditions of the community which contribute to the recalcitrance of the problem? The community may be geographically distant, isolated, or cut off by natural or man-made impedimenta—for example, rivers, railroad tracks, major highways—from the cultural, business, or industrial centers of the city or urban areas. The political articulation or influence of the community with the rest of the city may be extremely weak. Further, the community may have a peculiar sociocultural history of dominance of certain types of delinquency and crime. Gang fighting, thievery, or racketeering may be long-term patterns in certain areas, associated with particular socioeconomic conditions and ethnic populations. The community's basic structure, history, and traditions may, in certain instances, be regarded as resources as well as aspects of the problem itself. There may be important subcultural values and patterns of social relationship which may be used toward solution of the problem. For example, a strong subcultural interest in educational advancement for children and a tradition of mutual assistance constitute assets in delinquency-prevention and -control programs.

The commitment to social change or stability by the community work agency prescribes not only the worker's perception of the problem but also his intervention strategy. The agency's goals, policies, administrative and staffing patterns, program objectives, resources, and methods determine the scope of the worker's practice. For example, an indigenous organization, a branch social agency, a civil rights group, and an independent community action organization—each may approach the problem of race relations, slum housing, or delinquency differently. The community worker operates very differently in each of these organizational contexts.

The worker must study not only his own but other organizations and groups in the community. What are institutionalized arrangements for dealing with the problem? What community agencies and groups are concerned with the problem or parts of it? Which organizations and groups are potentially interested in the problem? What is the nature of their relationships to one another? How effective or valuable are the efforts of these agencies and groups in coping with the problem? What is the character of their relationships to the worker's organization? What significant patterns appear to militate against efficient and effective intervention in relation to the social problem—for example, inadequacy of resources, failure of coordination, absence of planning, misguided public relations, unrepresentative board, incapable administrative leadership.

The worker must be concerned with the locus of influence, authority, and control. Who are the influential persons, the decision makers, the power groups in the community? What are their sources of power? How is this power manifested, and under what conditions is it exercised? Power may be obvious or elusive, limited, or overwhelming. It may be moral, economic, physical, charismatic, technical, or normative. It may be used for good or evil purposes. The value placed on power may be largely a function of organizational "sets" or perspectives. The organizations and individuals who possess it may facilitate or impede. Then, too, power is often latent and conflicting; organizations do not necessarily combine their power, and may neutralize one another's influence. Power may exist in people and groups who do not know they have it but who can learn to use it.

The use of community power needs to be carefully mapped. Unfortunately, this is not easy. The existence, strength, and purpose of power may not be known until a specific test situation arises. Nevertheless, the worker must be constantly alert to clues which indicate its presence. A key procedure for determining the locus of power is to discover for whom the given social problem is functional or profitable and for whom it is not. The social agency, police department, delinquent gang, newspaper, civil rights organization, and individuals and subgroups within these organizations may derive profits—funds, staff, prestige, legitimation, additional influence and authority—from a delinquency problem or particular crisis.

The worker must also discover what roles, actual or potential, citizen groups play in relation to the problem. What is the nature of their interest, concern, and involvement in efforts to deal with the problem? How do other significant or powerful groups view this engagement? Who are the leaders of these citizen groups? What are their important characteristics relative to participation in the community work process? In other words, on what basis can citizen participation be initiated, developed, mobilized, or possibly impeded in relation to the problem-solving process?

The community worker, especially the professional, needs considerable clarity about the relation of the client or citizen's role to his own. The potential for role confusion and conflict exists, depending in part on the worker's interpretation of his role as professional and the consistency of the administrative structure patterning his and the citizen's or client's role relationships.

### Analysis

To solve or cope with a given problem, one need not completely understand it and, indeed, total comprehension is usually impossible in view of the complexity of the community situation and its varied problems. The specific analysis of a community problem will probably be guided by the organizational emphasis the worker gives to four values: opportunity, service, citizen participation, and control. If the problem is viewed as a basic structural one and if there is organizational commitment to institutional change, the worker may analyze the problem as essentially one of lack of opportunities. The delinquency problem, for example, may be viewed as occurring mainly in slum areas whose residents have inadequate access to educational, employment, housing, and other resources. The deprived community spawns many social problems, one of which is delinquency. The provision of more opportunities, especially educational and economic, for the general youth population in the area may be viewed as the major basis for reducing delinquency.

The service orientation often presumes that the social problem is of such complex and powerful origin that little can be done basically to prevent it but that much can be done to mitigate its course, especially within the individual, family, and small group. The aspect of the problem considered relevant is not so much its onset or incidence as its character and handling, once it is discovered. The community problem here is defined primarily at the level of failure of early identification, treatment, control devices, facilities, and resources. Under certain conditions, this approach stresses the administrative or structural aspect of agency services and procedures, recommendations for service saturation, and the addition of new types of programs, such as neighborhood service centers, joint agency arrangements, and coalition planning.

The commitment to citizen participation is based on a psycho-political analysis. The problem is viewed as one of disengagement of people from the institutional decisions which significantly affect their lives. Persons who have low incomes and reside in the ghettos of large urban centers are defined as hopeless and powerless to influence the organization which serves them. For example, the delinquent gang is viewed as alienated from major legitimate agencies—schools, employment, settlements—seeking to serve their members, even from their own families. The gang youth is an outsider and detached culturally, socially, and psychologically from local institutions. The problem is to be resolved not so much through efficient, extended, or increased services, or even the provision of basic opportunities as primarily through citizen or client action. Recipients of organizational service are redefined as constituents and helped to organize themselves into pressure groups so that change will occur.

The control orientation is fundamental to law enforcement agencies and many other organizations primarily concerned with delinquency and gang behavior. It tends often to be combined with a service perspective, but there are important differences and built-in limitations to such combination. Whereas a service orientation is concerned with the client or person immediately afflicted with the problem, the control agency is interested primarily in the protection of those others, mainly in the majority, who may not be immediately or directly affected. The function of control is to protect the rights and privileges of the members of the larger system. This approach stresses the importance of surveillance, isolation, suppression, and coercion of that minority of the population which would upset the normative and legal balances of most members of the system. The assumption here is that law and order are fundamental to the conduct of the affairs of the civilized community and that these should have precedence over any consideration of issues of individual self-determination, personal development, and social welfare. Further, the solution to the community problem tends to be analyzed in terms of efficiency of control procedures and measures rather than of the value of organizational goals and policies, which are ordinarily taken for granted.

None of these analytic schemes is necessarily exclusive of the others. There is, however, a tendency for one approach to dominate an organization's problem-solving efforts. Further, some of the approaches are mutually more compatible than others.[21]

## Goal Development

The goals, policies, and planning objectives of programs need to be specified. The general goals—for example, delinquency prevention, treatment, correction, rehabilitation, control—should be made explicit and assigned priorities. The development of policy or intermediate goals then follows. If, for example, the general or preamble goals are opportunities and services, a major policy goal might be to increase provision of economic opportunity for adolescent delinquents in the community. More specific operational goals or objectives might then be to develop educational upgrading, job training, counseling, and placement for a thousand hard-core adolescents from sixteen through nineteen years of age in a delimited geographical area during the next eighteen months.

The existence of multiple groups and organizations with competing or conflicting goals and programs for the same target population raises a question about the validity of goals. The claim is made that certain organizations are really not supporting relevant goals, or that they are implementing them poorly. Competing or conflicting goals of other organizations need not, however, deter the planning efforts of the community worker if he knows that the new, different, or additional program will be relevant by the standards of his own organization and can be supported by sufficient resources. In the decision about feasibility, however, the interests of other powerful and not so powerful organizations must be considered. Accommodation or conflict with these other organizations should be anticipated and planned for.

The sufficiency of resources available or potentially available for implementation of the goals must be clearly assessed before major decisions are made. The nature of organizational strength in terms of staffing, facilities, funds, leadership, and community appeal and support should be assessed. In other words, before determining the goals of his own organization, the worker should determine the amount of power his organization possesses in the pursuit of

21. See also Robert A. Dahl and Charles E. Lindblom, *Politics, Economics, and Welfare*, pp. 3–54, 369–526.

problem solving vis-à-vis other competing or conflicting groups and organizations.

The selection and development of goals also require some decision, explicit or implicit, about emphasis on task accomplishment or interactional process. The achievement of both instrumental and expressive goals may require attention to a problem-solving procedure. Nevertheless, it is likely that a focus on task accomplishment will probably require a greater degree of rational problem-solving effort. In any event, a commitment to expressive goals, such as group consensus or cohesion, may require less attention to the achievement of certain instrumental goals, such as the passage of a new criminal courts act. Instrumental and expressive goals, are never completely separable.[22]

### Planning of Intervention

The strategies of intervention are in part given by the organization. Nevertheless, some choice and certainly the way they are implemented remains for the worker to determine. Strategy and tactics constitute the major elements of the problem-solving process. The nature of alternate strategies will be briefly indicated here. The organizational determinants of strategies will be treated later in this chapter.

Strategy relates to general organizational intent and policy development, and is fundamental to the selection of objectives and resources for organizational achievement. Two general sets of strategies may be followed: social change, and social stability. Social-change strategies—advocacy and conflict—emphasize significant change in existing institutional patterns. Social-stability strategies—maintenance and development—emphasize the enhancement and protection of existing institutional patterns. Strategies are developed and implemented according to whether the organization is elitist- or constituency-oriented in its decision-making patterns.

At the planning stage, the worker must do four things. First, he must select the right combination of tactics or methods of intervention. Second, he must determine the programs and projects that are generally appropriate. Third, he must identify and select the poten-

22. See also Robert Morris and Robert H. Binstock, *Feasible Planning for Social Change.*

tial participants—organizations, groups, and individuals—who will facilitate problem solving. Fourth, he must plan the alternative patterns of connection among tactics, program, people, and strategy. In all this, the future development of the plan must be considered. For example, will one project lead to the next? Will the interests and concerns of the participants be sustained? Will a higher level of organizational unity be achieved? To what extent will all these planned objectives and efforts contribute to the larger ends of the worker and the organization?

### Intervention

In reality, the worker has been engaged in action from the very start of the problem-solving process. Perception, conceptualization, communication, and interaction are essential elements of each phase of problem solving. In a more restricted sense, we may describe intervention as those activities which result from previous study, analysis, goal development, and planning. We are consequently at the level of objectives and especially tactics or the methods of intervening. The chief tactics for the implementation of strategies are organizing, interorganizing, and intraorganizing. I shall give primary attention in this volume to the techniques of organizing and interorganizing. The tactics of influence underlies all these methods of community work. The methods or tactics take on different meaning and somewhat different form according to the various strategies employed.

Organizing is a method of stimulating, focusing, and mobilizing local citizen, client, elite leadership, or particular agency interest and concern toward problem solving. For example, a group of citizens—even delinquents—may be recruited by the worker to discuss, and act on an organized basis about, certain community problems that concern them, such as lack of recreation facilities or the unavailability of jobs for youths in the ghetto.

Interorganizing refers to efforts at enhancement, modification, or change in intergroup or interorganizational relationships to cope with a community problem. For example, the worker may seek to establish a committee of agency representatives to facilitate coordination at the levels of individual client service, major program, or general policy. Typically, an attempt is made by one organization to influence the practices of another. These efforts range from simple co-optive measures to sophisticated planning arrangements.

Intraorganizing refers mainly to the activities undertaken by the worker to carry out internal organizational or administrative functions. Its major purpose is to assure the efficient development of organizational effort in the areas of management, supervision, and staffing. Intraorganizing must, however, increasingly adapt to the presence of the client a constituent population as decision makers and staff members in the organization. The concepts of maximum feasible participation and new careers for the poor are relevant here. The way the ideas of maximum participation are put into operation and incorporated into agency or community group administration is still in the process of evolution.

The importance of the use of influence underlying each of these tactics needs to be stressed. For the community worker, influencing refers to his ability to combine or separate the interests of the members of groups and organizations to achieve the ends deemed worthwhile within the ethical boundaries of his professional and organizational commitment. The exercise of influence is not a one-way process; the practitioner is as likely to be influenced as are the other interacting parties. The outcome is the product of an extremely complex set of factors. Influence has both an interpersonal and a political character involving the appropriate use of legal, social, psychological, and economic sanctions, and is especially crucial in organizing and interorganizing. It may be exercised through such devices as education, persuasion, bargaining, pressure, the allocation of resources, and the threat of their withdrawal.

Methods of community work are interrelated. Each constitutes a way of doing different but interdependent parts of the problem-solving job. Depending on the character of the organization's strategy, one or more methods may be emphasized. A conflict-oriented worker may engage in more organizing than interorganizing activity. A worker committed to a maintenance strategy may emphasize interorganizing over organizing.

### Evaluation and Feedback

The results of a specific activity, course of action, or program must be assessed in relation to immediate objectives and long-range goals. Many questions may need to be answered. Did the action move the individual, group, or organization toward meeting its immediate objective? To what extent has the organization progressed toward its larger objective of service, opportunity provision, or citizen participation for delinquent adolescents from sixteen to nineteen years of age residing in the community? To what extent has the organization's larger goal of social stability or change been achieved?

If objectives are successfully achieved, the particular action or program may naturally terminate. If only one aspect of the problem is solved, the entire program may not have been successful. Then, a new set of objectives, tactics, and efforts must be devised and a new problem-solving sequence initiated. Ordinarily, certain organizational structure and procedures have already been established, and provide a pattern of action for the next problem-solving round.

The results of the organization's and worker's efforts may also need to be examined publicly. All members of the worker's organization, other organizations, and the community as a whole may need to be informed about the consequences of a project. This evaluation process may serve to knit organizations and groups together, particularly if the project outcome is successful, and should provide additional knowledge, understanding, and often stimulus for undertaking and supporting the next problem-solving effort.

These procedures of problem solving described have been utilized principally by the professional and more sophisticated worker. In varying degree, however, the process is employed by other types of workers and even by the problem-solving citizen group itself. The professional worker may employ the process not only to guide his own interventions but to sensitize, educate, and more fully involve members of the community to carry out their own work.

## Organizational Context

Few social problems, especially in urban areas, can be solved without the assistance of formal organizations. Most instances of political, economic, and social change are the results of the efforts of organizations, seldom of those of individuals acting alone.

This is simply because organizations become necessary when the achievement of objectives requires cooperative efforts, specialized roles, and the mobilization of capital, material, and human resources. Organizations are no more, in this sense, than the social invention, the method, for expending an individual's capacity to increase his value accumulation . . . beyond what he could do by himself.[23]

An organization may be defined as a social system that has an unequivocal collective identity, an exact roster of members, a program of activity, and procedures for replacing members.[24] Organizations are "collectivities . . . that have been established for the pursuit of relatively specific objectives on a more or less continuing basis."[25] Their distinctive features, which include, relatively fixed boundaries, a normative order, ranks of authority, a communication system, and an incentive system, enable various types of participants to work together in the pursuit of common goals.

The present study is concerned only with service and community work agencies. The service agency has a primary commitment to changing people, and may have an important secondary commitment to changing organizations. Even without this latter objective, however, it must inevitably relate to a variety of other organizations and adapt its services in some way to social problems and forces in the social environment. The community work agency is concerned primarily with efforts to stimulate people collectively or directly to influence other organizations toward more effective adaptation to, or change in, the social environment. The community work organization may also have an important secondary commitment to a service, particularly if it assumes that people change in the process of modifying organizational patterns or if it believes that people must first be made competent before they can participate effectively in social action. The functions of the service

23. Warren G. Bennis and Hollis W. Peter, "Applying Behavioral Science for Organizational Change," p. 294.
24. Theodore Caplow, *Principles of Organization*, pp. 1–2.
25. W. Richard Scott, "Theory of Organizations," p. 488.

and community work agencies are usually not completely separated.

I shall also distinguish between organizations and groups. The community organization is usually large, complex, formal, and enduring—for example, a welfare council, a school or neighborhood organization. The community group is usually small, relatively simple in structure, informal, and more transitory—for example, a block club, a PTA, a tenant's council.

## Response to Environmental Change

"Organizations exist in a changing environment to which they must adapt." [26] Adaptation to an environment may itself require modification of goals, decision making, and internal structure. In this view, organizational goals and programs are variable and even problematic. Without adequate response, sources of support may be cut off. The continuing interaction between the organization and the environment introduces an element of environmental control into the organization.

No organization can long endure if it ignores social forces and other influential groups and organizations in the community.[27] This is particularly true in an area of such sensitive concern as juvenile delinquency. For example, the administration of a youth correctional institution or Job Corps camp may, without due regard for community reactions, permit its inmates or residents to participate in the town's cultural or recreational facilities and activities—and local organizations, such as the American Legion post and the chamber of commerce, may object strongly, may mobilize other community groups to pressure the administration of the institution and local or federal officials to keep these youths out of the community. The organization may be urged to change its goals from rehabilitation to protective custody. A demonstration of outraged community interest and pride may force the closing of the institution or at least the removal of key staff. The organization

26. Mayer N. Zald and Roberta Ash, "Social Movement Organizations: Growth, Decay, and Change," p. 328; see also Eugene Litwak and Henry J. Meyer, "A Balance Theory of Coordination Between Bureaucratic Organizations and Primary Groups," pp. 33–58.

27. James D. Thompson and William J. McEwen, "Organizational Goals and Environment: Goal-Setting as an Interaction Process," p. 408; see also Amitai Etzioni, *Modern Organizations*, p. 8.

does not merely respond to environmental influences; it is critically dependent for its survival on the interests of other organizations and groups in the community.

## Organizational Interdependence

Every organization is dependent, to some degree, on other organizations and groups for the means—moral sanction, the legal right to exist, funds, clientele, and objectives—to achieve and shape its goals. The relations that result are, however, not always equally interdependent. The influence or power exercised by one organization may be greater than that of the other in regard to a specific issue, problem, or program. Thus a federal agency, such as the President's Committee on Juvenile Delinquency and Youth Development, may have exercised considerably more influence on the program of a local agency which it funded than did the local agency on the President's Committee. The PTA in a low-income community may be much more dependent on the resources and facilities of the local public school than is the local school on the PTA. In a reciprocal relationship, however, each organization needs the other to fulfill respective goals, though the larger, more complex, and diversified the goals and programs of an organization, the more likely it is to find alternative resources of sanction, funding, and objectives.

### *Salience of Organizational Need*

Organizational interdependence is also a function of the salience of the reciprocal needs to achieve particular objectives at a given time and place. Organizations are not required to have generally consistent goals to relate to, or coordinate with, one another. The output of one organization must, however, be the input of the other in relation to some issue, problem, or social circumstance. Cooperation or coordination between organizations occurs when the needs of an organization are served or at least not jeopardized by the other under specific social circumstances. Antagonism and conflict occur when one organization perceives the other as threatening its interests and need for goal achievement. It is thus possible for organizations with apparently dissimilar goals, strategies, objectives, methods of operation, and even with histories of previous conflict to cooperate. Further, organizations with reasonably similar characteristics and with a long history of cooperation may nevertheless engage in highly destructive mutual recriminations and attack. The saliency of perceived advantage or threat to organizational interests in a particular situation appears largely to determine the presence or absence of positive interdependency. The determinants of this saliency over time and its general pattern seem, however, to be a function of the organization's primary goal and decision structure, as we shall see later.

The inability of organizations to pool resources in the resolution of such a social problem as delinquency is wasteful. Essential democratic values are of course derivable from competition and conflict over goals and strategies of social intervention. Some differences and antagonisms among organizations may even contribute to effective community problem solving. Conflict between organizations serving delinquents, however, may reinforce norms and values of the delinquents, who are quick to sense their own antisocial advantage in impaired communications and ideological conflict between agencies, and who are occasionally in a position to play one agency against another and thus to defeat the purposes of both in regard to themselves.[28]

## Barriers to Organizational Cooperation

The relations between organizations are often characterized by resistance rather than open antagonism to the goal achievement of the other. This is particularly true where one organization is less dependent than the other in a given program. For example, a youth-serving agency, with a goal of rehabilitation for delinquent youths, developed a program of basic education and job training. The major task of job placement belonged, however, to the local office of the state employment service and to the personnel departments of local businesses and industries. The goal of the employment service was manpower development and its principal objective, job placement. Because of its difficulty in placing young people with arrest records, it gave preference to nondelinquents. In addition, there were other pressures on the employment service— from its higher-echelon officers, to show many job placements and from employers, to provide the most desirable candidates for jobs.

28. Gresham M. Sykes and David Matza, "Techniques of Neutralization: A Theory of Delinquency."

In other words, the local office of the employment service was more dependent on the sanctions of the state office and on the goodwill of local businessmen than on the youth-serving agency with its delinquent clientele, and the youth-serving agency was much more dependent on the local employment service for the achievement of its purposes than vice versa.

An organization may be handicapped by its own subunits in achieving cooperative relations with other organizations. The policy-making and administrative groups of a large organization may wish to cooperate with another organization in the achievement of a common objective, but lower-echelon staff may resist implementation of the policy. Relations between these organizations cannot then be genuinely cooperative or reciprocal.

Finally, it should be noted that interdependence between organizations may not assist in community problem solving. Organizations may deliberately band together to obtain or exchange resources for support of programs which may have little relation to the genuine achievement of such goals as rehabilitation or opportunities. Interagency relationships may serve primarily to support existing service arrangements or the status quo. In this interdependent process, goals, strategies, objectives, and methods bear only slight relation to technologically and socially changing conditions.

### Organizational Autarky

There is a natural centripetal movement of organizations toward self-sufficiency or independence from other organizations. This drive to autarky is a major cause of failure of efforts in community problem solving. Organizations operate under conditions of scarcity which do not permit the satisfaction of all appetites. Each organization and, indeed, each unit within the organization seeks to carry out their activities with as little dependence as possible on other organizations or units. Each tends to disregard the needs of other organizations in its effort to survive and develop.

The autarkic tendency is expressed more strongly in some organizations than in others. It stimulates excessive organizational loyalties, prevents the institutionalized staff member from making correct decisions, and restricts the intake of information and values available on the relevance of other organizational programs. The staff member's perception of client needs, social conditions, and the effectiveness of alternate strategies and methods for his own agency may be seriously narrowed.

Autarkic organizations may be characterized also by the formation of either highly personal, over professionalized, or extremely institutionalized practices and procedures, and by investments in facilities, equipment, and training for ongoing programs. Tradition and precedent—rather than an experimental approach—are the guides to program decisions. The organization is likely to recruit and retain persons sympathetic to its particular approach. Selznick describes the transformation of an organization:

> Day-to-day decisions, relevant to the actual problems in the translation of policy into action, create precedents, alliances, effective symbols, and personal loyalties which transform the organization from a profane, manipulable instrument into something having a sacred status and thus resistant to treatment simply as a means to some external goal. That is why organizations are often cast aside when new goals are sought.[29]

Many organizations dealing with the problem of delinquency are autarkic. They do not readily adjust to changing social circumstances, and they resist change because of the painfulness of altering habitual and accustomed ways of doing things. Original goals of some of these organizations have been lost, or inappropriate strategies and means now exist to achieve them.[30] This is the classic phenomenon of goal displacement. "It arises when an organization displaces its goal—that is, substitutes for its legitimate goal some other goal for which it was not created, for which resources were not allocated to it, and which it is not known to serve."[31]

Further, organizations are predisposed to turn all problems of policy into problems of administration and procedure. The conversion of social issues to social procedures may be explained by the fact that the sphere of activity of the professional or bureaucrat is

29. Philip Selznick, *TVA and the Grass Roots*, pp. 258–59.
30. Herbert A. Simon, Donald W. Smithburg, and Victor A. Thompson, *Public Administration*, pp. 392–93.
31. Etzioni, *Modern Organizations*, pp. 10–12.

limited by tradition and legal statute. The staff member, especially the executive, may fail to see that behind social principles and laws, and consequently behind every strategy of intervention, there lies socially fashioned interests and the *Weltanschauungen* of a specific social group. The professional or functionary does not understand that every administrative pattern or social methodology "is only one of many forms in which socially conflicting irrational forces are reconciled." [32]

The executives and practitioners in the autarkic organization are thrown into states of great confusion and disbelief during periods of rapid social change or revolution. Unable to meet change on its own terms, especially through development of new strategies and different procedures, they regard explosive events as isolated and untoward incidents in an otherwise highly ordered system "and not as the living expressions of fundamental social forces on which the existence, the preservation, and the development of society depends." [33]

In discussing the autarkic organization, I do not deny that voluntary and public agencies have "long traditions of social responsibility and humanitarian concern and do not deliberately convert themselves into seemingly irresponsible, semi-isolated enterprises." [34] But there does seem to be a natural tendency in organizations toward self-sufficiency, which defeats purpose and hinders program effectiveness.

## Organizational Opportunism

Opportunism, for my purpose, refers particularly to the flexibility and skill of executive staff in modifying organizational goals, strategies, objectives, and methods of procedure. This set of perspectives, attitudes, and ultimately behaviors emphasizes the organization's need to change as well as survive. The opportunistic executive may, if necessary, disregard organizational tradition, professional commitment, and even normative principles of conduct.

32. Karl Mannheim, *Ideology and Utopia*, pp. 118–19.
33. Ibid.
34. Alfred J. Kahn, *Planning Community Services for Children in Trouble*, p. 68.

There are various kinds of opportunism.[35] The first, tactical opportunism, arises out of a desire to enlarge the organization, even at the expense of partial modification of goals and program. If funds, prestige, and community support are to be derived from pursuing one set of agency goals at the cost of another, this route may be selected. If, for example, funds are available to youth-serving agencies for manpower training and community work activities, this course may be taken even though the consequences may be a withering of agency support for other services, such as recreation, gang work, and casework.

In a second kind of opportunism, the organization member "seeks to preserve the organization as an object of pride" [36]—the reputation of the agency must be maintained in the eyes of the larger community at all costs. The organization is dynamically responsive to social change. For example, a social agency may change its program emphasis within a generation from family service to settlement house activity to gang work to residential treatment to manpower training to community development. Change occurs not primarily for the sake of augmenting organizational size and resources but out of concern for agency meaningfulness and prestige in a changing community.

The third kind of opportunism arises from of a primary desire by the organizational member to protect or aggrandize his own position, power, prestige, or salary. His interest in and concern for organizational goals and objectives are clearly instrumental to personal, professional, or even partisan political advancement. The executive is probably the most opportunistic member of the organization. The higher his position in the hierarchy, the greater his sensitivity to pressures and influences from the environment. The executive may be more adjustive, more compromising, and is thus a prime target for community worker action. The executive obviously, has greater influence on his organization than other staff members do.

It should be noted that the opportunistic character or dynamic of an organization, particularly of its leadership, often propels it

35. Simon, Smithburg, and Thompson, *Public Administration,* pp. 392–97.
36. *Ibid.*

into new areas of policy, program, and interorganizational relationship, which were neither planned, anticipated, nor desired.

The exercise of administrative discretion gives life and meaning to the abstractions of policy and doctrine. The injunctions of a statute, the directives of a central management mobilize action on the assumption that common organizational goals exist and that these goals are effective in shaping rational administrative behavior. But the assumption breaks down as, in the exercise of discretion, officials are faced with the need to deal selectively with the environment. For as they come upon an existing social situation, individual administrators find it difficult to restrict their interest and involvement to the policy they are executing; they tend to be involved wholly, bringing to bear their own fractional interests upon day-to-day decisions.[37]

Thus, there may be a centrifugal, as well as a centripetal or autarkic, force in organizational structure and process which draws an agency into new areas of endeavor, participation in controversies it has not contemplated, and commitments which it would prefer to avoid and which may indeed be irrelevant to formally stated goals and objectives. Much depends on the character of the particular administrator or worker and the significant immediate organizational pressures to which he is subjected.

### Strategies of Intervention

The community worker's activity is a function of the organizational context of which he is a part. Each organization develops a major strategic orientation to its social environment, so that there is a generally prescribed approach or underlying philosophy of intervention which guides the community worker in the development of his role. This is not an immutable strategy, but is variable and often transformed in time. Pressures from both within and outside the organization make for realignment and shifts in basic orientation to action. Organizational strategy is principally a resultant of two variables—goals, and decision making. Specific

37. Selznick, *TVA and the Grass Roots*, pp. 155–56.

worker roles are largely determined by the interaction of these variables.

## Goals

Goals provide the basic vision and cultural thrust for community problem solving, and are central to organizational existence and struggle. In the Weberian tradition, organizations are expected to exhibit a "primacy of orientation to the attainment of a specific goal." [38] Goals are the official mandates, the formal yardstick against which effectiveness can be assessed. In a rational-systems model, they can be considered the functions performed for the larger society. Because internal as well as external influences create goals, they may be viewed as the commitments of persons and groups within the organization itself. Goals are also an evolving set of ideals which flow from the interaction of internal and external key groups and traditions. They are not always rationally or logically determined, but must provide integrative purpose to the efforts of the organization and must be attainable and related to the availability of means to achieve them.

Goals of service agencies or community work organizations may be part of a continuum of directed social change and social stability. The continuum may be viewed essentially as a political dimension of radicalism–conservatism. Each organization perceives, evaluates, and seeks to interact with its social environment. It may strive for large-scale, radical changes in institutional patterns that are regarded as basically defective. It may even urge revolutionary changes in the structure and purpose of other organizations. On the other hand, it may regard the present community system as generally desirable and seek only slight changes in policies and programs; then the organization's primary orientation is to maintain, enhance, and more effectively control the existing pattern of relationships in the society. Some organizations may become so firmly committed to the stability of the present system that means

38. See David Street, Robert F. Vinter, and Charles Perrow, *Organization for Treatment*, p. 17; Zald and Ash "Social Movement Organizations: Growth, Decay, and Change," pp. 333–35; Thompson and McEwen, "Organizational Goals and Environment: Goal-Setting as an Interaction Process," pp. 405–6.

and procedures are ritualized. The goals of most organizations are, however, probably somewhere between the two extremes.

### Decision Structures

A second significant factor which determines the organization's adaptation to the social environment is its decision structure. If goals create the basic thrust, the decision structure establishes the organization's problem-solving style. The decision structure reveals who makes the important decisions and on what basis. It consists of the positions in the organization responsible for the determination of action priorities and the values and norms which govern their relationships.

Several factors are involved in an organizational decision structure. The first is the relation between the decision maker and the organization's constituency or clientele. The decision makers may be legislators, politicians, bureaucrats, or business leaders who have no direct relationship with the organization. They may be board members, top executives, middle-level managers, or members of the constituency or clientele. They may represent upper-class, lower-class, middle-class, professional, special-interest or community-wide groups. The second factor is the basis of power. Decision makers influence decisions because of the legal, economic, political, or social power they possess in the community. The third factor is the degree of centralization. The process of decision making may be centralized in the hands of a few, or decentralized and diffused so that important decisions are made by many persons. It may be a formal or informal process, democratically or authoritatively determined.

The key factor in decision structure is who makes the decisions and whose interests are thereby expressed. Decisions can be made by an elite group acting on behalf of people without their direct or indirect involvement—this is the philanthropic decision structure. The best interests of people may be represented by others who may be distant geographically, economically, or socially. Decisions can be made by the constituency or by persons directly representing or highly identified with the affected population—this is the self-determinative decision structure. Most social agencies, public and voluntary, have a philanthropic decision structure, in which critical decisions are made by persons identified by dominant groups in the larger community as having superior social, economic, political, moral, technical, or professional endowments. Many militant organizations and neighborhood groups, including some youth and young adult associations, have a self-determinative decision structure. These organizations, usually identified with lower-class problems and concerns, insist that critical decisions be made at the grass-roots level by persons directly representing client or constituent interests.

Goals and decision structures may be interrelated and types of organizational strategies thereby derived. The practitioner generally uses the strategy which is most consistent with the dominant goal and decision structure of his organization and which is compatible with professional values and norms. Social workers are usually employed by organizations committed to maintenance and contest strategies, but they may occasionally find organizations committed to conflict and development. A worker with a primary organizational commitment to any one strategy may employ other strategies on a secondary basis.

### Maintenance

The maintenance strategy is characterized by systematic support of existing institutional patterns. Slow incremental progress is sought; radical or utopian schemes are rejected. Primary effort is to increase the efficiency of present programs and services. This strategy assumes that the present system is the best possible within the limits of reality as perceived by decision makers who represent the dominant structure in the community. Policy and program decisions are made by elite or professional groups fully sanctioned by the middle-class and official society. Organizational effort is mainly to expand the program, contain competition, and to fend off serious attacks from other organizations. The approach is often conservative, authoritative, and respectable, and serves to maintain community stability and cohesion. Most social agencies and service organizations use this approach. They range from boys' clubs and youth commissions to publicly sponsored community action programs, family and children's service societies, community welfare councils, and public assistance agencies with extreme commitment to social stability and control.

### Contest

Contest is a strategy of intervention characterized by the advocacy of social policies and programs which seek to change existing institutional patterns. Some examples are: discrimination in education, housing, employment; police brutality; juvenile court procedures; public assistance practices; political patronage. Its concern is with changing key institutional patterns causing major social problems in the urban community. The decision to contest existing institutional arrangements is made by an elite or professional leadership group. Methods of action are legally sanctioned, legitimate, and approved by the norms of the middle-class democratic society. The struggle for social change is carried on in an idealistic, fervid, yet respectable and restrained manner.

### Conflict

The conflict strategy is typified by a strident insistence on social change and radical modification of existing institutional programs and policies. Its concern is not only with significant problem solving; it seeks at times to substitute new or utopian alternatives to present arrangements for distributing social and economic opportunities and resources. For example, demands may be made for: complete and immediate integration of all public schools, public and private housing, and employment; submission of the police to a civilian review board; abolition and replacement of the public assistance program. In this approach, there may be insistence not only on change in the nature of programs and services available to the poor, the deviants, or the residents of ghetto neighborhoods but in the decision-making pattern for allocating and developing these programs and services.

### Development

The development strategy is exemplified by local efforts to develop distinctive human and organizational potentials, to protect against the expansionist programs of larger, more powerful organizations or the "depredations" of extremely deviant members of the particular community. Development strives for indigenous "culture building" in its attempt to solve significant problems, and is a strategy usually followed by minority groups or socially deprived populations with limited access to funds, facilities, expertise, and middle-class standards. Organizational leadership is indigenous and sometimes charismatic, particularly in the initial stage of development. Decisions may be made autocratically and paternalistically but in full accord with the norms of the indigenous population.

The style of action may be quasi-rational, impulsive, and occasionally based on suspicion and unreal perceptions of reality. The organization often has a weak structural foundation, and may devote a great deal of energy and time to problems of survival— membership recruitment, fund raising, and meetings. The result may be an organizational subculture that is, only partly related to the norms and values of the larger culture and that compensates for the lack of access to prestige, opportunities, and power withheld by the dominant society. The organization may also serve the intimate personal and social service needs of its members.

The strategy of such organizations is often to protect the limited gains made by the organized, aspiring, and ambitious members of the lower-class population. Although this organization is ready to attack those who seek to deprive it of organizational status and community stability, its strategy tends to be conservative, emphasizing stability over social change. Its pattern of activities is respectable by its own standards but often quasi-legitimate by the norms of middle-class society. Such organizations prefer to be left alone to pursue the development of their own social and cultural patterns.

## Variability and Transformation

Although organizations tend to be committed to certain primary strategies of intervention, they also support subsidiary, and at times incompatible, strategies of action. Thus, an organization may tolerate or encourage internal differences and conflict over goals and decision patterns. For example, a social settlement committed to various kinds of individual and group services may encourage advocacy of low-income housing legislation, although its board of directors may be lukewarm or split on the issue. On the other hand, a civil rights or neighborhood organization committed to a militant reform or conflict approach may still sponsor, or at least cooperate in, job training and day care service.

Organizations with one kind of strategy may allocate part of their energies to encourage and develop another kind. For example, an antidelinquency organization may energize a grass-roots organization in its protective or defensive efforts against landlords or the threat of urban renewal; a youth gang may assist a civil rights organization in its demonstration against discrimination in housing or even in political efforts to unseat a reactionary state legislator. As indicated earlier, the strategies of different kinds of organizations may be compatible because they are complementary in given issues and programs.

Further, organizational goals and decision-making patterns may be transformed over time. Old strategies die and new strategies arise. Radical strategies generally tend to become conservative as conflict and contest are transmuted into maintenance orientations. For example, if an indigenous, militant organization survives, charismatic leadership may be replaced by professional staff or bureaucratic functionaries. Leadership becomes oligarchic. Decision making is routinized and increasingly serves the interest of a dominant, more active faction. Reformist goals are replaced by an accommodation to the general society. The major concern of organization can become the maintenance of membership, funds, and other requirements of organizational existence.

On the other hand, under certain conditions, organizational goals may be transformed in a radical direction. Leadership splits may occur, organizations coalesce, and coalitions develop which may result in a complete change of organizational strategy. New social problems, new perceptions of old problems, access to additional resources, and new societal goals may bring changes in organizational goals and decision structures. Goals may be radicalized, and grass-roots leadership rise to transform strategies from maintenance and development to contest and conflict.

The strategy of one organization both influences and is influenced by the strategy of other organizations and by social forces in the larger society. A conflict strategy against a maintenance or development agency may stimulate a counter strategy of conflict. The provision of resources by a maintenance-oriented organization to a contest- or conflict-directed organization may serve to co-opt its program and to transform its strategy.

In a period of rapid social change, when traditional values and institutional patterns no longer adequately serve community problem-solving functions, alternate strategies are born and tested. In a transitional period of a democratic society, competing and conflicting strategies strongly contend for community support. Each new radical orientation may, however, stimulate, to a certain tolerance point, more radical alternatives to troubling social problems. The organization is thus a key instrument for change and stability in the community. Further, its strategy of intervention conditions the nature of the role played by the worker in the community problem-solving process. Before the roles of the community worker are discussed, however, it is important to look more closely at the general problem of delinquency. The nature of the community problem itself may condition the way problem solving, organizational strategies, and roles are carried out.

## The Community Problem

Delinquency may be considered the result of the failure of various general systems of society and the community—cultural, social, economic, political—or as the result of the breakdown of certain specific systems—individual person, family, peer group, school, employment, recreation, social agency, courts. The distinctive contribution of the community worker to the problem of deliquency is the wholeness or interrelated nature of his view and efforts in regard to these failures. At the same time, his strategic attention to certain systems and conditions is most significant in the modification of the problem in a given community.

In other words, the community worker sees juvenile delinquency as a problem not only of individuals and families but of social organizations and social conditions in dynamic interaction with one another in a particular place and time. It is a problem not only of children who have weak egos and poor impulse controls but of the parents who have been inadequately socialized; not only of delinquent gangs but of inadequate agency facilities and services; not only of youths who are dropouts and unemployed but of lower-class culture and race discrimination. Further, these systems and conditions are interdependent and feed back upon each other. For example, the construction of a low-income housing project in an isolated and undesirable section of the city draws families of limited social and personal resources. The male offsprings who have feelings of powerlessness and resentment band together to commit acts defined as delinquent, thus making the housing project more undesirable, further depleting family resources of cohesion, control, and satisfaction increasing the anger of these youths and intensifying their commitment to groups which have delinquent norms.

The delinquency problem is also a consequence of a basic community ambivalence about the dignity and worth of the individual human being. The typical urban slum is as much committed to the production of social disease, abnormality, and destruction as it is to social health, normality, and creativity. The operation of public and private institutions in slum communities seems to be based on dualistic and contradictory premises. Each slum is organized as much to hunt and harass certain types of youths as to help them grow into positive human beings.

In effect, two types of communities exist in our society: the authentic, and the inauthentic. The inauthentic community, producing a high rate of delinquents, operates at best on the principle of equal opportunity for those with unequal abilities and background. Social rewards are accorded to those who can readily meet the expectations of the dominant members of the society. Theoretically, equal social, cultural, and educational opportunities are provided to all. In truth, only those who meet certain criteria of color, academic performance, manner, and motivation are fully able to meet the challenge of equal opportunity. The authentic community—and it may exist in precarious form in isolated, usually suburban, corners of the larger society—operates on the principle of the fulfillment of human needs. Each person in this community is to be given equal consideration for the full realization of his potential. An attempt is made to create the varying conditions under which each person's life would be equally fulfilled. Thus,

A community can require differential contributions to social welfare or make differential payments to individuals so long as it views these individual differences through a concern for equal fulfillment.[39]

The inauthentic community operates on the assumption that men and organizations are basically in mortal combat with other men and organizations, that one man's health, normality, or creativity can thrive amidst the illness, deviance, or the destruction of his fellows, that one organization's success is another's failure. In such a community, men attempt to develop individual, group, and organizational identities in relative unconcern and isolation from one another. The authentic community requires a higher level of rational coordination of human and organizational endeavor. Men and their organizations are so much a part of one another that these conditions of social environment and social systems cannot be ignored. Men develop their identity and human potentials by the high degree of concern and sensitivity they manifest for one another in their respective patterns of group and cultural organization.

Delinquency is thus a function not only of economically and socially depriving systems but of a community committed to the wrong values. In certain communities, people are bereft of concern for their fellow men. If they do not actually create harsh and brutal systems and social conditions, at best they are ambivalent, ignorant of, or acquiescient to their existence. The delinquency problem in the inauthentic community may be seen, as a series of extraordinarily intricate, dynamic, yet intractable patterns of community breakdown. These distinctive community patterns are distance, stigmatization, failure of opportunities and services, and "politics." These master mechanisms articulate social systems in the development and maintenance of the delinquency problem, and must be understood before adequate strategies and action programs can be developed by the community worker.

## Community Distance

The inauthentic community is divided and divisive. Significant groups and organizations do not understand or accept one another. Patterns of divisiveness are a significant cause and sometimes a

39. Richard Lichtman, *Toward Community: A Criticism of Contemporary Capitalism,* pp. 27–28.

consequence of the delinquency problem. The major kinds of divisiveness in the urban community today are ethnic, class, intergenerational, spatial, and subcultural. The underlying problem is essentially one of corporate and institutional distance, and has not yet been adequately studied in social science research.[40]

The ethnic or racial schism between white and nonwhite groups or between groups of different cultural background—for example, Italians, Puerto Ricans, Mexicans, Appalachian whites—is a condition of threat for those immediately concerned. The tension that arises between opposing adult groups is a basis for the development of interyouth group antagonisms. Adolescents are the eyes and ears, the sensitive antennae, and the volatile embodiment of the temper of people in a neighborhood. They act out the attitudes and feelings of adults. Unfortunately, these consequent actions of youth groups may be violent and destructive, and lead to delinquency; these abate as the ethnic schism is reduced, usually as one of the groups leaves the area or as people in the area no longer sense a major schism with those immediately outside it.

Class, also a divisive factor, may not be so immediately destructive as ethnic or racial division but may eventually contribute to isolation and stigmatization of lower-class youth. Class differences especially afflict the Negro ghetto, and the consequences are both pathetic and tragic. There may be little connection between the haves and the have-nots. The energies of the middle-class Negro tend to be directed almost exclusively to escaping his immediate environment. Middle-class residents attend meetings of garden or block clubs and religious groups, seek membership on important committees of citywide civil rights organizations, or escape to friends and relatives living outside the ghetto or even in the suburbs. They send their children to private schools and to out-of-town colleges, and usually have enough money to vacation away from the neighborhood.

The professional, the white-collar employee, and the businessman in the ghetto may not provide the leadership or join with low-income groups to improve conditions of the immediate com-

40. For a discussion of social distance from a basically individualistic or psychological point of view, see Edward S. Bogardus, "A Social Distance Scale," and more recently, Edward O. Laumann, *Prestige and Association in an Urban Community.*

munity. Funds and human resources—for example, to support youth services—derive largely from outside the community. Middle-class residents tend to accept limited responsibility for the development and staffing of opportunity-providing or remedial programs. They do not seek to become role models or engage in positive interaction with potentially delinquent youths. Mutual suspicion, hostility, and open antagonism usually exists between middle- and lower-class elements in the ghetto.

The distance between the generations, even at the same class level, is particularly wide in the ghetto or the inauthentic community. The struggle for survival by many adults is so intense that little time and energy remain for the socialization of youth. The scarcity of adult interest, warmth, and affection stimulates in youth

> the impression, unfortunately often very accurate, that there is nobody really in the adult generation who either cares for them or can do anything effective for them in relation to the problems they are facing. So they turn their backs on the older generation and do what they think makes sense to them. Their activities are often regarded as antisocial.[41]

Distance and conflict among the generations may be heightened as a result of competition for the same kinds of nonskilled jobs. With the demands of industry for increased educational and vocational preparation, both dropout youths and unskilled adults are placed in competition for the same limited job or resource-producing opportunities. Relations between the generations are also aggravated when adults, especially males, do not derive status and security in their role relations with their male children. For example, the poorly educated adult Negro male is likely to have feelings of worthlessness and loss of status if his male children obtain a better education than he has. The youth loses respect for his father when he becomes aware of how little his father knows. Then too, the youth who is a dropout but has obtained an eighth-grade education believes that he has done better than his father, mother, and other adults around him, and that he is qualified to meet the occupational demands of the larger society. His awakening in the

41. All illustrative material hereafter not identified by source has been obtained through interviews, case material, and agency documents. Identifying data have been disguised.

reality of the job market is rude and painful, and does little to improve his relationships with adults in the immediate or larger community.

The distance and tension between the generations are further aggravated by the different culture each may subscribe to. There are varying and sometimes conflicting expectations and values between the youth and adult cultures among certain low-income first- and second-generation ethnic groups—for example, Italian, Polish, Mexican, Puerto Rican, and Chinese. This culture gap between the generations may be regarded also as partly a function of scarce opportunities and institutional defects which fail to provide an adequate education, good jobs, and personal security— necessary conditions for adult understanding and acceptance of youthful points of view.

Spatial distance, whether physical or psychological, from objects of value leads to status loss and feelings of deprivation and may also contribute to delinquent patterns. If the place of residence does not provide access to expected satisfaction or if its location is defined as undesirable, then feelings of resentment and anger and a readiness for combat may be stimulated. The low-income housing project, for example, may not only be an out-of-the way gathering place for deprived families but may also provide a condition favorable for the creation of conflict between those in and those not in the project. The problem is how to remove the isolation from the low income project and the larger community in order to facilitate communication, travel, and interchange between these highly differing worlds. Actually, no project or ghetto community can be completely isolated—especially for teenagers—in our large cities, but the problem of the sense of difference and isolation remains. Its consequences may be conflict, especially when youths leave their own territory to make use of facilities and resources elsewhere.

The most serious problem of the ghetto is probably economic, rather than social or psychological, isolation. One aspect of the economic problem is spatial distance—people may not have easy physical access to adequate sources of livelihood. The ghetto may be a long distance, in time, physical space, and convenience, from where resources are available. An extraordinary amount of motivation, energy, and money is required of the residents of the ghettos to participate meaningfully in the life of the rest of the city. No wonder that resentment, anger, and fury can build up in these areas.

The delinquent subculture,[42] a summation or product of harmful social conditions and system breakdowns, is a characteristic of the inauthentic community. For the period during which youths are delinquents or gang members and defined as such, they tend to be isolated from effective relations with family, school, church, employment, conforming peer groups, and other types of organizations. The members of the delinquent group are likely to be meaningfully connected with only a small sector of the adult world. Delinquents may accept the validity of only certain types of adult attitudes and behaviors. Their role models are pimps, prostitutes, thieves, and racketeers. For the younger delinquent, the available role models may be even more limited. Children in the slum areas often aspire to be like older delinquents.

> Over and over again when you ask the young kids, 9, 10, 11 years of age, what do you want to be when you grow up, the answer is a Ranger, a Vice Lord, a Disciple. It depends on what part of the city he is from and how active the gangs in his area have been.

The delinquent selects from the kind of values and norms available to him. A big car, sharp clothes, and a fat bank roll may be what truly counts on the streets. The values of education, a steady job, and stable marriage are not fully accepted; nor are the means to these values really accessible. The delinquent subculture is the mechanism for producing alternate means to status, otherwise denied to many ghetto youths. For example, the fighting gang in the worst areas of the city may be committed to aggression and violence not for its own sake but to create reputation, dignity, and self-respect for its members, albeit in terms distorted and meaningless to the outsider.

## Stigmatization

Delinquency is more than a general response to the breakdown of community systems and moral commitment, and consequent

42. See Albert K. Cohen, *Delinquent Boys: The Culture of the Gang;* Richard A. Cloward and Lloyd E. Ohlin, *Delinquency and Opportunity;* Irving Spergel, *Racketville, Slumtown, Haulburg.*

adaptation to destructive social conditions. It is represented by more than the incidence or prevalence of deviant actions, however defined. It is more than the sum or representation of specific antisocial acts committed. A particular kind of community interactional and communications process, delinquency is a function of a specific identifying and labeling or stigmatizing process.

A great many persons in all walks of life in our communities commit antisocial acts, some extremely ser?ous by any standard. These persons are not necessarily delinquent—more precisely, they are not labeled delinquent. The status of delinquency is not automatically attributed to everyone who engages in an unlawful act. Whether such an act—for example, assault—is reported to the police, or whether it is regarded as a peccadillo or major offense, may depend on several variables.

> These include the community's tolerance for violence, the provocation which started the conflict, the injury which results, the formality of police-community relationships, the size of the police force in relation to the size and density of population, the skills and interests of lawyers for the defense and prosecution, and many other factors.[43]

In the assignment of the status of delinquent, actual offensive behavior must be treated not merely as the phenomenon to be explained but instead as one of a number of circumstances contributing to a stigmatizing process.[44] Dress, manner, race or color, neighborhood, immediate situation, family income, and occupational status—all are variables determining whether the suspect will be categorized as delinquent.[45]

For example, the differences in the police treatment of minority-group and white middle-class youths congregating on the street corners of their respective neighborhoods are too great and consistent to be ignored. An alienating and criminogenic process may be initiated for the members of one group but not for those of the

43. Daniel Glaser, "National Goals and Indicators for the Reduction of Crime and Delinquency," p. 108.

44. Albert K. Cohen, *Deviance and Control,* pp. 21–25; Austin T. Turk, "Conflict and Criminality," p. 341; see also Edwin M. Lemert, *Human Deviance, Social Problems, and Social Control,* pp. 42–44.

45. Irving Piliavin and Scott Briar, "Police in Encounters with Juveniles," *American Journal of Sociology,* pp. 205–14; Carl Werthman, "The Function of Social Definitions in the Development of Delinquent Careers."

other. The stigma commences and develops with arrest, detention, court appearance, trial, sentence, imprisonment, and parole, and is sustained later through a series of interactional encounters and institutionalized acts of degradation by significant persons at home, at school, on the job, and in the neighborhood.

Stigmatization is the result of a highly coercive and irrational process which discriminates not so much the erring from the unerring as those thought to be, or tending to be, errant. The act of delinquency is usually immoral; the inconsistency and insensitivity of the institutional reaction to it are also immoral. Stigmatization is itself a major contributing factor to the delinquency problem. The "cure" may be worse than the illness, and indeed tends to contribute further to the progress of the social disease. Evidence suggests that both youths and the community may profit from elimination of many "curative" institutional processes. Support for this notion probably arises more often from cases involving middle-class rather than lower-class youths. Undoubtedly the quantity and quality of positive community influences are greater in the white middle-class area than in the lower-class ghetto. The point at issue is that middle-class youths do commit serious acts, are probably less frequently stigmatized, and are therefore less likely to become delinquents and comprise a problem.[46]

Stigmatization may result not only from overzealous and discriminatory law enforcement procedures but from preventive and treatment procedures by social workers, teachers, psychologists, and other professional helpers, particularly if they are closely related to law-enforcement and traditional control agencies. The helping process often has unanticipated consequences. The effect of identifying and treating an individual or group as delinquent, or even potentially delinquent, may offset the positive values of well-intentioned efforts. Treatment or prevention may create a complex interactional situation in which the awareness of delinquency for the youth and other affected persons, especially adults, heightens negative meanings and actions. The youth identified as delinquent is provided with a tag which negatively modifies his views of himself and reinforces rather than reduces alienation from acceptable values and behaviors.[47]

46. See Edwin H. Sutherland, *White Collar Crime.*
47. Leslie T. Wilkins, *Social Deviance,* p. 96.

Stigmatization may be viewed as a process of communication or information feedback which increases the likelihood of continued deviance by anyone identified as deviant. The action taken by the courts, schools, and assisting personnel results in the self-perception of the youth as delinquent and leads to his isolation and alienation from other youths. It constitutes the first part of a "deviation amplifying system," and it is "hardly to be expected that people who are excluded by a community will continue to regard themselves as part of it." Youths may defensively band together and develop their own opposing value system, resulting in additional delinquent acts and further or stronger definitions of delinquency by official groups. The whole system may continue "round and round again in an amplifying account."

The "deviation amplifying system" can, however, be avoided or modified by the provision of greater access to opportunities for legitimate acts, by the minimization of sanctions or punishments (so that they do not become devalued by excessive use or misuse), by defining as deviant the minimum number of actions possible, and by insuring that the definers of deviant acts and persons are clearly aware of the reactions to such definitions by the deviants themselves. Delinquency itself, it must be emphasized, is often only a transitory adolescent phase, especially if not reinforced by inappropriate institutional and adult reactions.[48]

In the final analysis, the delinquent is a product of a legal definition, according to which he is a violator of local, state, or federal laws that apply specifically to juveniles. For example, some ordinances or laws relating to truancy, running away from home, curfew violation, and ungovernable behavior apply only to juveniles. The laws that relate especially to juveniles are subject to a wide range of interpretation and enforcement. The violation of these laws accounts for a surprisingly large proportion of juvenile delinquency cases reported in the United States. "In 1963, for example, 55 per cent of the referrals to court in the case of girls and 20 per cent in the case of boys, were for offenses applicable to juveniles only." [49] It may be entirely possible to reduce the number of delinquent acts by defining some of them as behavioral problems

48. *Ibid.*, pp. 102–3.
49. U. S. Department of Health, Education, and Welfare, Children's Bureau, *Juvenile Delinquency Prevention in the United States*, pp. 3–4.

and dealing with these not through such a punishment- and highly control-oriented institution as the juvenile or youth court but through a less control- and more treatment-oriented institution as a public welfare or other community social agency.

The stigmatization process is not only fundamentally coercive; it serves, intentionally or unintentionally, to augment vested organizational and professional interests. The larger the number of youths who are defined as delinquent, the greater the need for expansion of organizational interest and professional service to deal with the problem. A broad base of crime and delinquency in a community guarantees the existence of many organizations, professional associations, and community groups in which bureaucrats, professionals, subprofessionals, and ordinary citizens can find work, outlet for their energies, and moral justification for vocational or avocational interests. In other words, a great many organizations and groups have developed not only a rationale but a functional need for the perpetuation and growth of delinquency. Traditional organizational efforts to deal with delinquents and delinquent acts may therefore produce the unanticipated consequence of increasing rather than reducing the persistence and incidence of delinquency. A workable plan to limit the delinquency problem may require a real test of—and even challenge to—certain accepted approaches as well as a more efficient coordination and augmentation of existing effort.

Nevertheless, it is probably necessary that a minority of the community's members be identified and labeled as deviant in order to assure the commitment of the majority to legitimate norms and values. The cohesiveness of the community is reestablished through such actions as attack, punishment, concern, and treatment for certain persons in the community. Also, the destructive impulses of a great many respectable persons may be fulfilled vicariously when crimes of delinquency are identified as committed by others. There may be a need to suffer vicarious guilt and punishment for these crimes through expression of indignation, anger, concern, and forgiveness for offenders.[50] It must be empha-

50. Reverend Bert A. Anderson (Statement), Subcommittee to Investigate Juvenile Delinquency, of the Committee on the Judiciary, U. S. Senate, 86th Cong., 1st sess., S. res. 54, pt. 2. *Juvenile Delinquency*, pp. 1055–56; Emile Durkheim, *The Rules of Sociological Method*.

sized that these speculations do not deny that the same sociological functions and psychological needs can be provided through less coercive and stigmatizing processes and applied to fewer persons.

## Failure of Opportunities and Services

A key aspect of the delinquency problem is the failure of social opportunities and services to meet the needs of youths identified as delinquent.[51] This is really a double failure. Not only are delinquent youths ordinarily subjected initially to limited access to social resources but, once they are identified as delinquent, even fewer opportunities and services are available to them. For our purposes, social opportunities can be described as access to means, whether economic, social, cultural, or psychological, by which to achieve meaningful or respectful status by the standards of the larger society. Social services can be generally regarded as mechanisms which link basic opportunities and enhance their utility.

The distinctive importance of the correlation between limited economic opportunities and delinquency has been stated many times.[52] Fleischer recently said: "In areas of high tendencies toward crime, a 10 per cent rise in incomes might well result in a 20 per cent decline in delinquency." Unemployment is also a significant factor: a one per cent increase is associated with a .15 per cent increase in delinquency.[53] The lesser importance of distinctively psychological factors and the relatively greater significance of social factors in the development of delinquency or any deviant adaptation should also be recognized.[54]

The lack of adequate social opportunities has generally been associated with many characteristics of the delinquent: a poor self-image; a greater sense of powerlessness; a more fatalistic attitude towards life; a lack of future orientation; nonverbal, anti-intellectual, and primitive conceptual ability; unrealistically high and fanciful aspirations and, at the same time, depressed expectations for achievement and success; and, finally, a greater potential

51. See Cloward and Ohlin, *Delinquency and Opportunity;* Spergel, *Racketville, Slumtown and Haulburg.*
52. See, for example, Belton M. Fleischer, *The Economics of Delinquency.*
53. *Ibid.,* p. 117.
54. Marc Fried, "Social Problems and Psychopathology," p. 441.

for antisocial behavior.[55] In other words, the lack of economic and social opportunities creates a condition of relative social deprivation associated with a range of maladaptive attitudes and behaviors, including delinquency, to be found in low-income areas.

The unavailability of social and economic resources has thus probably contributed to the evolution of nonconformist or deviant cultures and subcultures. The deviant social systems survive and maintain themselves through a process of alienation from the larger culture. A major means for institutionalizing the unequal distribution of social opportunities is "skimming."

## Skimming

Skimming is a process of organizational avoidance of social problem solutions through not providing services or the provision of inappropriate, inadequate, or irrelevant opportunities and services. In recent years considerable interest and resources have been expended on additional services and in devising new opportunities and services for preventing and treating delinquency and for eliminating the more inclusive problem of poverty itself. Many factors have contributed to the limited value of most of these programs. For example, organizations funded to meet the needs of delinquent or poor youths for education, job training, job placement, cultural enrichment, and leadership development may have failed to reach the right clients. Only the less deviant may be accorded access to these additional opportunities and services. Delinquency prevention and antipoverty programs tend to serve the "responsive" or "deserving" poor, the upward-striving rather than the resistive, persistent, or hard-core delinquent. Political pressures and inappropriate public policies have placed priority on one set of programs rather than on another or have failed to view the interconnectedness of problem solutions and the need to carry out several kinds of efforts simultaneously or in sequence. It may be deemed preferable, for example, to invest greater resources in preschool and early-school cultural enrichment programs than in educational and job opportunities for delinquent or "difficult to serve" adolescents. The younger child is less deviant, easier to reach, and there

55. Jacob R. Fishman, *et al., Community Apprentice Program, Training for New Careers,* p. 1.

are perhaps more powerful organizations and groups interested in him.

Certain bureaucratic pressures also contribute to the skimming process. Organizational policies and procedures often negate basic goals of the programs. Federal bureaucratic processes have been responsible in some measure for this form of local agency goal displacement. Manpower development projects, for example, are required to show evidence of success at the end of a given time period. In order to "deliver" and then to be in a position to obtain funds for additional training, counseling, or job placement programs, local agencies must demonstrate a record of success with clients served. To meet this federal demand, local agencies sooner or later recruit the "best" and sometimes exclusively the "most promising" youths.

Antipoverty funds have sometimes encouraged a process which makes local agencies less effective in reaching and serving hardcore delinquents than they may have been in the past. Agency personnel previously assigned to delinquent groups may now be engaged in general service efforts to large numbers of adolescents and children, most of them nondelinquents. A diminishing number of hard-core delinquents tend to be involved in many of these mass programs for a variety of organizational reasons. Another variant of the failure of opportunities and services is the provision of irrelevant resources by agencies. In one major city, a multimillion dollar teen post program has been established primarily to provide recreational services to low-income, particularly delinquent, youths. Although a great many delinquents have apparently been served through this kind of program, it may be argued that more relevant to delinquency reduction and improved social adaptation might be literacy training, job-counseling, job-placement, and job-development programs. Indeed, overemphasis on recreational activities may deter and distract youths from concentrating on their studies and effective job preparation.

In the entire process of opening opportunities and services for delinquent youths, the potential of involving delinquents in program determination and execution has generally been overlooked. The history of the involvement of adolescents—let alone delinquents—in significant decision-making processes and of the development of service programs and community projects has not been auspicious. The traditional involvement of youths in such activities as youth councils has been characterized by adult manipulation, paternalism, and authoritative control. In general, these councils have been ephemeral and of little consequence. They have served primarily as vehicles of recreational, athletic, and limited educational purpose or to satisfy predetermined agency decisions and needs. The rationale underlying the failure to involve youths in important programs of services either for their own immediate personal value or for community problem solving has been that youths in general and delinquents in particular have little capacity, self-discipline, and desire to do so. Recent experiences—of a pilot nature—in several large cities suggests that this may not be a valid argument.

In any efforts to deal with the problem of delinquency, it is essential that the failure of opportunities and services be clearly identified. The elements which need to be confronted are the lack of adequate resources, their low priority of allocation to delinquents, organizational reluctance in providing available opportunities to delinquents, irrelevant programming, and a traditional unwillingness to permit delinquents to determine their own social needs and programs.

### Politics

The persistence of juvenile delinquency in our society may be due in some measure to its importance for certain political or organizational purposes, as suggested above.[56] The problem of delinquency is more than the variety of psychological, social, cultural, educational, and legal effects on the delinquent. Unless we understand the uses of delinquency for organizational and political ends, we shall not grasp an essential element of the problem. The term "political" in this context is meant to suggest that he who wages battle against delinquency in the community may accrue power or influence in decision making related not only to delinquency control, prevention, or treatment programs but to other community issues and problems. Power derives from the fact that whoever successfully engages in reducing delinquency, or creates the myth that his program is curtailing delinquent activity, gains

56. Irving Spergel, "Politics, Policies, and the Delinquency Problem."

the respect, prestige, and gratitude of the community, which rewards the particular leaders for their efforts.

There is a reservoir of deep psychological and moral concern in urban communities over the problem of delinquency. Delinquents, especially aggressive gang youths, are regarded with fear and considered evil incarnate. They symbolize fundamental human conflicts over good and evil. The hard-core gang youth or the notorious delinquent may serve as the projected image of the community's concern with its own impulses to commit murder, mayhem, and violence. These impulses are more readily stimulated in a period of rapid societal change, when deep frustration and failure result from the inability to understand or adequately to cope with the myriad of new and complex problems of daily living.

In other words, the program which is successful in engaging and controlling delinquents represents, in moral and psychological terms, a reordering or reestablishing of the human condition. Everyone shares in the surcease of anxiety and dread when a delinquency crisis has been resolved and the world seems right and under control again. When the battles are successful—and they are almost always claimed to be successful—the principal warriors are accorded a special lien on the community's goodwill and the reward of public prestige, salary increases, opportunity to expand programs, public acceptance, and even commitment to a social cause. On the other hand, when the community or its representatives view a given program as no longer successful, extreme hostility, denigration, and even destruction of positions or the agency itself may occur.

At least four major political roles have recently developed in response to the problem of lower-class delinquency. Each role has become—or is becoming—socially structured, and provides opportunities for the achievement of the political ambitions of its occupants. These roles are: the civil rights leader, militant or otherwise; the new politician; the former, or sometimes present, gang leader; and the agency executive.[57] These relatively new roles influence the nature of the cause as well as the solution of the delinquency problem. The community worker will need especially

57. For a discussion of the classic links between politics, crime, and delinquency, see Herbert Asbury, *The Gangs of New York: An Informal History of the Underworld;* Frederic M. Thrasher, *The Gang.*

to understand these roles if he is to deal effectively with the problem of delinquency at the local community level.

## Civil Rights and Militant Leaders

Civil rights and militant leaders have attempted to use delinquent gang members to support and sometimes to staff their movements. The evidence is clear, for example, that the Southern Christain Leadership Conference (SCLC), the Student Non-Violent Coordinating Committee (SNCC), certain Black Power groups, and even the pro–Chinese Communist groups in at least two metropolitan areas have occasionally sought to use gang members. Gang youths, delinquents, and other members of the *Lumpenproletariat* have reputedly constituted a significant component in many political revolutionary efforts. They can be useful as the shock troops, the *putschist* elements, the essence of the rabble or the mob which attacks and serves to topple the existing political regime or at least seriously to threaten the existing political structure. Certain extremist leaders, for example, have sought to capture these youths, probably because of their availability, their vigor, and especially for their willingness to participate in violent action. Extremist groups may see gangs as a useful means of influencing and controlling low-income populations in an urban area.

Highly sustained and controversial attempts at cooptation—controversial in the sense that they were opposed by most authorities and social agencies in the city—occurred in Chicago in 1966. A former gang-work researcher and director of a radical community action group attempted with little success to interest gang youths in his highly militant, possibly revolutionary, program. Workers from various militant groups have sought to establish relationships with leaders of warring gangs in a number of cities. The effort has been to redirect intergang hostility into controlled anger against the system. At an early stage, staff strategy was to stimulate participation in protests, sit-ins, tent-ins, and vigils in relation to schools, housing, welfare, and other problems afflicting inner-city ghettos. Significant involvement by gang youths in these activities has not yet materialized, although on several occasions individual gang youths and subgroups have participated in marches as guardians or

disciplined protectors against hostility and attack from white onlookers. More recently, efforts have been made by extremists to
engage gang youths for violent revolutionary or pre-revolutionary
attacks on the symbols of established authority.

### The New Politician

The new politician is usually an executive of a gang control
agency, community action group, or neighborhood organization
who uses his connections with the delinquency problem for his own
political advancement. These leaders often think of themselves as
directly or indirectly heading a youth or young adult movement
whose object is legally to force a change in the political structure,
in particular to drive out incumbent councilmen, assemblymen, or
congressmen who are opposed to civil rights or progressive social
legislation. These new politicians consider corrupt or inefficient,
officials or elected leaders as the cause of the social problems
which afflict low-income communities and contribute to delinquency. They consider also that the capture and assumption of
political power are the *sine qua non* of remedying defective public
leadership.

The new politician has certain characteristics. He is very sensitive to, and familiar with, the problem of hard-core delinquency in
the slum. He is articulate, intelligent, ambitious, and highly committed to a progressive social point of view, and sees his own direct
experience with delinquents and people in the ghetto as his best
qualification and as the basis for an effort to change the system.
These new politicians have not yet developed viable organizational
machinery and have not acquired support from dissident elements
within the established political or governmental structure. They
tend toward self-deception about available staff, organizing ability,
indigenous neighborhood support, and the strength of the opposition, and toward a certain quality of fantasy or unreality in their
plans and actions.

### The Gang Leader

A third emerging community leader is the present or former
gang leader. Traditionally, the leader of a gang has sought and
claimed wide influence over delinquent youths in the community.

If he is talented and ambitious, he may attempt to extend his hegemony to other gangs and areas of the city. In the past several years many of these gang leaders have obtained positions as program directors, aides or community workers performing many recreation, social welfare, and organizational tasks, particularly with other youths. Agencies, churches, and community action programs have attempted to capitalize on the influence of these young men for their own organizational purposes, but, highly sensitive to their own interests and quick to learn community organizational techniques, they may decide to build their own organizations. They often play a complex simultaneous game of serving an agency, building their own following, and planning political advancement or wider influence in the community.

### The Agency Executive

The development of the political role of some agency executives —and it has not been so recent as that of the other roles—has been a direct function of the ignorance of the community about the causes of delinquency and the effectiveness of agency remedies. The agency administrator may perpetuate this ignorance by systematically avoiding any evaluation of his program. Extensive publicity of agency activities, frequent fund-raising campaigns to sustain the program, and ingenious stimulation of crises and playing on community fears about delinquency constitute the stock-in-trade of the successful executive; the board of directors of the agency, the newspapers, and citizen groups play a collusive role in purging the community of fears and anxieties. Together these activities serve to maintain collective inattention to the forces which make for and sustain delinquency.

Efforts at gang control are usually initiated and sustained with a great deal of publicity. More public attention has been centered on gang control efforts in the past twenty years than on any other welfare activity, with the possible recent exception of the antipoverty programs. Many gang programs have been devices to acquire funds for other agency projects—for example, community organization, recreation, casework, referral, day care. Many organizations traditionally not engaged in service to gangs have recently enlarged the scope of their activities to capitalize on the community's concern with gangs. At the same time, there is sufficient evidence, dating from the Cambridge-Somerville study [58] before World War II, to indicate that most existing community–based delinquency control, treatment, and prevention programs, particularly those concentrating on recreation, intra- or inter-personal approaches, may be of limited value.

58. Edwin Powers and Helen Witmer, *An Experiment in the Prevention of Delinquency: The Cambridge-Somerville Youth Study.*

# 2

# The Role of the Community Worker

The roles of community workers in recent years have evolved in three distinct yet overlapping traditions: social service, social reform, and community development. These traditions both produce and interact with particular forms of organizational structure.

The social service tradition—represented by social agencies and welfare councils—has contributed the notions of professional leadership, democratic process, enabling, and reliance on consensus to achieve reequilibration of a problematic social situation. The activities of the social service worker have included fact finding, planning, public relations, community education, coordination, standard setting, consultation, and, occasionally, the development of policy statements on public issues. More recently, the activities of organizing and stimulus for direct service innovation have been added in particular instances.

The social reform tradition—represented by political and union activists, early settlement house leaders, and currently by civil rights, some black power, some community action, and antipoverty workers—has contributed the ideas of militant organizing and political change. More concerned with radical social change than with improvement of agency program efficiency and effectiveness, it has encouraged political and legal action as well as mass organizing, stimulation of crises, and use of pressure tactics to force concessions from established community leadership.

The community development tradition—represented by public and voluntary agencies and local community groups, and most recently, by certain black power groups, and derived in part from foreign experiences—has contributed the ideas of grass-roots or indigenous social and cultural development, sometimes with the aid of outside resources of leadership, expertise, and funds. Emphasis has been on building stronger, more viable local cultures through maximum utilization of indigenous talent, norms, values, and motivations. Radical change has not been encouraged; rather, the emphasis has been on the slow building of local community leadership and citizen involvement around a whole range of social and educational activities as well as in relation to such social problems as delinquency.

### Enabler

The role of the enabler derives from the social service tradition. Such a worker, usually a professional, is expected to guide, advise, and assist representatives of community groups, often representing the dominant interests of the community, to work together to solve various agency and community problems. In this process the group, and theoretically the community itself, is expected to achieve a higher level of moral or value integration. An indirect rather than a direct leader, the worker should stimulate the group to make its own decisions and to assume maximum responsibility for the implementation of these decisions. Then too, he should try to balance, as feasibly and efficiently as possible, community resources and the needs of the people. His commitments are to his social agency and the social work profession; usually, there is a little conflict in the strategies and tactics espoused by these two reference groups. He works more often and more successfully with middle-class rather than lower-class groups.

### Advocate

The role of the advocate arises in part from the social reform tradition in part from a newer social service or broader welfare tradition. In this role, the worker directly represents or persuades other members of professional and elite groups to represent the interests of an estranged, deviant, or less powerful and usually less articulate sector of the population. He performs a vigorous mediating or ombudsman function on behalf of the dispossessed group—whether delinquents, public aid recipients, tenant unions, or simply slum dwellers—in their relations with public and voluntary bureaucracies as well as with political structures. He is partisan in favor of the significant change of organizational structures, procedures, service patterns, and legal institutions, and is usually engaged in contest with the established order on specific issues by means of normative processes of change rather than through generalized conflict. He is more interested in innovation and plans for effective services, usually through the medium of demonstration programs, than in traditional services. This worker insists that organizations provide their clientele or constituents with the service rightly due them, and is more concerned with the expeditious resolution of a social problem than with the nature of the interpersonal process by which it is accomplished. In other words, he is more interested in the achievement of specific ends than the facilitation of a group process of social development. His interest in the building of sustaining community or local organizational effort may be less than that of other types of workers. Usually committed to the ideals and norms of the liberal or radical wing of his profession, as represented by social work, law, or psychiatry, he operates within the context of progressive social, civic, and religious organizations.

## Organizer

The role of the organizer is strictly within the social reform tradition. Such a worker usually has strong ideological commitments and is concerned with the general change of a social system, whether at a neighborhood, city, or national level, so that the people concerned may more fully achieve their human potentials. His organizational activity is largely mobilized around antagonism or conflict with an important or dominant organization or power structure in the community. He may be less interested in such limited problems and groups as delinquency and delinquents than in such larger problems and groups as poverty, the slum dweller, and the Negro. The organizer is often charismatic, and may operate more effectively with large, loosely structured than with small, tightly knit groups. He is especially attentive to the sociopsychological factors which bind group organizational action in support of a program. His tactics are often militant, including protest, picket, boycott, propaganda, or even violation of certain laws, but usually stop short of violence. He stimulates community groups, usually of members of a dispossessed class, not merely to express differences with the organizations in power but to neutralize and destroy the capacity of the opposition to generate certain policies and programs, although he may not have an alternate institutional system to substitute. Not usually committed to the established tenets of any professional organization, he operates from the base of a social movement, people's organization, or political organization that is often financially weak.

### Developer

The role of the developer depends on the resources, motivations, values, and institutions for self-help of an indigenous population, usually in a low-income urban area. This worker's major aim is to nurture and develop the integrity of the community's pattern of adapting to social conditions. His purpose may be only secondarily to assist people in the community to solve serious social problems —he is more concerned with process than with content. His role is highly integrated with the daily life of the population. He intimately knows and shares the trials and tribulations, the joys and sorrows of a large number of individuals and families in his area. He is also a mediator and a protector of the local population in its dealings with formal organizations and the larger society. Although he may protect the group from hostile, external influence and interference, he also fosters a sense of group cultural identity and achievement somewhat compatible with the norms of the larger society. He influences the group in its decisions and program development through a process of persuasion and leadership which may or may not be democratic or always viewed as legitimate by middle-class standards but which is consistent with the traditions of the indigenous population. This worker may have nominal affiliation with, and economic support and sanction from, an outside agency; but his allegiance and primary identification are with the immediate community. His orientation is essentially toward adaptation and culture building rather than contest or conflict.

## Worker Roles and Community Problem Solving

Each worker—whatever his own role—must know the nature of other roles in a complex community situation. Not only will he confront workers playing other roles in relation to such a problem as delinquency but he himself may, within limits, occasionally need to play other roles.

### Problem Identification

The nature of the delinquency problem is perceived differently by different types of workers. In specific practice situations, these differences may seem of small degree or little importance, but, analytically and in terms of long range effect, the differences are major. The enabler sees the delinquency problem as centralized in particular individuals and groups of delinquents, contributed to by such persons as parents and neighbors, and aggravated by inadequate social resources and inefficient agency arrangements. The advocate sees the problem primarily as the breakdown or failure of particular institutional patterns. Lack of educational or employment opportunities, rather than the delinquents themselves, may be the major problem. The organizer views delinquency least specifically. Delinquency, poverty, unemployment, slum housing, and discrimination are not separate or different problems but symptoms of a basic political, economic, and social failure in the allocation of dignity, respect, income, and services by the larger society. The developer sees the problem as originating mainly in the defective behaviors of the delinquents and the insufficient interest of the adults in the local community. It is a failure of will, on the part of delinquents and the people in the immediate community, to develop their own human capacities and social opportunities.

### *The Enabler*

The enabler often initiates his intervention at the point at which some segment of the community is concerned with the actions of a particular delinquent group.

Mrs. Milanzo, president of the Turner block club, approached the worker with the problem of the kids in the neighborhood. Matters had moved beyond the talking stage. The adult residents had almost lost control of the neighborhood. The members of the gang were throwing garbage cans up and down the street, breaking banister posts, tearing antennas from the cars. The neighbors would peep out of the windows and be afraid to come out.

The enabler may also see the problem as a lack of sufficient concern on the part of the local population.

All that these people were interested in was to get more police protection. They felt whenever they called the police, they should come in, pick up the kids and take them away to jail. When you start moving beyond this, these people don't see a role for themselves. The attitude is, "We pay our taxes, let the police take care of these kids." When you start talking about their extending themselves to help the kids, they can't see it.

Also, because these kids have been so indifferent and disrespectful, they just don't want any involvement with them at all. These are the attitudes you have to break through.

The problem is also with the established agency systems at the local level.

The settlement houses, boys clubs, family agencies—they're all weighed down with administrative technicalities. Their programs are too dull and traditional. They don't reach out to these kids. They're always screaming about more money for staff but they never get around to serving these kids.

At the interagency or coordinative level, the enabler may see the problem as lack of adequate communication and sufficient services for certain types of cases. Each agency pursues its own program objectives without clear attention to what impact the programs of other agencies have. Agencies may thus be working at cross-purposes. Not all seriously delinquent youths or groups are reached, and those who are reached may receive services which are inadequate or not complementary.

## The Advocate

To the advocate the delinquency problem is mainly the result of the failure of particular institutional arrangements by such organizational systems as the courts, police, or public housing projects. The advocate may seek to defend or extend the rights of the particular delinquent or his parents against the arrogant, illegitimate, or illegal practices of a large organization. Each case is useful for achieving institution change.

> The antipoverty center's legal aid lawyer saw Manny Díaz, and decided that he would do what he could to prevent Manny and his brother from being dispossessed by the housing authority. The lawyer said that the authority had no right to dispossess Manny just because his parents were dead. The lease had been made out to his mother, but she had recently succumbed to a fatal disease. Manny, aged twenty-one, had a long record of juvenile delinquency, but had been in no trouble during the past two years and now held a steady job. The lawyer, along with the community worker, saw the case as a means of forcing the public housing authority to develop a more enlightened policy in regard to admission and retention of families with members who had delinquency or criminal records. It wasn't Manny alone they were interested in."

The advocate may frequently identify the problem operationally at the community, educational, or political level.

> We will improve the whole climate of juvenile corrections in the state, if we can get some of the key organizations such as the Children's Protective League and the Educational Committee of the State Association of Commerce and Industry to endorse a bill to bring the commissioner under civil service. Most of the legislators don't give a damn one way or the other how the vote goes. This is not a partisan political problem. It is a problem of getting the right information to the right organizations and important people who can apply pressure.

The advocate may also see the problem as a basic failure of existing service patterns, which may be irrelevant, outmoded, and beyond remedy, and may recommend new service structures and technologies. Further, the advocate is more likely than any other type of worker to define the problem on the basis of research findings and systematic data.

### The Organizer

The organizer sees the delinquency problem as symptomatic of basic defects in the whole structure of society and not in the delinquent himself, who is forced into his behavior by the conditions which society imposes upon him. Thus, delinquency is strictly a defensive reaction.

> We have gangs because their mothers and fathers are out hustling bread to beat the system. There ain't nobody home to take care of them. These kids are not delinquents. They are our future leaders.

The problem is seen as the failure of the power structure to deal with the conditions which enslave the slum population. A great many organizations may be at fault, but the police are usually regarded as pivotal in the larger community's attempts to keep down the deprived population, including delinquents, and to prevent it from effectively organizing.

> So we structured a gang convention which we held at the S——— Hotel. The three basic issues we selected were housing, employment, and police brutality. You have to understand the special role of the police in the Negro community. The mayor is the pimp, and the police are his helpers in maintaining prostitutes, who are all the people in the slum, including the delinquent, to make sure that as long as the prostitutes are good they won't get hurt.

The problem may be in the existing leadership of the minority group.

> The problem is that local leaders are ineffective. The Negro leadership, mainly middle-class professionals and businessmen, are absentees from these neighborhood efforts. They don't understand. They don't get involved. Mr. S. was bitter about this.

The problem may be of such enormity as to be beyond rational comprehension. Demons may be invoked as elements of the problem. The white woman may the the cause of the Negro male's downfall.

> Miss M. noted that some of the Civil Rights organizers are especially leery of white women in the movement. They're regarded as corrupters of black men and are there mainly to trick them. Indeed, this is one of the instrumentalities of the white power structure to seduce and weaken black men—to make them delinquents, lazy, and unconcerned with the things that really count.

For the organizer, the problem of delinquency may be seen as part of a philosophy concerning the condition of man in the universe. The Negro youth may be regarded as the chief victim of society's failure to respect and dignify individual man. The only solution for Negro youths, especially delinquents, is somehow to seize the reins of their own destiny.

> We take the position, first of all, that racism and delinquency result from the realities of the universe. Man is more important than material resources. The resources are to be utilized for man's creative fulfillment and development. But this is not the way of the universe. Instead, we have racialism— white boys go to college, but Negro boys go to jail, you know.
>
> The gangs, as we understand them, have no relationship with any positive institution, with men's values. They are locked in. Negro boys can't get a good education, a good job, a decent house. They can't be astronauts. The Harlem and Watts riots were based more on this bread-and-butter fact than on police brutality.
>
> One of our many problems is to get these kids to clarify who the enemy really is. They have to come to grips with their own manhood. They have to use their gang organizations to control and govern their own community so they'll have the right to a good education and job. Otherwise, they'll still be hitting the policemen, robbing the milkman, and hitting and killing each other because of the whole question

of self-emasculation. If the society doesn't respect these gang kids, they in turn don't respect themselves. It becomes a perpetual contest of the survival of the fittest.

The problem then boils down to the fact that a delinquent has to come to grips with his own manhood, because slaves can't run institutions.

The rhetoric of the organizer may not be logical; nor does it always provide for easy definition of a problem. But it reflects a sense of profound social disorder.

### The Developer

The developer sees the problem of delinquency as individual, group-related, and linked to social influences in the local community. Accordingly, delinquency is essentially a habit resulting from certain attitudes and traditions which are prevalent in the community. The delinquency problem resides in the delinquents themselves, in the local residents and organizations which have not learned how to deal constructively or, indeed, how to prevent the problem. A key aspect of the problem is the lack of involvement by significant indigenous leaders.

> We see the problem as mainly in a whole range of adults in the community, the parents, the storekeepers, the ex-cons, the policemen, the teacher, and even the men who hang out on the street who don't take an interest in these kids. These youths, especially the boys, are constantly on their own. They play hooky, they steal, they get into gangs and have fights. They're in sexual difficulty with the girls. But no one seems to take the time to stop and talk with them, or teach them otherwise.

The developer in the low-income area sees the delinquent as having limited access to economic and social opportunities and all slum dwellers as having no participation in the culture and activities of the larger society. But these are not critical determinants of the delinquency problem. The developer believes also that the culture of the slum may have many positives. The slum may provide a fairly adequate, if minimal, system of rewards for its members. Further, it can be made a decent place in which to live and grow up. The problem is to maximize existing opportunities and to develop the natural potentials of the people to make the most of the situation.

> John said that the organization was started about nine years ago when he and his friend Martin and another person got together and decided they might as well stay in the neighborhood and make the most of it. There really was no way out for them anyway. They decided that the streets had to be cleaned of garbage, the houses fixed up, and a respectable way of life developed. It was very important to solve the youth gang problem. The first thing was to organize people on a block basis. A young adult was selected on each block as the captain. One of his major jobs was to get the kids and organize them into different leagues, depending on age of the kid, and different sports for each season were established.

Delinquency presents many small and large problems for the developer. Almost any problem of the youth in growing up is of interest to him. He has difficulty in determining which kinds of youth problems have priority. He sets off in many directions on the assumption that the slum community is organic. If the problem is defined in one sector, it is reflected in another. It doesn't matter so much where you start or what you do, so long as the residents themselves are involved in a general way in helping young people.

### The Study Phase

The study phase may be approached in limited or extensive, simplistic or sophisticated, haphazard or systematic fashion by the worker. Much depends on whether he is a professional or nonprofessional. The enabler and the advocate are likely to engage in more extensive, sophisticated, and systematic study efforts; the developer, in more simplistic and haphazard efforts.

#### *The Enabler*

The enabler is usually a stranger to the community, and moves cautiously in any direct involvement with it. He probably spends a great deal of time becoming acquainted with its people, particularly its formal leadership, and its delinquency problems. As a professional, he has access to many sources of data about the community—agency reports, studies, and documents. Because the enabler does not represent any basic threat to the existing system, he usually has easy access to key staff persons of other organizations.

Depending on various factors—not the least of which is the cost and critical importance of the potential project or program—the enabler may engage with a team of experts in a systematic and extensive study of the community delinquency problem and the available resources for coping with it.

The enabler may also in time take to the streets to become personally acquainted with the people and the delinquency problems. These initial informal talks also become the basis for later organized intervention.

> Certainly as you are out in the community, as you stand and talk to a great variety of people, you begin to sense and get a real impact as to what the dimensions of the problem are— what it really means for kids to hate the cops and vice versa, for agencies to be confused about who it is they are really serving, for so many adults and citizen groups to be frightened of gangs.
>
> One thing you really come out with in gathering first hand information about delinquency is the wide scope and intensity of concern that exists among almost all groups and organizations in the low income area.

One of the unanticipated consequences of a thorough study of the community is that it provides the enabler with an important source of authority and control. At the end of the study, he may know a good deal (about delinquency) that is current and relevant to the community. He may be sought after not only for data about the delinquency problem but about other agency programs and general service impact on delinquents. He fills an important knowledge gap, at least temporarily.

### The Advocate

Of all workers, the advocate usually undertakes the most extensive, sophisticated, and systematic examination of every aspect of a problem. He must accumulate data on the political, legal, and administrative aspects before he can propose changes in policy, objectives, and patterns of services. Because of his commitment to legitimate procedures and the acceptance of middle-class norms, he must base his recommendations on facts and reasons acceptable to the system itself.

The study phase is important for the advocate in that it often provides a response to the pressures of funding agencies, whether public or voluntary, to guarantee that their investment in "progress" or social change is well based and will have maximum pay-off potential.

> The agencies joined together and wanted to develop a project which would demonstrate their knowledge, their experience, and methods of work. The foundations and the federal government, at first, wouldn't buy their program. They had to try something new. Some rearrangement of services was important, but even more a whole new approach to social action was recommended. Wherever they went, they were also told two things:
>
> 1. You've got to have a theoretical framework, a system of rationales much beyond the traditional program of the agency.
> 2. You have to be willing and competent to develop plans and programs subject to evaluation. This means whatever you do, you have to equip it with solid data, based in a research art.

Whether at the grass-roots, city, state, or national level, the advocate must command the basic facts to challenge institutionalized ways of doing things. The study process offers the opportunity to examine new ideas and innovate programs which have been used elsewhere and to consider their potential for adaptation to the current situation. If the advocate personally does not command the skills or expertise required, then he hires them.

### The Organizer

The organizer tends to be limited, unsystematic, and at the same time sophisticated in his approach to the collection of data. For the organizer, the study process is closely tied in with a preset strategy of action. Specific types of knowledge—usually of a political and organizational nature—which reveal key leverage points for action, are required. The nature of many of the problems of the community may be taken for granted. A vast array of facts and a thorough investigation of many organizations and their programs are not required. What must be known are the key elements, organizations, influential persons, and situations, and techniques which will produce the desired change. This highly dynamic and complex approach attempts to capture the meaning of social events in motion and to make them usable for organizational purposes and objectives at the right moment, and requires a high order of political sensitivity.

> Well, they sent me in, and the first thing that I did was to case the joint to find out who was who and why, to determine what you could expect of these various people in a pinch. We had to determine what the political make up of this community was really like, how it would react, and what we could feasibly hope to accomplish. Bitter experience had taught me long ago that the most powerful leaders and organizations are powerful so long as they are never asked to exercise their power; once they try to exercise it, it falls to pieces in their hands.
>
> You know when you begin a study of this kind you're going to have to approach it the way a master diamond cutter does. You're only going to have one blow with the hammer and chisel, and you're either going to shatter the diamond or you are going to come out with something useful, and sometimes beautiful. We studied this thing from many points of view to get the angle for our desired results.

The study process for the organizer is an exercise not so much in the systematic gathering of data as in the intuitive sizing up of situations to serve the purposes of his organization. The gathering of observations is done under great pressure because of time limitations and the fear that opportunities for action may be lost. The general public-relations impact, the morale of the constituent membership, the attitudes of the local community—these are some of the elusive but critical variables which must be sensed before analysis is made and a plan of action determined.

Potential community reaction and intervention must be carefully forecast, and earlier experiences with a given strategy must be considered. The study process blends imperceptibly into assessment, goal formation, planning, and intervention. All these phases must be subtly monitored and centralized if the organizer is to achieve even limited success in his sometimes grandiose goals.

## The Developer

The developer, although he is often quickly immersed in action projects, may be interested in some limited form of study, usually of a fairly simple and diffuse variety. The developer is, nevertheless, engaged in a continuing "natural" study phase by means of informal conversations with local people. His objective is to

> learn about local persons who are concerned with juvenile problems. Only by persistent and intensive efforts can the worker discover who is concerned about youth. The worker may discover an important lead by chatting with a local grocer or by attending a PTA meeting or by "shooting the breeze" in a teen-age hangout.

> The developer involves himself in action as he circulates in the community. He spends a great many hours on the streets rather than in an office. The study and the action phases thus seem to merge.

> The worker is encouraged to use the "house-to-house" method to . . . arouse concern for the problem of delinquency. This personal informal approach has proved itself time after time in building a maximum of local participation. The worker, therefore, must maintain his freedom of time to circulate in the neighborhood.

Often the developer has the best intentions toward, at least a quasi-systematic, data-gathering process, particularly involving formal organizations, but his lack of familiarity with agency protocol and his discomfort in dealing with professionals may impede his good intentions. He does make some contacts with agency representatives, but he gets most of his information about delinquency problems from informal, intimate associations with the delinquents and those nearest to them.

The study process may at times directly involve indigenous persons themselves. Grass-roots organizations may assist in carrying out a simple survey process, and delinquents may gather data on such matters as gang membership, housing conditions, number of liquor stores and bars, or the availability of part-time jobs in the neighborhood. For the development worker, the involvement of his constituents is a major accomplishment and an end in itself. It may require a great outpouring of indigenous organizing energy, self-discipline, and consequently personal and group satisfaction, if the job is to be perceived as well done.

### The Analytic Phase

The analytic phase comprises the application of values to the data and the conceptual refinement of the problem. For each type of worker, the process is basically the same but the content is quite different. Established organizational strategies or commitments, explicit or implicit, well or poorly developed, have ordinarily guided him in the identification and study of a target problem. The general nature and outcome of the study process are inherent in the organization's approach, and determine the development of certain types of objectives and actions. Nevertheless, the worker's personal disposition, earlier experience, and especially his professional commitment may afford greater latitude in some instances than in others. The data themselves may, however, be constraining and capable of only limited interpretation. In general, the nature of organizational strategy seems to be the dominant factor in the selecting of the significant values which will guide the analysis.

### *The Enabler*

The enabler tends to evaluate the delinquency problem as a breakdown in individual or family functioning, organizational services, or interorganizational arrangements for implementation of these services. In the final analysis, he is concerned with improving operational procedures and adding services, whether his target is the individual client or the organization. Although he may be concerned with the inadequacy of services available to the delinquent and his family or on the meager resources available to existing agencies, he will be concerned mainly with improving the efficiency of the existing system of the delivery of services. Increased opportunities—not so much in relation to basic resources of income, education, and jobs but through improved counseling, recreational, and public relations—are emphasized directly and indirectly in the analysis.

The lack of services and poor administrative technology are highlighted. The absence of remedial reading help; special vocational rehabilitation facilities and equipment; inadequate case finding and referral arrangements; the low level of staff training; the absence of interagency conference committees; the breakdown of communications among the agencies concerned with the delinquent at the policy, administrative, and program levels—all these may be noted. The lack of involvement by delinquents, parents, and citizens in agency programs may be suggested by the data.

The principal factors in the analysis are the basic adequacy of the existing structure of services, the need for additional staff, facilities, and equipment, and the importance of developing improved administrative or communications procedures. Major innovations in services are not implied except in the call to increased professionalism and stronger adherence to certain accepted standards.

## The Advocate

The advocate is, first of all, a reformist. He is seeking new policies, structures, programs, and patterns for dealing with a social problem like delinquency. His analysis generally assumes that the problem is much more serious than is contemplated by the community at large and by organizations in particular. He may engage in an extensive analytic demonstration of the ineffectiveness of existing institutions to reach their goals.

The inadequacy of basic particular organizational structures is emphasized. It is not merely that the staff is poorly trained or that poor facilities and equipment exist, but that there are major gaps or faulty assumptions in service patterns. For example, the advocate may conclude that correctional institutions are committed to custody rather than to rehabilitation; that there is too much emphasis on professional and routinized casework and too little on community work and the use of indigenous nonprofessionals; that political patronage and shortsighted governmental pay scales guide the selection of personnel in the administration of public programs on behalf of juveniles; that punitive and illegal practices of the police and courts contribute to the victimization of the delinquent and his family; that the history of abortive attempts to change institutionalized patterns may be reanalyzed in the light of the influence of corruption, community apathy, and agency resistance. The costs of inadequate attention to a serious problem may be carefully and fully itemized. The effectiveness and efficiency of several organizational patterns may be compared. Implicit in the analysis is the assumption that a major overhaul in particular opportunity- and service-providing systems is essential.

### The Organizer

The organizer is committed to revamping a major segment of the community structure, and is convinced of the correctness and justice of his position. The problem is obvious, and needs little clarification through the use of data, which are used primarily for their emotional or rhetorical appeal. The content of the analysis is not so important as its style. The problem is analyzed in its starkest, most shocking terms: analogies are made with totalitarianism, slavery, and revolution; dire predictions and threats are implicit and explicit at every turn; sweeping charges are made, often unsupported, about the complete failure of a total system.

The analysis springs also from a vision of the good society, the competent community, the full man, the conquest of justice over injustice and of love over hate. A total rearrangement of the structure of control over resources as well as of organizational purposes is implied in the assessment. Comparison may be made with positive accomplishments in other communities, usually by some affiliate of the militant organization. An underlying militance and dogmatism create a picture which has few shades of gray or indeterminateness.

The posture of justice and righteousness taken by the organizer and his organization in relation to the problem is guaranteed, intentionally and unintentionally, to precipitate opposition in all who would take the slightest exception, to the arguments presented. The analysis is usually calculated as a step in the strategy of action itself, and may be presented by means of the mass media, protest marches, or formal demands of the power structure.

### The Developer

The developer assumes that conditions in the community, particularly the delinquency problem, is serious but can be ameliorated through attention to the personal, social, and cultural strengths of the local populace. Emphasis in the worker's analysis may be not so much on aspects of the problem as on the individual persons, groups, and organizations in the community who are interested, concerned, and can be mobilized to improve the situation. The nature and scope of potential strength in the community, rather than the problem itself, have been assessed. The ability of the various individuals and groups to work together is evaluated. The delinquency problem itself seems to be taken for granted.

> The worker, for example, must cultivate (from the start) support of a cross section of residents. Despite the varied political, religious, social, and moral beliefs of the people, the worker must enlist their concern, without clashing with their beliefs. The worker must appeal for help on behalf of problem youngsters, not condemnation. Thus, the worker must be a shrewd judge of character, and he must get to know the local adults thoroughly, so as to relate the appropriate adult with each individual delinquent, or a group of delinquents.[1]

The worker's analysis must clearly demonstrate his identification with the hopes, aspirations, and values of the majority of members in the slum community, and is essentially a distillation of what the people themselves see as the problem and in what circumstances they are prepared to do something about it.

His analysis, like his data collection process, is simplistic and obvious, and is attuned to the expressed needs and interests of the community sector concerned with the problem. It tends to focus on the potential for program development by grass-roots individuals, and only secondarily considers the problem as it relates to, or can be coped with by, agencies and groups outside the community. The analysis builds on the notion of what the people themselves can do about delinquency and only secondarily expresses concern about failures in formal organizational structures or the lack of basic opportunities which can and should be provided through outside resources.

### Goals

The development of goals at different levels, especially at the policy level, is of crucial importance in the problem-solving process. The worker may, however, also specify not only what goal or

1. Ray Raymond, "The Role of the Community Worker," p. 17.

objective he recommends but those of which he disapproves. Negative goals may occur, whether or not he makes the process explicit. Goals, particularly at the policy level, may be developed in two dimensions: task and process. The worker must decide not only what he wants to achieve but generally how he wishes to achieve these ends and whether the necessary resources of structure, facilities, leadership, expertise, and funds are available. Organizational goals and decision structures usually provide the strategic context in which the community worker operates. Certain general limits of purpose and the nature of community involvement are given. It is at the level of strategic goals, especially in the more specific planning objectives, that workers exercise choice.

### The Enabler

The enabler, by definition, is concerned with achieving goals of maintenance and social growth through involvement of local or communitywide leadership, often elite persons, in a middle-class democratic decision process characterized by consensus. Small active groups, relatively adequate facilities, professional expertise, and fairly sufficient funds are generally available to achieve goals and objectives.

The enabler may also seek to bring about neighborhood or community change by reaching out to individual clients, groups, and agencies and assisting them to resolve problems of service or organizational efficiency. The agency may see its general purpose and the role of the worker in relation to multiple goals, even including a change orientation.

> It reaches out into the neighborhood, seeking to help people resolve problems by giving group and individual help and guidance, curbing delinquency, facilitating the use of leisure time and working with its clients to improve family life and bring about neighborhood *change*. Our role is to work with people to enable them to live fuller lives in a better community.

Operationally, however, the worker tends to view his objectives in the following terms:

> Identify and help youths from seven to seventeen who have become involved in the kind of difficulties which bring them

to the attention of the police. Help is offered by home visits, and discussion with both youth and family. The varied resources available in the church, the school, and the community are brought to their attention. Where the need for further help is indicated, youth are encouraged to avail themselves of the services of ministers, school counselors, and professional social caseworkers.

Develop projects and a program of speakers, trips, and films about youth problems which will result in a better-informed citizenry.

Direct police attention to chronic or developing conditions in the community which might lead to youth or adult delinquency. This enables the police to investigate and take action, where indicated.

Improve police-citizen cooperation.

At the interorganizational level, the worker may be especially concerned with communications, liaison, and consultation directed toward improving existing systems of service. A community work coordinative body may have the following types of policy goals and planning objectives, here specified as generalized and specialized worker roles:

### GENERALIZED

Develop effective communications and working relationships with and between the components of the corrections system.

Develop effective communication and working relationships between the corrections system and the treatment system.

### SPECIALIZED

Plan or participate in organizing meetings with youth officers, to develop common values related to the welfare of youth in the district or area.

Provide feedback to youth officers in areas in which their preventive or enforcement efforts can be made more effective.

Relate youth officers to other components of the correction system, such as probation and parole officers.

Act as liaison with local workers of the local department of public aid, family agencies, settlement houses, churches in their follow-up on families in trouble, clusters of problems, and the development of resources to solve problems.

Establish communication and priority with work training, Job Corps, Neighborhood Youth Corps, community action, and other urban opportunity programs to insure opportunities for youths returning to the community.

The enabler is concerned with the process of achieving goals and objectives even more than with the achievement of specific programs and structures. If he is a social worker, he is concerned with certain principles of individual and group acceptance, recognition, and self-determination of those participating in the various projects. For example, the worker may be interested in a range of social or interactional experiences for the parents of delinquents, the delinquents themselves, or other community members defined as clients:

. . . parent discussions; parent projects in the household arts; health; child care, as well as trips with their children, and projects in community service. Organizational structure should be informal, in keeping with membership understanding and skill. Intensive guidance and support would be given to help the group identify common goals, learn new and more effective ways of working together, and begin to build new attitudes about, and new ways of, coping with the wider traditional institutional structure. The role of the worker is perceived as that of resource person, teacher, enabler. While action would continue to be a primary goal, greater attention would be paid to interpersonal relations. Members should be helped to develop new ways of resolving differences, to build attitudes oriented toward change (of themselves) . . . such experience is seen as providing a bridge between present alienation and future readiness to identify with socially acceptable attitudes and traditional institutional structures.

The above statement clearly emphasizes the social-maintenance purpose of the approach of the enabler, who is concerned primarily with improving the capacities of people to fit into the existing institutional structure. He may at times be so much concerned with his process mission that the tasks of community problem solving are given secondary importance. It is not specific or general change in the external structure but general change in intrapersonal and interpersonal functioning which is required. The key goal is the development of a more adequate sense of individual and group selves.

> The real problem is keeping them together and helping them to recognize the need for themselves to do—and this is not in itself terribly important—what they want to get done.

The enabler also focuses on process objectives in his relationship with other organizations, particularly if his strategic goal is to improve the delivery of services more adequately to meet the needs of clientele. He seems more concerned with generalized process objectives than with task objectives.

The enabler, further, is concerned with certain goals and objectives he does not want to support and may even want to counter. To know what he stands for, he may have to be clear about what he is against.

> Well, I think we ought to be clear on one issue here. At the present time in community organization, there appear to be two fairly distinct models of action. The protagonist and the cooperative models. We have to be clear about that; as a social agency, we are obviously not working on the basis of a protagonist model.

Another worker justifies his opposition to the conflict or advocacy strategy in terms of process or personal development.

> In relation to the community organization program of the Youth Council, she said that their major purpose was to get kids involved in community-wide social or political action, but these kids are not ready for this kind of thing. They first have to develop capacity to make effective decisions about their own affairs.
>
> We discourage young people from participating in protest, because we believe that young people cannot control themselves, and they would undoubtedly get involved in aggres-

sive or counter-aggressive activities should they be subjected to attack from onlookers or participants. We are more interested in changing the attitudes of these kids so they can take advantage of existing opportunities and programs.

At best, the enabler may take an equivocal position in regard to the objectives of contest or conflict strategies. The problem of cooperation with other groups engaged in militant social action may often be resolved in terms of personal sympathy for, and acceptance of, the position of the advocate or organizer. But the enabler may not actively encourage members of his groups, whether they are youths or adults, to participate in such activities. For example, the nonviolent civil rights movement may be occasionally viewed as an educational opportunity, but community group members must make their own decisions. The worker may not commit himself in his official capacity to support social-reform or radical-change objectives and activities.

## The Advocate

The advocate is concerned with goals of social change through the legitimized challenge of established institutional patterns. This process tends to be primarily a specialized professional one involving other experts and key influential persons representing particular pressure or interest groups. Involvement of persons at the grass-roots level is minimal or of secondary importance. The efforts of the advocate may even be based in establishment- or maintenance-oriented organizations, and he and his small group of associates may represent a faction or special cadre interested in social change. Special demonstration projects, often financed by large federal grants, may support their efforts.

The advocate is most concerned with specific-task, rather than with general-task or process, goals. In approaching the problem of police records and youth employment, for example, he may have the following planning objectives:

1. Bring the story of arrest records and youth employment problems forcefully to the attention of the employers at the policy level, so they will want to: (a) accept the social and financial responsibility of helping youth with arrest records to

find employment, and (b) take a look at what arrest records mean and what they do not mean.

2. Recommend that the court seal arrest records for minor offenses after a one or two year interval, instead of the five years now required.

3. Apply auto-pool bonding principles to employed with arrest records, thus spreading the risk to all bonding companies.

4. Endorse legislation which sees to it that all records of minors arrested or convicted of misdemeanors are sealed.

The above objectives are task-specific, and only generally imply the nature of the process required to achieve them. Work processes are ordinarily seen as merely means to a more important end. The processes are normative, and tend to be taken for granted. For example, public relations, persuasion, and political activity concerning the passage of legislation are regarded as essentially neutral in themselves, although they are critical for the attainment of specific objectives. The process of changing basic institutional patterns—in this instance, court procedures legislation—will of course meet with considerable resistance, and requires carefully planned and executed procedures of intervention.

The contest strategy requires a great clarity and the sophisticated understanding of opposing strategies, particularly those developed by the enabler.

> You have to be on guard against those people who say that it is only the lack of saleable skills that keep youths with or without arrest records from the kinds of jobs they want. Our evidence clearly indicates that few employers care to risk a skilled and trained youth with an arrest record. They prefer a less prepared youth with a clean record. Also, we get into a lot of trouble with schools, the employment service, and even some social agencies who want to focus on training and education, without attention to the pay off of whether all kids who are equally educated and trained are going to get an equal crack at available jobs.

The advocate is much less concerned with the goal process of other strategies than with their substantive objectives. He is less antagonized by the protest and militant tactics of the organizer than is the enabler; nor is he annoyed by the paternalism and consensus approach of the enabler, as is the organizer. He is concerned with the achievement of the objective as expeditiously and efficiently as possible. He may therefore give relatively little attention to grass-roots support or the involvement of any group of persons a priori unless there is a clear connection between such support and task achievement. The effectiveness of specific program efforts, rather than the inherent value of certain organizing processes, is of paramount importance to the advocate. He sees the value of organizing as strictly a means to an end in relation to a particular issue or problem.

### The Organizer

The organizer proposes social change goals which must be achieved as soon as possible. Normative middle-class or legitimate procedures are of little concern in achieving these goals, but grass-roots participation, often on a mass conflict basis, may be a major instrument. Adequate facilities and funding are serious and pervasive problems. Public or major voluntary funding is usually not available.

The organizer is committed to the achievement of a new kind of community and society, and believes in social, economic, and political revolution, but not necessarily through bloody combat or violence. He is a blend of the utopian, the revolutionary, and—occasionally—the realist.

> Fundamentally, my goal is to free politically, economically, socially, and psychologically the millions of enslaved Negroes in the South, but also in the North today.

The organizer tends to speak and think not so much in goals and objectives as in the essential beliefs and underlying rationales of his organization or social movement. His creed is usually simple and fundamental.

> I believe every man must be reached. I believe in the dignity and worth of every individual; I am committed to the creation of those institutions in which each person can express that which is in him.

These ideas are not pious aspirations mouthed by the organizer for the benefit of his constituents or supporters. They guide him in his daily practice.

> The worker said that he was devoting all of his time to the organization, a local militant store front organization in the heart of the slum. He was given only an allowance to live on. "We have to be open all of the time. We have to take care of all the needs and all of the problems of people coming to us, whether it is for food, clothing, money, or to solve housing, welfare, or police brutality problems."

At the level of policies and objectives, the organizer tends to be highly political. He sees voter registration drives, the building of an electoral apparatus, and pressure against public bureaucracies as the keys to freedom. He may give high priority to the development of local leadership, the creation of the consciousness of Black Power, the exploring and testing of new patterns of business development and self-employment.

On a general level, the achievement of objectives is often through some kind of mass action. Decisions for such action are reached either by a small group of leaders or through full and extensive discussion among many groups of constituents or supporters. In either instance, the leader or organizer—the terms are occasionally used interchangeably—is assumed to have a special empathy and identification with the needs and aspirations of his constituents, or the latter may feel that it is in tune with the decisions made by the leader. This sharing of ideals, feelings, and hopes, whether freely or sometimes ritualistically developed, constitutes the generalized concern with process. The values of the interaction of persons on behalf of a cause are recognized but not specified.

The commitment to change is massive and pervasive. The problem of delinquency is merely one of many interrelated problems of the ghetto to be solved in the process of creating a new ideology, a new political order, a new social system. At the same time, intermediate goals or planning objectives tend not to be developed with any great degree of specificity. Protest and demonstration are evolved almost as ends in themselves. The link between immediate actions and long-range or larger goals is not developed in detail.

The focus is on negating the plans or actions of other organizations without specifying the desired alternate strategic objectives.

Our objective is to get all our groups in the community to develop pressure against the Housing Department by marching on the Mayor's office next Tuesday morning. We want them to build their housing project somewhere else.

We want the school system to remove all the mobile class rooms in the slums. We are going to picket every mobile unit, until they are all removed and a commitment is obtained from the Board that permanent facilities will be available.

The strategy of conflict is fraught with many internal as well as external organizational hazards. The absence of intermediate goals creates an opportunity for many contending points of view. At times, the involvement of many subgroups in making key decisions may lead to unclear objectives and conflict, internal and external. There is little normative restraint on the kind of objectives or projects which may be selected.

F. S., one of the organizers engaged in a low key diatribe against his organization, felt his organization wasn't doing enough, particularly in the area of jobs for young people. He suggested several schemes to solve the problem. One would be to picket all loan shark operations in the area, until they each hired one, two, or three young guys. These youths, many of whom were presently members of gangs, or ex-gang members, could provide protection for the stores. These would not have to be full time jobs for the kids.

Jack said that his organization had been much more effective in reaching low income Negroes in their neighborhood than the Civil Rights people. The Civil Rights or civil dollar boys were outsiders and middle class Negroes who were more interested in changing the school system, or getting middle class type jobs. On the other hand, they wanted more welfare rights, especially improved aid payments, right now.

The problem of the serious lack of funds by militant organizations may at times severely compromise conflict strategy. Internal struggles seem to flourish when even token remuneration cannot be made for long hours of work done and risks taken. Then too, establishment organizations sorely tempt militant groups by their promise of funds in exchange for the cessation of protest activities. The ideals of militant organizers may wear thin under the constant pressure and bickering within the organization and attacks from outside.

> There aren't too many of us who really have solid commitments. Most of us are just waiting for the real good job with the poverty program to come along.

Integrity is, however, not necessarily so easily compromised in all militant organizations.

> Jack rambled on. He was slightly drunk. He sat in my car for quite a while before joining the marchers. He spoke about the efforts of the various organizations to capture his group. The city anti-poverty board had offered them $350,000 to conduct various service programs, if they would desist from their diatribes against the city administration. One of their church sponsors didn't like their campaign on slum housing and refused to renew their grant. They, therefore, had to curtail a job counseling and placement program they had started. This meant some staff had to leave. Some of them were bitter about this.
> The "Z" Family Fund also tried to interfere and tell them how to run their programs. They refuse to knuckle under the whims of other people. This means they are forever operating on a shoestring. They want to be independent, but "most people don't know what headaches we got when we refuse money. Some of our staff are up in arms."

The most serious challenge to the moral authority and goal commitment of militant grass-roots or civil-rights organizations comes from established organizational and political structures. The competition for community loyalty and support is often won by the organization that most effectively distributes resources or pays off to key people in the low-income community.

> We were able to meet with the leaders of the major gangs throughout the city. We had a convention at which all these leaders were present. We set up a program and these guys and their groups were ready to implement it. But we didn't

have any money or jobs for these guys. We couldn't compete with the Poverty Program. They dumped money. They prostituted people. We couldn't compete with the political machine and the social agencies. They undermined what we tried to do. They pulled the kids away through a street work program. They had two million dollars for recreation and job training. We couldn't compete with that.

The street workers began to talk with these kids. So after a while when we again met with the gang leaders and discussed their participation in the Civil Rights marches, they asked, "Now, if we get put in jail, who's going to take care of our children?" I knew we had lost right then. In a non-violent movement every man stands on his own. "Who was taking care of your children before we came?" Then we got to squabbling about the whole question of economics—that is, bail money and pay for their work with us.

### The Developer

The developer aims mainly at a series of specific process objectives directed to social stability. He believes that the effective solution of any community problem depends on the constructive efforts of local persons who want to make the best of things and move ahead slowly. The achievement of the specific task goal may be less important than simply getting people to work together effectively on very limited projects. The social involvement of people in matters which intimately and directly concern them is the strategic objective of the developer, who believes that "people themselves can do something about their own problems, if they are stimulated and guided, banded together, and given a definite program of action."

The developer is sensitive to the norms and values of the low-income population and to their needs for guidance and direction in achieving their expectations and aspirations. There is little complexity here. Community work is almost anything which brings people together to give them a sense of personal and cooperative accomplishment in relation to some immediate neighborhood problem.

In this group, we have developed a Little League. Some people say it is a baseball group, but to me it's community organization. In a sense, any time you can organize people, what's the difference between organizing people around the problem of delinquent youngsters or organizing them around a baseball program?

Also, I'm a firm believer in solving the little problems; to heck with the big ones. Let them take care of themselves. If I can make these different activities of the group effective, that in itself is a worthy occupation.

The developer and his community group may frequently sense a threat to their integrity from larger organizations. Although it may be difficult to fight superior force, opposition must somehow be developed.

The main problem, right now, is the Housing Authority. They're adding the new buildings to the project. We have trouble enough without facilities. There is no high school, shopping center, or real good recreation program. We've been concerned about these things, the past two or three years. And now the project is to get larger. We've contacted all the important agencies concerned—the Planning Commission, the Housing Authority, the Board of Education. There's been a lot of talk. We're not clear yet as to what's fully involved, and we don't have a program of our own to recommend. We just want something done to ease the problem that is going to get worse, and it is bad enough now.

The developer is threatened not only by aggressive and expansionist establishment agencies but also by militant or radical organizations. The basic "go slow" maintenance, adaptive philosophy may even be challenged from within the organization.

The worker said that he spends a lot of time with some of the members of his organization who are drawn to certain "Black Power" ideas. He has tried to counter their approach, but doesn't know how successful he's been. He tells the people that the militant "Black Power" groups only want to use them as instruments. They simply want to take over the neighborhood and the government. He says if these kinds of "Black Power" people take over, Negroes will be third-rate, not just second-rate citizens. He said that Negroes are not now in a position to take over political control or run anything. They don't have the confidence, training, or skill for these things yet."

The developer operates from day to day, often on an individual youngster or family or organizational crisis basis. The mutual support and cohesion derived from simply working with others may be his most important achievement.

### Planning

Each worker must make decisions about projects, methods, participants, and the schedule or timing of his efforts. Each worker is constrained by organization strategy to develop certain types of plans of intervention. Although all workers make use of tactics or techniques of organizing, interorganizing, and intraorganizing, the priority and emphasis by which methods are carried out will tend to vary. Thus, the enabler will be relatively more concerned with interorganizational and administrative problems than the developer or organizer will be. The advocate will emphasize problems of interorganizing. The organizer will obviously concentrate on problems of organizing. The developer will focus on problems of organizing and, to some extent, of administration. Interpersonal influence is exercised by each worker, although with different emphasis on its elements. For example, the enabler may be more concerned with techniques of education and persuasion; the organizer, with bargaining, pressure, and threat. The methods may be carried out at different levels of sophistication and of course for different purposes.

As indicated earlier, the enabler and advocate are more likely to work with elite, professional, or middle-class leadership in the execution of their tasks; the organizer and developer, with grass-roots and lower-class leadership. The enabler and the developer are more likely to concentrate on the provision of field services; the enabler, on attempts to improve services of other agencies; the advocate, on legislative and administrative studies; the organizer, on protest and political action. Whereas the advocate and the organizer will be concerned with maximum feasible speed in the accomplishment of objectives, the enabler and the developer will tend toward slow, deliberate action. Each will attempt to relate particular methodologies, participants, and projects to some larger concept of organizational goals.

### The Enabler

The enabler approaches the planning of his complex job within a framework of consensus and accommodation. He organizes his community or facilitates its mobilization around a specific problem or issue with the idea of solving it amicably and achieving some sense of greater cohesion among the group members and with organizations in the community. He is concerned with community improvement in terms of a framework of social stability. For the enabler, the problem-solving process tends to stress the study or planning phases.

> One of the major problems you have is that as soon as you get a group together to look at, say a bad sanitation or police brutality problem, the first thing some people want to do is get up a petition or go down and picket. But this is not going to solve their problem. This is a one-shot deal, so you try to get the people to study the problem and invite the sanitation inspector or police captain to come down to your meeting. You let him know how you feel about it and understand his problem. You might even develop some program which shows that you are doing something to combat the situation and are set to cooperate. Then you are in a better position to call on him for additional services or improvement in what he's already doing.

The enabler and his group are extremely concerned with persuading other organizations to extend services in the slum community, whether in intensified police coverage, additional recreational services, or enriched school curricula. Continued and repeated efforts are made to reach, communicate with, and educate such officials as the alderman, school principal, agency administrator, or police commissioner about the problem and what specifically is required to solve it.

The enabler may plan direct, often case-coordinative, services. He provides internal and external organizational referral or mesh-

ing services to support individual clients. The distinction between
the caseworker and the community worker may become blurred.

> Mrs. L. is a new staff member. She has a college degree. Her
> job is that of liaison person with the girls who are in the
> Neighborhood Youth Corps project run by the agency but
> located in the Welfare Department. This program was set up
> for delinquent girls or street girls so they could learn how
> to adjust to the job as well as to perform certain duties
> connected with occupations such as typist, assistant homemak-
> ers, practical nurse, etc. These girls will be assisted to com-
> plete their duties, to get to work on time, not to get frus-
> trated, not to get into arguments. She will counsel the girls,
> assisting them with literacy problems and developing perma-
> nent job prospects for them. Mrs. L. will also have to work
> with the administration in interpreting the needs and prob-
> lems of the girls. She is to be a kind of mediator and publicist
> for these girls.

The planning phase of community problem solving is clearly
controlled—if not directly determined—by the enabler. He is
usually very influential in the selection of community leaders to
implement the various programs, and may even sit on important
committees or boards.

> Mr. F., the director of the agency, said that he had made
> prior decisions as to who would be the best people to have on
> the board. When a few of the key people had gotten together
> with him afterwards, they came to the same conclusion. A
> specific slate of officers was decided upon. He was not really
> ramming certain people down the throats of the community.
> He was sensitive to community process. If he had selected
> people who would not fill the bill, then he would have had
> some kind of negative response. Apparently, they were
> pleased with what he had done.

The enabler sets the limits on the community problem-solving
process by advising on appropriate methods, structure, timing, and
focus.

> Many members of the group have mentioned the necessity of
> clearing off abandoned cars from the streets and alleys of the

community. But I feel that these things can be handled at the proper time. Our major agency focus is on delinquent kids. You can't permit these people to spread themselves too thin in terms of the great many interests and activities that attract them.

The enabler has many abilities and techniques—making speeches, arranging basketball tournaments or tutoring programs, drawing up proposals for funding of various projects. He may even, on a limited basis, and as a last resort, engage in protest activities, which are usually highly circumscribed and are planned to avoid open clash with authority. The following are instructions by a gang work agency on the planning of "peace squad" activities after an outbreak of serious delinquency.

> The worker should fully understand this mission. The group should not be allowed to talk or answer hoot calls. The spokesman (usually the worker) is the only person authorized to talk to the press or interested individuals. The protest march should last from 30 to 45 minutes and no longer . . . night marches should not be planned, and the best time is from 1 P.M. to 5 P.M. None of our groups should be encouraged to miss school unless agreed upon by the director, and written permission is received from the school and parents of boys under 21 years of age.

The police, social agencies, and established community groups are informed about these protests and invited to cosponsor them. Further, awards may be given for outstanding participation or effort in these demonstrations. An instrument devised to challenge the establishment is thereby turned around in order to serve and maintain it. Protest may thus be domesticated and become another legitimate program activity.

### The Advocate

The advocate plans his job on the basis of his commitment to social change, and is prepared to wage a battle on behalf of an individual, group, or issue, using accepted channels of redress. He selects those key systems—education, welfare, or housing—where his activities can be most useful and often where there is already some readiness for a change.

Father Smith spoke of the need to be constantly alert to break down in the school system. Many kids are kicked out or transferred for no good reason. They have, however, developed a procedure whereby if any kid complains of getting a raw deal, a staff member immediately goes out to investigate. If the youngster has been kicked out without due process, for example, one of their lawyers goes after the Board of Education. They have generally been successful in keeping kids in school and in some cases getting youngsters sent to real good schools in the city. The main point is that the school system is much less willing now to kick any kid out. We believe our pressure may have contributed to this.

Conflicts among subgroups or staff of the organization oriented to advocacy are more likely to occur at the specific planning than at the goal development stage. The issue often arises of the extent of planning and implementation of program by non-elite groups.

The discussion was between Mrs. Selznick, the supervisor, and Jack Tanner, the worker, assigned to solicit the aid of a group of youths in improving police-community relations. Captain Jones of the local precinct had decided to go ahead with Mrs. Selznick's idea of setting up a store front manned by the police to improve communications and relations between the police and community. This was to be one of two pilot units for the entire city. Mrs. Selznick and Captain Jones had worked out most of the details of the program. But Jack objected. He said that the matter should not have been arranged at this top level. One of the representatives of the youth group should have been involved in the negotiations. They had expressed such interest in participating from the start. It was apparent that Mrs. Selznick was quite "enamored" of her own accomplishments, and convinced of the correctness of her approach. She was reluctant to go along with Jack Tanner's point of view. "These were delicate complex operations. Maybe the kids could be entrusted at some other level." Jack was still unhappy.

At the planning stage, the advocate is always alert to the use of other organizations and programs to serve his organization's purposes. His access to, or control of, large resources of expertise, funds, and power often makes it possible to co-opt the energies of other organizations in relation to specific projects. Representatives of federal, regional, and local antipoverty organizations and *ad hoc* citizen's groups may play this advocacy and co-optive role. Certain militant organizations or agencies capable of service innovations are often the targets of such efforts.

> Larry Atkins said that after the riots, one of Shriver's aides contacted them and some of the other Black Power organizations. They were asked to meetings at the regional office of O.E.O. Larry said most of the fellows who went were young, in their early twenties, and were very naive. "We were promised a lot of projects and jobs. Some of them came through, but most of them didn't. Meanwhile, we held our breaths and tried to quiet things down in the neighborhood."
>
> Larry added he guessed the federal boys were able to embarrass the mayor and some of the local bigwigs. They were interested in some changes, but didn't want things to go too far.

If we were to categorize planning objectives and goals in political terms, we might label the advocate an aggressive liberal, the organizer a left-wing radical; the enabler as a middle-of-the-roader, and the developer a conservative. The advocate may be under constant pressure from organizations representing an accomodative approach, on the one hand, and a radical approach, on the other. He is under special pressure because of the flexible and innovative character of his organization and the substantial resources he commands. To maintain his integrity, the advocate must exercise a great deal of discipline and perseverance in the exercise of his plan. The advocate's dilemma is to decide at what point negotiation and compromise obtain realistic organizational change and at what point continued pressure by him results in negative feedback and open conflict with other organizations. Further, he is often placed in a precarious mediating position between the enabler and the organizer, and, as a result, is in danger of either opposition or co-optation from the dominant and stable power position of the enabler and the radical ideology and appealing methodology of the organizer.

## The Organizer

Although the organizer is militant and seems less concerned with the nature of means selected than with the achievement of significant goals, he may in practice be as much—or more—concerned with certain means for achieving objectives than with the objectives or goals themselves.

A civil rights organizer, with a special responsibility for the organization of gang youths and their incorporation into the civil rights movement, explained his plan of action as follows:

> One of the major problems we see is that a lot of money is taken out of the slum neighborhood, but very little is brought back in. This is particularly evident on the issue of slum landlords. We want these landlords to donate money back to the community. So we planned housing co-ops in which the tenants would not pay their rent directly to the landlord but to a special co-op agency. Some of this money would go back into repair of the buildings and stay in the community.
>
> One of the ways of bringing about recognition of these coops by the power structure was to get all the gangs of the city together to march on the Mayor's office. We could do the same over the issue of police brutality.
>
> This kind of action galvanizes these kids. It would give them a sense of their own power, even if they didn't win out the first time. It would deal with the whole frustration and apathy business. Just the dynamics of getting together and going down to the Mayor's office would set in motion a whole lot of very good things.
>
> I have no illusion that marching by itself will solve the problem. But it does raise the issue. You've got to keep demanding that the man atone. You've got to keep it up till the whole rotten structure begins to change.

Organizing in relation to one problem could lead to organizing on other problems.

> We would assign each gang to an area for inspection of buildings. We would find out who owns the buildings, what

condition it was in. The gangs would assign their own building captains to keep tabs on what's going on in respect to each slum structure. We would develop information and files on the tenants. We would then be ready to organize the tenants in each building for a whole variety of purposes: voter registration, improving schools, solving the public aid problem, jobs, etc.

The planning of action is often elusive and *ad hoc,* and there may not be appropriate follow-through. Expediency may determine the nature of the action, and unintended consequences may result.

Father Hughes spoke of his tactics. At one point, they were picketing one of the local stores. He had forgotten the reason why. But it turned out they were marching in front of other stores nearby. Apparently, the picketing was keeping people out of these stores as well as the one they were specifically concerned with. Father Hughes said this was a gimmick he had stumbled on. It was a way of increasing power and pressure. These other stores could then bring their own pressure to bear to get the target storekeeper to change his practice. "This is an approach we are using fairly frequently now."

Mr. Vinson of the local welfare council office noted that not long ago one of the Black Power organizations got a lot of young people together to march on the police station to protest some problem of police brutality. Before they got there, though, they smashed the windows of a couple of stores and threw a Molotov cocktail into a liquor store.

The great amount of attention given to problems of organization may also result in less attention to interorganizational problems. There may be little communication, interaction, or joint planning with other organizations in relation to a given problem. The tactics and activity of militant protest occasionally create pressure for greater militancy, greater self-determination, organizational self-realization, and exclusive participation by the population affected by the problem, and the scope of interaction with other like-minded individuals and groups may be narrowed as a result. In one form, this becomes an issue of black power.

> "Our organization stands for Black Power." Jackie and Lennie, former gang leaders, agreed there are too many middle men around. They are the so-called leaders, the preachers and the clergy who try to speak for the community.
> "If they live in the ritzy, new integrated neighborhood, who do they think they're speaking for? They're living on easy street. They're not experiencing it anymore. The same frustrations—they can't feel them. It's time we stopped being defined by others."

At the same time, the more extreme the commitment of the organizer and his organization to change, the more likely he is to avail himself of those elements in the community who are most dissatisfied, rebellious, and deviant. A primary source for new members and leadership is the delinquent gangs, who are considered by some as the most powerful potential instrument of pressure on the system.

> Every organizer of a Black Power or even of some civil rights and neighborhood organization believes that if he can get the gangs behind him, he will have tremendous bargaining power. First, gang leaders can control these kids, and all we have to do is hire these leaders. These kids are a threat to the community and the power structure. They create more disturbance and antagonism than any other group. We can capitalize on the threat. These kids can furnish help to us, if we just channel their energy and time. If worse comes to worse, these kids would constitute the ideal nucleus for any urban guerrilla warfare.

### The Developer

The key planning objective of the developer is to bring together those who represent the indigenous interests of the community to do something on their own terms about problems which concern them. An essential element of his organizational role is his personal familiarity with, acceptance of, and influence over a wide range of individual persons in the community. Ideas for projects and the rationale for their accomplishment are personalized or developed on an informal basis.

> Mrs. Jameson announced at the meeting that she had an idea for solving the truancy problem. She had talked about it with the local public school principal and had already gotten his support. The project called for appointing a half dozen or more parents to patrol the school area each morning especially to see that children were not truanting. Any child who was on the streets or known to be in his apartment and playing hooky—while his parents were working—would merely be escorted to the school principal's office.
>
> She had spoken with other members of the neighborhood organization and with a few people on the outside and they were willing to give it a try. What she wanted now was just a formal okay for her idea from the steering committee.

The developer is constantly seeking to involve local citizens in the activities of his organization.

> For those who indicate that they cannot become active, the worker can suggest such forms of indirect help as giving financial aid or serving in advisory capacities or becoming interested in a particular case of delinquency, e.g. playing the role of big brother or big sister. The enthusiasm of the worker is essential in relating each community individual to some activity of the group. A good worker is constantly striving to persuade local people to assume some specific responsibility. He strives to fit each person to a task which it appears the person can do. Prospects are almost tailor-made to the interests of people. Perhaps one of the most frequent remarks characteristic of a good worker is, "Will you do this?"

The personalization of the community work process does have its hazards. Formal organizational procedures may not be clearly established and understood. Planning itself may be haphazard and at times nonexistent. Organizations and workers tend to drift from one activity to another. The organization may be held together by the personal involvement of a relatively few persons. Subgroups may attempt to control the organization for their own personal interests. There is limited concern for interorganizational effort.

Although the community organization is theoretically open to all members of the lower-class community, it tends to attract only those who are stable. The genuine lack of attention to social issues fails to attract the more militant persons of the community; the group's commitment to respectability or, at least, to acceptable lower-class norms and values tends to close the group off to more deviant or unstable lower-class elements. Whether the community group comprises mainly property owners, tenants, young adult graduates of delinquent gangs or whether it is a block club, improvement association, social and athletic club or PTA, it sooner or later sets norms of appropriate community conduct which it seeks to enforce through its activities and projects. The worker's and the group's major function is, therefore, a socializing or stabilizing one. The major means of the worker for exercising influence are persuasion, education, and group pressure. He tends to avoid conflict as too threatening to the normative structure and viability of the group. His major orientation is coming to terms with the local environment, not substantively changing it.

With the advent of the antipoverty program, some development organizations have been converted to quasi-social agencies. With an increase in funds, the developer is now able to plan for many additional projects and services for the use of social workers, lawyers, and health personnel. The basic grass-roots character of the organization is, nevertheless, retained.

> Mr. Wiley, the director of the area organization, said that a lot of the money was going directly into improved facilities, but some was going into upgrading staff as well as hiring two part-time social workers. They were Department of Public Welfare workers, not trained, but good people, who grew up in the neighborhood. They would be doing special counseling with the tough kids.
>
> But mostly they would be doing what they had in the past. Much of their work didn't require special training. They would continue to organize baseball and football teams among the youths. They would expand their block programs to other streets. No great skill is required, only that people

know the neighborhood, "who was in it, and what problems people had." To some extent the advent of the antipoverty funds meant that volunteers who had been doing much of this work for nothing would now be getting paid.

The roles of the enabler, advocate, organizer, and developer are not necessarily mutually exclusive. One worker may plan activities which are characteristic of another approach. Admittedly, the purpose of the activity planned may be quite different. Futhermore, the roles are not necessarily incompatible in any given community problem-solving situation, particularly where immediate objectives are complementary.

## Intervention

Problem solving is a complex, overlapping series of stages and processes. Identification, analysis, goal setting, planning, intervention, and evaluation—all are interrelated, and each has its own action process. Then too, each type of worker has his own specific approach, professional background, and personality, and consequently may have his own characteristic limitations. The enabler may be paternalistic or overconcerned with the value of services; the advocate may have difficulty in distinguishing advocacy from protest; the organizer may select means which are self-defeating; the developer may find himself developing his own capacities rather than those of the community he is serving.

### The Enabler

The enabler educates and persuades his group to engage in some kind of action. But he structures situations—he sets the stage and establishes general plans and objectives. He is also especially concerned with the development of relationships—his own with the group, and those of the group with other individuals, groups, and organizations in the community. He urges his group toward goals of service.

I wanted this community group to take more responsibility in programming for delinquent youths. I had gotten to the point where the group had asked the police for increased patrol service and gotten it. At this point my problem was to get the group to understand that this was only a temporary or limited answer to the problem.

It was possible that police coverage might diminish when you have youth who are acting out. They will move from one corner to another as long as there's police pressure, but as soon as the police move on to something else, the youngsters return and the problem of vandalism, extortion, and disturbance reoccurs.

I told the group that what we have to do now is to try to get ourselves to relate directly to the kids. We have to help these kids who have no respect for us, and no concern for our property. This was a difficult point to get over to the group. I said that one of the things needed was attention and support from them as neighbors. What did I mean by this? Well, they might start in by just speaking to the kids rather than ignoring them. Perhaps the group might plan some activity that might involve them with the kids. Just off the top of my head, I suggested a trip or a picnic, organizing and supporting a softball team. In some cases it may be possible to get these people to counsel some of the kids, to explore with some of them why they hung out on the street corners. They might go to their homes and visit the families of these kids.

The enabler serves as an intermediary between needy people and available services and, in so doing, exerts influence on both the client and the service agency.

> The community group is very concerned with the lack of recreation and group work facilities acceptable to these youths. They requested the worker to contact the lone church which had a well-developed youth program, mainly directed to the middle class or good kids, in the neighborhood. The worker contacted the church and in the course of discussion and subsequent negotiations between the church and the community group, the church agreed to provide a room and a youth worker for the group. The community group agreed to provide certain types of gym equipment and to subsidize 25 percent of the youth worker's salary.

## The Advocate

The advocate is concerned with establishing a new set of structural conditions which may eliminate the basis for a problem or at least significantly modify it. Although he usually operates at organizational, interorganizational, and legislative levels, he may also be innovative in the direct delivery of services to clients or constituents.

> Dr. Y, a psychologist, with a large grant from the National Institute of Mental Health, spoke enthusiastically of his project: "The bearded admirer of Summerhillian philosophy sees his role as a 'non-authoritarian' one. He is there to support the kids and make sure the activities stay within legal bounds. He explained that the organization attempts to take pressure off boys and girls who have been pushed around for much of their lives, by parents, by police, and by a 'custodial school system' which is more interested in discipline than in education. They have a great deal of freedom in devising their own educational and social action activities."
>
> The psychologist also has secured assistance from lawyers in fighting police brutality cases, affecting the youngsters in his program. The newspapers, under his goading, have exposed conditions in the local schools. He has made contacts with state and national legislators, demonstrating the need for new understanding and new legislation especially in the area of employment and education.
>
> Dr. Y sees himself as a pioneer and hopes that his experiment, at least in parts, will be emulated in the ghettos of other cities.

The advocate is often a social reformer, utilizing all manner of legitimate means to prick the conscience of the community. He is a professional, often with a full range of research tools at his disposal and with important connections with change-oriented power centers in the various local, state, and national systems. He seeks to modify old patterns or at least to invigorate them, but prefers not entirely to replace them, merely to shake and bring them up to date. Although he is relatively free to attack many of the organizations in the community which are slow to change, he usually does so within certain legal and legitimate constraints.

### The Organizer

The organizer is an idealist, a charismatic leader, a man of the people. He is in a hurry, angry, often intolerant of opposition. His ideology of radical change requires that he have the capacity to engage people in some new, deep, even transformational experience.

Well, I think that a person dealing with non-violence has got to understand himself. He's got to understand his strengths, his weaknesses; he's got to know where he's going. He needs a profound passion for people, in spite of what they do for him or to him. In spite of what happens and how long it takes, he has to love them. He's got to know how to deal with the frustration of people, how to create conflict, and yet turn it into an act of love.

His actions are guided by his belief in the innate potentiality of people—they are not only what they are but what they can be. To him, the terms "delinquent" and "criminal" are meaningless, if the deviant can demonstrate his commitment to a social cause; further, how he helps the cause is less important than the mere fact of his commitment.

Frank O'Connor pointed out one of the fellows, in his early twenties, who was just driving away in a sharp, red, foreign sports car. Frank said that the fellow was a volunteer on the program and came around periodically. He had been very helpful. He had a great many contacts in the community and the fellows and girls look up to him. He used to be the toughest youth gang leader in the area. He was now a highly successful pimp, with a lot of girls working for him. This fellow carries a minimum of $500 in cash with him at all times. If the organization ever needs a crowd for a rally or a protest march, if ever kids are to be recruited for some program, or a gang fight stopped in a hurry, this is the man to do it.

### The Developer

The distinguishing characteristic of the developer is his identification with the life style of his constituents and his personal investment in the social and cultural development of the community. He has to interact with his constituents in the simplest of programs and in the most down-to-earth manner.

> If the community committee does a painting job, for example, the worker may lend a hand. He would do so not only to help the committee, but also to keep the respect and confidence of the committee. He writes letters, and may even lend money out of his own pocket to people in the organization. He is part of the community.

In a lower-class community, he may function as a bookkeeper, an officer of the organization, a recreation supervisor, a personal counselor. He may make crucial decisions for the group. His diverse abilities and intimate knowledge of the community may be truly astonishing. He may evolve into a kind of politician without portfolio.

> We have a man uptown who is one of the most skilled community workers in the city. The man is about fifty. He's been in the particular community for six years, now. He knows every crack in the sidewalk. He knows thousands of people. There's nothing this guy can't move locally, the agencies as well as the people, everyone. This man may take kids shopping, if their parents are not available. He goes to weddings and funerals. If there is an emergency or a crisis, he is one of the first people to be called. He doesn't want to leave the community. He gets a tremendous kick out of his job. He's become a landmark.

Because of the enormity of the problems faced by the lower-class community, and the general lack of resources and developed human capacities to deal with them, there may be excessive dependence on the skills of the developer. As a result, the talents and interests of others in the group may not be fully developed, and the apathy and weakness of the community may be perpetuated.

### Evaluation and Feedback

Community workers do not often systematically and meaningfully evaluate their own efforts. To most workers, evaluation and feedback comprise merely simple case histories and general evaluative statements, which often reflect a lack of clear or full understanding of agency goals, objectives, and priorities.

In general, sufficient evidence does not exist to establish the comparative effectiveness of any of these approaches. It is important still that we look closely at these approaches, particularly at specific elements which appear to give some promise of utility or success. This is essential, if we expect ultimately to specify and then assess which models of intervention are successful under which conditions.

# 3

# Influence

In community work, influence—that is, the general act of producing an effect on another person, group, or organization through the exercise of a personal or organizational capacity—underlies the worker's organizing, interorganizing, and intraorganizing efforts. Like the term "relationship" in casework or psychotherapy, influence may indicate the effect of a direct interpersonal interaction. More important, in community work it suggests an indirect effect upon persons and groups who may not be in immediate contact with the worker or his organization. Influence usually depends less on the purely interpersonal aspects of relationship and the satisfaction of direct personal need than on meeting organizational and collective expectations and needs.

In community work, influence is directed toward stability or change in group, organizational, interorganizational, and community systems rather than in individuals per se. The community worker is of course concerned with the interpersonal functioning of individuals, but he deals with it in terms of its consequences for solving community problems.

The concept of influence assumes that key components of the community work system—individuals, groups, organizations, and workers—are connected by a formal or informal communication system by which information is sent and behavior modified. It assumes that the components of the system have preferences, mainly explicit, about social choices, and that the system has a procedure for rendering choices or making decisions. Further, the concept of influence assumes that there exist various media of exchange whereby individual components seek to arrange agreements on advantageous choices. Finally, it assumes that each component has certain values, knowledge, and skills relevant to a problem of social choice and that the system has criteria for solution. Influence therefore assumes a process by which the organization calls forth and organizes knowledge and skills as systematically as possible to reduce the difference between present and preferred position in relation to other organizations.[1]

## The Nature of Influence

In the exercise of influence, the worker attends to two kinds of circumstances—first, a series of social events which have or will acquire a set pattern and recur regularly; and second, those events which are and will continue to be in a process of becoming, "in which, in individual cases, decisions have to be made that give rise to new and unique situations."[2] The first circumstance requires what may be called a more routine or administrative exercise of influence; the second, the organizing and interorganizing or largely political aspects of community work. The boundary between these two classes of influence is rather fluid, however, and at times vague. "For instance, the cumulative effect of a gradual shift of administrative procedure in a long series of concrete cases may actually give rise to a new principle. Or, to take a reverse instance, something as unique as a new social movement may be deeply permeated with 'stereotyped' and 'routinizing elements.' "[3]

The kind of influence circumstance we are mainly concerned with in this chapter is the political. The worker develops a point of view based on a set of values which he communicates and attempts

1. James G. March, "The Power of Power," pp. 65–66.
2. Karl Mannheim, *Ideology and Utopia*, pp. 112–13.
3. *Ibid.*

to have others accept in relation to a specific community issue or problem. Others in his organization or an allied organization join and interact with him to produce a point of view representing some common group or organizational interest. The worker with the aid of the group, or vice versa (since the decision process may be initiated by others, also), then attempts to educate, persuade, negotiate, bargain or coerce other groups and organizations to accept a position. A situation of interorganizational cooperation, competition, or conflict may ensue.

Community work in American society is concerned with a market process by which various individuals, groups, and organizations with either different or similar programs and interests compete, contend, and sometimes cooperate to achieve particular ends which bear on the solution of a problem such as delinquency. In order to achieve his own end or that of his organization, the worker must select an appropriate form of influence. For example, in the solution of a community crisis resulting from a series of juvenile gang killings, the worker and his organization may seek to develop a job training and employment program in cooperation with other organizations. Or he and his organization may compete with organizations whose projected solution to the problem may be different, that is, they may prefer psychiatric facilities or tougher police enforcement. Even organizations which start out cooperating toward an objective, may end up competing for funds, community support, and control of the program.

Implicit in the use of influence is the notion of power—ability to establish control over another group or organization. The notions of influence and power for our purpose may be used interchangeably. Power is perhaps a more effective or stronger influence. The idea of authority must also be noted in any discussion of influence. Authority, as used here, has a broader meaning than ordinarily employed. It is viewed as a legitimate right to make decisions and bind a collectivity. In this sense, all members of groups or organizations may have authority to exercise decision-making power.[4] Rather than differentiating between those having and those not having authority, we are distinguishing between those who have relatively more and those who have relatively less. Thus, when we

4. Talcott Parsons, "The Political Aspect of Social Structure and Process," p. 76.

speak of an organization that is philanthropically oriented, we are referring to a situation where professionals and bureaucrats have relatively more authority than clients or constituents to make decisions to bind the organization. So, too, in a self-determinative organization, constituents and indigenous members have relatively more authority than professionals or bureaucrats to make decisions.

## The Value Base of Influence

Inherent in the political character of the influence exercised by the community worker is the desire to ameliorate, control, or prevent the occurrence of a social problem—say that of delinquency. Influence, therefore, is always connected with some comprehensive view of the world, and its use is founded on and therefore implies a "definite conception of history, a certain mode of interpreting events, and a tendency to seek a philosophical orientation in a definite manner." [5] Influence, in its organizational form, and in all its community work uses is partisan. In the final analysis, it contributes to political education.

A commitment of the community worker to the values of the democratic society, moreover, may compel him to transcend the norms and goals of the particular agency or organization which employs him. Of course if the goals and objectives of the organization are consonant with his or his profession's conception of democratic values, there is little problem; but if the practices of the organization, and indeed the community of which it is part, reflect an inconsistency or antagonism toward democratic values, a good deal of tension may arise. (We are suggesting here that there is or should be a basic democratic value component to the worker's role and his exercise of influence which is not and should not be strictly a function of a particular organizational approach. The commitment to democratic values, in its political or influential sense, presumably is inherent in professional training, at least in the United States.)

The difference between a worker representing strictly an organi-

5. Mannheim, *Ideology and Utopia*, p. 148.

zational interest and one representing a community interest is illustrated in the following remarks by a maintenance-oriented worker.

> Yes, but at first I wasn't an organization man. I was a community man. I have changed my point of view because I've got to look out for my own security and future. You know for the worker in a social agency or any organization, there is always a dichotomy. He works both for his organization and the people. The best interests of the organization are not always the best interests of the people in the community. I don't care what you say. Organizations go into an area and set up programs for a variety of reasons. Somebody wants to run for office. The board of directors want to feel they're doing good—but on their own terms. Somebody is looking for a grant and money to expand staff. Another guy is in it for the publicity and prestige. There are all these things and more. The people in the community—the clients—they know that organizations are in the neighborhood for the good of the organization and only partly for the good of the people in the community.

It is my opinion, then, that the community worker ought to enter upon his job with a clear commitment to democratic political ideals. The worker may need to pursue a process of change within his own organization, despite its strategic orientation, and for him to effect such change may require a great deal of time and effort. (For example, he may need to persuade his organization to accept greater participation by clients or constituents in significant decision making.) Closely connected with the democratization of power is the pursuit of those goals and objectives which serve to increase dignity and respect for each individual in the community. A worker may not necessarily be effective in his efforts at internal organizational change, but it is important that he realize he is not solely a creature of organizational goals and structure.

Since the conception of social and economic welfare in a democratic community is incompatible with the notion of an unbridled free market system, the exercise of influence in community work requires commitment to a more equitable allocation of social and economic opportunities. Whatever differences of race, character, intelligence, or wealth distinguish the delinquent from the non-delinquent magnify themselves under conditions of unrestrained competition. "For every advantage that an individual derives from competition only simplifies the additional piling up of advantages. It is as though after every race the runners were permitted to start again from the position in which they found themselves at the termination of the previous race." [6] Unequal social and economic status of the delinquent results in the possession of unequal authority, which in turn simplifies the procedures for denying him social prestige and income-producing opportunities. Once a dominant group—in this case the middle-class members of the urban white community—has increased its relative status beyond a given point, it becomes progressively easier to incapacitate minority member lower-class youths and their families, in the process, further enhancing the dominant group's position. The unchecked free market system, therefore, tends not only to protect inequality but to increase it.

What we are arguing is that the community worker's influence needs to be a function not only of organizational structure and community practices (often determined by an extreme free-market ethos), but also by commitment to a set of beliefs about basic human welfare inherent in the democratic society. The worker, therefore, may need to influence the very organizational structure out of which he operates to implement his own social democratic values, since he must take a certain political or partisan position in support of the social welfare interests of that segment of the population generally defined as socially inferior, especially the delinquent—and this may place him at times in conflict with his own organization.

## The Reality Structure of Influence

Although this idealistic position is essential for the worker, it is insufficient for the day-to-day exercise of his influence. Abstractions of social and political democracy may be legitimately opera-

6. Richard Lichtman, *Toward Community: A Criticism of Contemporary Capitalism,* pp. 16–17.

tionalized in different and contradictory ways, but the worker is compelled to operate within a framework of individualistic as well as social democracy. His dilemma is how to reconcile organizational self-interest and interorganizational rivalry with the welfare interests of the client or constituent population.

A community is not cohesive; it is a series of individuals, groups, and organizations in varying forms of individualistic communication and interaction. In the more pragmatic conception of reality confronting the worker, he must deal with a system of dispersed inequalities.[7] There are many kinds of resources for influencing people and organizations, but they are generally unequally distributed. In this view, it is assumed that individuals and organizations best off with respect to access to one kind of resource may be badly off with respect to other resources. No one type of influence necessarily dominates all others in every or even most decision situations, and influence may be effective in some areas and in relation to certain issues but not to others. There are, in reality, sufficient leverage points to achieve many organizational ends for a great variety of people in our society. The individualistic or pragmatic position, however, provides a beginning point for the exercise of influence that the social democratic or idealist position does not, under present community circumstances.

Conflict is produced in such a system. There is constant struggle for the achievement of organizational objectives, often at the expense of other organizations—and without necessarily contributing to the welfare of a client or constituent population.

## The Resources of Influence

Effective influence or power depends on the availability of resources to enforce decisions. An influence resource may be defined as " 'anything' that can be used to sway the specific choices or the strategies of another individual," [8] group or organization. Resources may be classified into at least four major categories:

7. James M. Buchanan, "An Individualistic Theory of Political Process," pp. 26–28; Robert A. Dahl, *Who Governs?*, p. 228.
8. Dahl, *Who Governs?*, pp. 225–26.

normative, economic, coercive, and conditional. These are heuristic or suggestive categories, yet possibly useful in clarifying distinctive meanings of influence. Normative resources include the worker's professional knowledge, experience, and skill; his agency's legitimacy, sanction, or reputation; the social, moral, and political standing of the members of the group or organization which supports or represents the point of view of the worker; and the right to vote or express an opinion. In this form, influence operates on the intentions of the person to be persuaded and through positive channels. It tries to convince him that acting as the persuader desires is in his own and the collective interest. It relies on the acceptance of the intrinsic argument, or on the prestige, the expertise, the moral or traditional standing of the person or group presenting the argument.

Economic resources include access to funds, credit, facilities, staff, services, jobs. Coercive resources include a variety of means, which have in recent years been regarded as militant, for example, a boycott, a strike, picketing, sit-ins, protest demonstrations. It may depend on the application, or threat of application, of psychic, social, or economic force which results in deprivation, but generally, coercive influence avoids the direct application of physical sanction. It seeks negatively, through embarrassment, annoyance, and discomfort, to control the decisions of a target group. Finally, the fourth category of resources, conditional, serves to enable or condition the use of the other resources; conditional resources would be availability of time, energy, intelligence, friendship, popularity, personal esteem, or charisma.

The resources may be used conjointly and, even more important, they are interactive and indeed may stimulate or augment each other. Thus, the professional expertise of the worker may be functional for the acquisition of economic resources, while the use of coercion may initiate a process whereby members of the organization acquire prestige and consequently access to the political structure.

All of these propositions assume, of course, that influence resources are effectively used. Where the worker or organizational members are not successful in their influence attempts, a deflationary resource spiral occurs. Lack of economic resources lowers the prestige of the organization and vice versa. In other words, resources well expanded produce other resources; poorly used, they represent an expenditure without a return.

In a number of respects, influence resources, whether they are normative, economic, coercive, or conditional are like money.[9] They may be borrowed to expand the system's power capacity or the effectiveness of its influence, and they can be contracted for from some higher or more general level of organization or system of control.

Influence, ordinarily, is not increased alone by the manipulation or improved management of the internal resources of the organization; an exchange of resources with some part of the environment is required. The organization borrows resources but promises, implicitly or explicitly, to return the resource or its equivalent, with a dividend. A federal agency's funds are utilized successfully by a local organization and in return the federal agency justifies its existence and may demand additional funds from Congress for its own organizational expansion. The prestigious member who lends his name to the organization's program or cause derives added prestige and personal satisfaction from the successful outcome. The community members who participate in a boycott of an unfair merchant may obtain lower prices on goods which are sold to them. Staff who successfully expand the organization's influence may get increases in salary or professional satisfaction.

The influence process, therefore, is carried out as an exchange relationship.[10] It is consummated through an agreement, implicit or explicit, in relation to the solution of a given operational problem. The size of gains made may depend on the strengths, relative and absolute, of the parties to the transaction. This assumes, further, a patterned set of relationships (or nonrelationships) between organizations characterized at various times by competition, conflict, or cooperation. In a community system characterized by competition and conflict, there may be losers as well as gainers in the transaction.

Finally, it should be noted that the worker does not stand at the peak of a pyramid in the influence process. The worker negotiates, cajoles, exhorts, beguiles, charms, pressures, appeals, reasons,

9. Parsons, "The Political Aspect of Social Structure and Process," pp. 96–97.

10. Buchanan, "An Individualistic Theory of Political Process," p. 33.

promises, insists, demands, threatens, but he is also responsive to and needs the support of others.[11] He must acquiesce or may even succumb to the influence of others in his own organization or outside of it. In the process of negotiating with representatives of his own and other organizations, his attempt at influence is inevitably modified.

## Patterns of Influence

Influence is also organizationally patterned and takes on certain characteristic institutional forms. The normative, economic, and coercive kinds of influence expressed in particular actions become patterned and recognizable as cooperation, or competition, or conflict. Emphasis in this section is on conflict as currently one of the basic modes of influence in our highly competitive free market community system.

### Cooperation

Cooperation suggests a condition of mutuality of influence efforts in relation to goals, objectives, and procedures. It allows for a state of peaceful, smooth, and positive interplay of influence efforts in a joint enterprise. While this condition often characterizes the stable family and the cohesive peer group, it is less commonly seen between formal groups or departments within organizations, even less so between independent organizations. Cooperation, however, does take place between organizations. It may occur through agreement on basic goals and norms, such as on the right to life, liberty, health, a job, a decent education for all, and on rules governing discussion, dissent and voting. While this kind of interorganizational cooperation may seem often to be largely ceremonial and ritualistic (except during major crises, such as war, flood, and pestilence), it serves, nevertheless, an important purpose in the resolution of community problems. It provides a sense of solidarity in regard to basic values among a wide range of organizations and their membership, thus permitting competition and conflict to occur within acceptable bounds. It also provides an

11. Dahl, *Who Governs?*, p. 204.

initial or terminal point for other patterns of influence and mitigates their potential destructive effects. (Organizations may also cooperate frequently in minor ways, more to exchange general information and concerns or to stimulate use of slack organizational resources than to exchange significant resources.)

A significant form of cooperation is most likely to occur among two or more organizations under perceived attack from some third party or coalition of organizations. For example, in the aftermath of riots or serious gang fighting, social agencies tend to develop common objectives and procedures of action (at least temporarily) to withstand attack or threat of attack from various other organizations or sectors of the community, such as the newspapers, grassroots organizations, the legislature, or the police department. The organizations most likely to cooperate are establishment- or maintenance-oriented organizations, since they have most to lose in any radical shift of public opinion.

We should note that, in general, change-oriented organizations appear to have less to gain through cooperation than do social-maintenance–oriented organizations. Alternately, change-oriented organizations may have less to lose by not cooperating with other organizations. Finally, it would appear that over the long run, organizations with similar goal orientations are more cooperative than organizations with dissimilar goal orientations.

## Competition

Competition is a scrambling for resources, which may include clients or constituents, funds, facilities, and other means to achieve individualistic organizational objectives. It refers, nevertheless, to a complex network of relationships and "nonrelationships" of individuals, groups, and organizations tied to each other in seen and unseen ways, and it indicates a rivalry of persons and organizations for resources which may or may not be known to each other in the complex community system. In every case of competition, however, "a third party makes a choice among alternatives." Two or more organizations attempt to influence that choice through some "type of appeal or offering; and choice by the third party is a vote of support for one of the competing organizations and a denial of support to the others involved." [12]

12. James D. Thompson and William J. McEwen, "Organizational Goals and Environment: Goal Setting as an Interaction Process," pp. 410–11.

Competition is the most typical influence pattern employed by organizations in their relationships or interactions with others. It is often, but not always, a form of struggle in which organizations are vying for a "prize that is not under the control of either, where efforts are therefore parallel rather than offensive and defensive."[13] It has a limited socializing or "civilizing" effect in the sense that competitors have to adapt to third-party organizations or interests; sometimes these third parties represent a public sector. The implicit agreement among competing organizations is usually that they will abide by certain rules of conduct in order to capture the funds, support, or other prize for which they are vying. Goals, objectives, and the means of organizations are thus open to partial control by the environment. "One of the values of competition is that it may prevent unilateral or arbitrary choice of organizational goals" or "correct such a choice if one is made," and it makes it sometimes possible for the community to eliminate "not only inefficient organizations but also those that seek to provide goods and services the environment is not willing to accept."[14]

Competition and conflict have in common the fact of struggle, but they differ in the main objective of the struggle.[15] For the worker engaged in a competitive set of influence relationships, the objective is to appropriate scarce resources; for the worker engaged in a conflict set of relationships, it is to defeat the opponent organization. Conflict and cooperation have in common the direct interaction and involvement of organizations with each other—but for different purposes. Further, contact is indispensable for conflict and cooperation but not for competition. There is an impersonal quality often found in competition which is not common to cooperation and conflict. Conflict particularly "evokes the deepest emotions and strongest passions and enlists the greatest"[16] influence efforts, but it tends generally to be more intermittent than cooperation or competition.

Each pattern of influence may be converted to the other. Competition becomes conflict when organizations clearly identify each other as opponents and attempt to impair the other's influence in

13. Robert C. Angell, "The Sociology of Human Conflict," p. 101.
14. Thompson and McEwen, "Organizational Goals and Environment: Goal Setting as an Interaction Process," pp. 410–11.
15. Angell, "The Sociology of Human Conflict," p. 113.
16. Robert E. Park and Ernest W. Burgess, *Introduction to the Science of Sociology*, p. 574.

relation to the same, but not mutual goal. Competition ordinarily assumes an absence of, or limited, communication. Therefore, if communication improves, there is the possibility that competition will turn to conflict or cooperation. The end result of either competition or conflict, however, may actually be quite similar: program or agency destruction.

### Coalition and Cooptation

Coalition and cooptation are means of averting threats to the stability or existence of organizations or groups standing alone, means for enforcing cooperation among previously competitive groups which have now joined together to engage in rivalry with other nonmember organizations.[17] We may describe their influence patterns as forms or subtypes of competition as well as of cooperation, however, since they are utilized primarily to enhance or increase the strength of the organization or organizations in the competitive struggle over scarce resources.

More specifically, cooptation operates through a "process of absorbing new elements into the leadership or policy determining structure of an organization as a means of averting threats . . ."[18] Influence is exerted formally and informally to diminish the opposition of leaders of other organizations. In effect, organizations coopt each other through a process by which goals, objectives, and procedures of action are mutually modified. Cooptation may be regarded as a device both for preventing a competitive struggle from breaking into open conflict and also for strengthening organizations in their competitive struggle vis-à-vis other sectors of the community.

Coalition is a more durable way of solving a competitive situation. It strengthens several organizations in their efforts to obtain resources, usually for a common or related program. Coalition has been described as a "joint preference ordering"[19] on the part of a number of independent organizations. For example, various organizations estimate that they have more to gain by competing collectively for a grant to serve delinquent youths through a joint pro-

---

17. Thompson and McEwen, "Organizational Goals and Environment: Goal Setting as an Interaction Process," p. 412.

18. Philip Selznick, *TVA and the Grass Roots*, pp. 13–14.

19. J. A. A. Van Dorn, "Conflict in Forward Organizations," p. 118.

gram of counseling, manpower development, and street work than by competing separately. Common, or at least similar, objectives and procedures are worked out. Coalition, however, is still an unstable system, since the needs and the power of organizations shift over time, and greater gain may be perceived by a member of the coalition, if it acts alone. Bargaining may restore the balance, however, if a new agreement can be arranged whereby resources are reallocated differently.

Both cooptation and coalition are usually conscious and rational processes. Workers from each organization must determine whether relative costs are higher or lower through use of cooptational and coalitional devices than straightforward competition, or even conflict. The organization which elects to maintain its strictly competitive stance may lose the prize. On the other hand, cooptation and coalition may involve a surrender of some organizational integrity and a partial sacrifice of goals and objectives, and therefore of some individual organizational influence. Thus, the worker must carefully calculate and guide his organization in either surrendering autonomy and augmenting resources, or not doing so when in a projected final accounting such surrender may prove unprofitable.

### Conflict

Conflict is struggle for mastery of resources possessed or controlled by another individual, group, or organization, defined as an antagonist. Conflict arises when there are mutually exclusive goals, objectives, or norms espoused by the contending parties such that if the goals, objectives, or norms of one are fulfilled or dominate, it will be at extreme cost, or threaten the survival, of the other. It occurs when divergent interests cannot be compromised. Conflict may also occur within an organization. In this case it may result from "empire building," [20] that is, the extreme efforts of an organizational unit to enhance its jurisdiction and authority, or overly strong identification by members with subunits of organization.

Conflict appears to be an influence pattern of increasing use and community concern. The growing awareness of extreme difference among sectors of the population has created great tension. Im-

20. Herbert A. Simon, Donald W. Smithburg and Victor A. Thompson, *Public Administration*, p. 297.

proved media of communication have, in part, contributed to rising cultural aspirations especially among lower-class minority groups. With increased hope and desire for success status but without improved access to opportunities, alienation and despair—especially in urban ghettos—develops. Conflict, planned or unplanned, violent or nonviolent, becomes the natural order of the day.

Conflict is probably not an influence pattern of preferred choice by any organization. It tends to occur when organizations are far apart not so much in their goals or means, but in their immediate objectives, and when normative and economic resources for the exchange of influence are not present or used. Coercion may be the only influence resource which is not in scarce supply. Furthermore, the use of coercion may be used to stop the flow of other resources.

## Perceptions of Conflict

Conflict in previous decades has been viewed primarily in psychological and social-psychological terms. It is only recently that explanations of conflict have returned to an older sociopolitical tradition. In general, organizations oriented to social stability still tend to view conflict in psychological terms; organizations concerned with social change are prone to view it in political terms. It is likely, furthermore, that during periods of major change and crisis which threaten the basic social order, the sociopolitical aspects of conflict are given more emphasis. Organizations support new or old programs according to these differential perspectives. In the final analysis, however, even the psychological perspective implies a political point of view—social maintenance.

Social-stability organizations see conflict as a result of an irrational set of attitudes and behaviors. It signifies a "disorderly and inconsistent value system, faulty calculation, an inability to receive messages or to communicate efficiently." [21] Its purpose is the release of collective anxiety and hostility. In this view, conflict is precipitated by people and organizations which project their own hostility onto other, "actually nonthreatening," [22] organizations, usually of a social maintenance or control character, which then see themselves as unjustly subjected to attack, accused of practices which are misconstrued and of policies for which they are not

21. Thomas C. Schelling, *The Strategy of Conflict*, p. 16.
22. Ross Stagner, "The Psychology of Human Conflict," pp. 52–54.

basically responsible. Conflict is thus seen as internal anger, arising for a variety of reasons, which now becomes attached to an objective—organization or individual—perceived as "devil." In this process, important evidence goes unnoticed, and an exaggeration of attributes, which otherwise seem only slightly good or bad, takes place. The conflict situation may also be explained as the result of previous competitive failures by an unequal population for scarce resources. The unsuccessful resolution of previous situations stimulates an overflow of hostility and leads to generalized antagonistic, destructive, and possibly violent behavior.

This psychological view denies the legitimacy of certain forms of conflict, for example, violence. In addition, although violence is not regarded as an appropriate channel for release of hostility, alternate means for its constructive release (or the provision of significant means to avoid frustration) are not provided. The problem of prevention and later of controlling the build-up of community hostility is not solved within such a strictly psychological framework. Frustration and hostility are merely submerged, a state of apathy rather than stability is created, and cycles of hope, frustration, violence, and apathy may occur with increasing intensity.

Unlike the psychological perspective in which conflict is negative, something to be avoided or controlled, the sociopolitical view is that conflict may be as important or more important than cooperation or stability for the production eventually of a viable social system.[23] The conflict pattern, even if destructive to particular individuals, groups, and organizations, contributes in a larger historical sense to positive social development.[24] According to this tradition, conflict and controversy are the "lifeblood of a democratic community and their suppression would be the antithesis of democracy and freedom."[25]

Conflict viewed in this light is essential to the approaches of both the advocate and the organizer, but in the view of the advocate, conflict or contest must be bound according to com-

23. Georg Simmel, *Conflict*.

24. Park and Burgess, *Introduction to the Science of Sociology*, pp. 583–84.

25. William Kornhauser, "Power and Participation in the Local Community," p. 489.

monly accepted rules and regulations; they are a prelude to compromise by the "ins" and "outs" of the system. The advocate assumes that basic values are legitimate and ought to be kept intact, but that they need to be more fully realized, and that this can occur through regulated conflict. Under no circumstances is the sanctity of life to be violated, and property rights are to be modified only according to due process. For the advocate, conflict is an expression of vitality in a democratic community.

For the militant organizer, conflict and even violence may represent the only device for individual and collective liberation from a system which must be changed. Basic norms and values may be questioned, and legitimacy itself may no longer stand for a process founded in community or societal consensus. The established norms and the laws of the community are regarded as a response to the will of the dominant group and are techniques of oppression rather than an expression of basic social compromise.[26] The militant and his group regard themselves as excluded from norm- and law-making processes and must appeal to nonlegal, "more abstract principles," such as justice and natural law. For the militant organizer, conflict may take almost any form, may ebb and flow. It temporarily subsides when resources are depleted and resumes when support is again available—until the community is basically changed and a new value system is institutionalized.

## Positive Functions of Conflict

For the advocate, above a certain, not clearly delimited threshold necessary for the basic cohesion and stability of the community, the more conflict, paradoxically, the more stable the relationships among individuals, groups, and organizations, and the closer the state of community relations to the values of the democratic society.[27] It is essential in any community that there be struggle over ruling positions, challenges to organizations in power, and shifts of parties in office. There must, however, be consensus on the "peaceful" play of power, the adherence by the "outs" to decisions made by the "ins," and the recognition by the "ins" of the rights of the "outs." [28] Furthermore, it is essential that conflict

26. Austin T. Turk, "Conflict and Criminality," pp. 346–47.
27. Angell, "The Sociology of Human Conflict," p. 99.
28. Seymour Martin Lipset. *Political Man,* p. 1.

be crosscutting and shifting in the alignment of groups. Numerous conflicts that crosscut each other prevent their "cumulation to form a basic line of cleavage." [29]

Social and political conflicts under these constraints have important positive values. At the personal level, they make us "feel that we are not completely victims of circumstances." [30] They give vitality to relationships among individuals, groups, and organizations. They serve to preserve relationship, or indeed to constitute it, which without conflict would dissolve into organizational apathy and indifference to community interests. If there were not power and right to oppose other organizations, groups would be "driven by desperation" [31] to total conflict and complete destruction of relationship. Where there is no organized opposition, riot, chaos, as well as apathy are potential outcomes of severe social disparities.

To the extent that conflicts can be organized and legitimized, they may be regarded as socially unifying. The civil rights movement, for example, through its conflict engagements, has constituted a unifying force, and it may be hypothesized that the aggressiveness of Negro (or other minority group) warring gangs should be diverted and politicized, and controlled conflict established, particularly in relation to key social issues of community development. Gang fighting theoretically may be thus reduced, since it represents a less politicized and a more unregulated form of conflict.

Relative to the delinquent, the gang, the poor, or any socially deprived population, conflict in a democratic society serves the major function of developing pressure for the reduction of "inequality and status ascription" which occurs in any community over time. "The only groups which have an 'interest' to modify and reduce inequality are the underprivileged" and those which support them. "The only effective restraint on the power of the dominant class is counter-power." [32] And the primary instrument of such restraint is conflict, manifested in such organized devices as the strike, boycott, demonstration, and finally the vote.

29. James S. Coleman, *Community Conflict.*
30. Simmel, *Conflict,* pp. 19–20.
31. Park and Burgess, *Introduction to the Science of Sociology,* pp. 504–5.
32. Lipset, *Political Man.*

Conflict even in its undisciplined form acts as a danger signal and a catalyst. If it is clearly regarded as evidence of hatred and envy, want and desire, then the very outbreak of violence may be a first step in removing the conditions which have produced it. Conflict of a disorganized nature may be viewed as a symptom of a disease and indeed as an effort of the community organism to free itself of the disorder. Thus, conflict may be the precondition for efforts at resolution of a problem, the means—particularly if it is planned and controlled—for bringing to bear a range of competence to its solution.[33]

### Conflict Resolution—Bargaining

Community organizations in their day-to-day operations tend to be engaged in two types of conflict, episodic and continuous. Sometimes, there is transformation to a third type, terminal conflict.[34] We have said that conflict is waged not so much in relation to differences over goals and norms, but with regard to particular interests or objectives, to secure scarce resources in relation to these objectives. Episodic conflict tends to develop periodically, particularly over economic resources, at times of budget hearings, elections, or the passage of legislation. The point of the struggle, of course, is to secure an advantage in the distribution of rewards which are available only periodically. Continuous conflict arises out of competitive day-to-day struggles for resources, both normative and economic. It tends to be controlled, delimited, and low-keyed. Examples include organizational rivalry for clientele, staff, and community prestige.

In general, continuous and episodic types of conflict are held in check because of the specificity of interest and the crosscutting affiliations of staff, board, and clientele or constituents with other organizations. The antagonists on one issue may be allies on another, and neither party can destroy the other without jeopardizing some of its own interests. The militant civil rights organization which attacks the youth-serving agency for its failure to provide adequate services may yet join with it to petition or accuse the local school superintendent of a policy of student segregation.

In terminal conflict, the object is a single redistribution of power

33. Lewis A. Coser, "Some Social Functions of Violence," pp. 8–18.
34. Theodore Caplow, *Principles of Organization*, pp. 331–57.

and resources, and the outcome is relatively permanent, inasmuch as one of the organizations or its program may cease to exist. This type of conflict is infrequent, but it does occur, even between maintenance-oriented organizations, often in response to a sudden shift of power and search for new resources. Police and youth-serving agencies have in the past decade engaged in this kind of struggle over the issue of control of resources to do something about the problem of delinquency. Invariably, the police have been successful, with the youth-serving program occasionally destroyed in the process.

Conflict, however, must at some point be replaced by an accom-modation or a cooperative pattern of influence. The process of terminating conflict may involve bargaining. Bargaining refers to the negotiation of an agreement for the exchange of resources. The exchange, of course, may not be an equal one. Bargaining is inherent in all conflict, some competitive, and indeed all coopera-tive situations. In any explicit negotiation, whether between friends or enemies, the threat of reduced cooperation or increased disa-greement is either implicit or explicit, and gains and losses are implied in these threats. The term threat does not necessarily connote aggressive or hostile actions, however, at least not at the conscious level. Bargaining, however, is not necessarily the diver-sion of some fixed quantity of resources such that the gains of one party are the losses of the other. Bargaining sessions are not only "constant-sum" but also "variable sum gains," so that "The sum of the gains of the participants involved is not fixed so that more for one inexorably means less for the other." [35]

Bargaining may require the sacrifice of freedom of choice through explicit commitment to a position. The power to constrain an adversary depends paradoxically on the power to bind oneself.[36] "In bargaining, weakness is often strength, freedom may be free-dom to capitulate, and to burn bridges behind one may suffice to undo an opponent." [37] The power of the commitment depends on communicating it persuasively to the other party; the problem arises when the opposition's commitment is also strongly held, and an impasse is reached or a breakdown in negotiations occurs when

35. Schelling, *The Strategy of Conflict*, p. 5.
36. *Ibid.*, p. 22.      37. *Ibid.*, p. 28.

neither side has the ability or willingness to modify its commitment.

There are certain institutional conditions which affect the bargaining situation.[38] For example, the worker as a bargaining agent for his group or organization may be given specific instructions that are difficult or impossible to change, or he may be given some freedom to operate, with the likelihood that his negotiations will be acceptable to his group. On the other hand, the worker may have an incentive structure of his own which differs from that of his organization, and the resolution he achieves may be acceptable to him but not to his constituents. Also, the commitment of an organization, particularly a public organization, may be narrowly circumscribed by law. For example, only a certain amount of money is available to the local antipoverty agency and much of it is earmarked for certain kinds of programs. The director of a CAP program is limited by law (and priorities) to certain commitments.

Another kind of condition which affects bargaining is the presence of a contingency issue and the potential use of it to influence the outcome on the issue or problem under consideration. For example, when a worker seeks funds from a board of education for improved educational facilities in the ghetto community, his hand is strengthened if his antagonist knows that the issue of integrated education on a citywide basis could be raised. Finally, the condition of threat or actual use of power from a higher system of authority affects the bargaining situation. The pressure, seen or unseen, from the mayor or an important legislator, may make a significant difference.

The fluid nature of bargaining needs to be considered. The variability of information and attitudes is a key dynamic in negotiations. Thus, new information and changed attitude may be brought to bear in an interaction situation such that alternatives satisfactory to both contestants may be revealed. Additional factors are introduced into the relationship which open up new opportunities for trading and further benign moves,[39] and basic norms and values may be uncovered which serve to integrate seemingly disparate interests. Differences can be integrated and compromised among conflicting and competing parties, and, thus, even where the

38. *Ibid.,* pp. 28–29.
39. Kenneth E. Boulding, "The Economics of Human Conflict," p. 177.

resources of the participants are clearly unequal, the outcome is not foreordained. Conflict thus may be of critical value in the achievement of objectives by relatively weak organizations. It may serve the purpose, moreover, of workers from all kinds of organization. It is of special value in the achievement of change objectives by the advocate and the militant organizer. Workers usually differ not so much in whether conflict is employed but in the manner and frequency of its use.

In general, the enabler and the developer are more oriented to the use of a cooperative form of influence and depend heavily on normative resources for the achievement of agency objectives; the advocate and organizer tend to be more committed to the use of conflict and coercive resources. The competitive pattern of influence appears to be widely employed by all types of workers. Finally, as we shall see in the next chapters, these various influence patterns are the building blocks of the worker's basic methods of organizing, interorganizing, and intraorganizing for the solution of a community problem such as juvenile delinquency.

# 4

# Organizing the Local Community

## *The Social-Stability Approach*

The community worker engages in both organizing and interorganizing activities. The geographical scope and functional complexity of the organization, as well as its strategic commitment, determine which method he emphasizes. Thus, the worker with a neighborhood organization is concerned primarily with organizing; the worker with a metropolitan welfare council, with interorganizing.

## The Significance of Local Organizations

Since at least the time of Tocqueville, the institutions of local self-government and voluntary associations have been regarded as integral to the success of the American democratic system. Local organizations

> inhibit the state or any single source of private power from dominating all political resources; they are a source of new opinions; they can be the means of communicating new ideas to a large section of the citizenry. They train men in

128

political skills and so help to increase the level of interest and participation in politics.[1]

Tocqueville and others feared certain trends of modern society —industrialization, bureaucratization, nationalism, apathy, the absence of meaningful citizen participation, and especially the lack of organized opposition to the power of the central government. Local and voluntary organizations were viewed as countering the negative consequences of the mass society. Centralized power was regarded as fundamentally evil, and the ideal society was predicated on the diversity of organized interests. The expression of local interests was expected to lead, through competition and conflict, to basic cultural and political unity.

In every community, no matter how apathetic or problem-ridden, there are untapped leadership, positive human resources, and institutions which can contribute to the well-being of both the local and the larger community. Any local community organization effort may, therefore, be

> designed to reach even the most disorderly and disorganized community and seek out its constructive human resources. The reference here is to the islands of orderliness and normality which survive in even the most unfavorable social settings, and which are presented by self-sustaining social groups and by integrated persons of high morale. The forms taken by these groups differ from neighborhood to neighborhood. In some, they are found in the religious institutions; in others, in mutual aid societies, or clubs set up to promote the recreational sports, or socializing interests of its members. . . .
>
> Generally, these groups and persons are groping toward the goal of upward mobility, that is, the improvement of status in the wider social order. It is this activity together with sentiments of protectiveness toward their children which represent the social forces to be harnessed to the service of delinquency prevention. . . .[2]

1. Seymour Martin Lipset, *Political Man*, p. 52.
2. Henry D. McKay (Statement), Committee on the Judiciary, U. S. Senate, 86th Cong., 1st sess., S. res. 54, pt. 5, *Juvenile Delinquency*, p. 172.

A case has also been made *against* the value of local organizations in the solution of local problems, the charge being that most existing organizations, even indigenous associations in slum areas, are generally not concerned with the welfare of its most needy inhabitants. While the membership of a block club or neighborhood organization is lower class in many of its characteristics, its identification may be primarily with middle-class norms and values. A self-selective membership process rules out the problematic members of the ghetto community; home owners, white collar workers, business people, representatives of the stable, upwardly aspiring groups gravitate to such local associations, and they look down upon those persons who are deviant and especially upon families which produce delinquent children, regarding them as immoral, shiftless, and worthless.

Another criticism is that many of the organizations, albeit labeled grass-roots, tend to be undemocratic.

> . . . Very few of them regularly afford their members an opportunity to vote on the stands the group will take. Very often the leader will speak for the group without having consulted the membership. Many of the organizations consist of small cores of local activists who have no significant following and little status in the local community . . .[3]

Further, it is argued that local organizations are inherently limited and usually exaggerate their influence.[4]

Nevertheless, despite serious questions about the viability and value of local organization, sufficient evidence has accumulated which indicates that local community organizations under certain conditions can be effective social instruments.[5] They can dissolve apathy and stimulate interest in local problem solving; they can provide low-income membership with new perspectives about their own capabilities; they can afford significant experiences in self-help, develop political leadership, and provide important social services.[6]

3. J. Clarence Davies, III, *Neighborhood Groups and Urban Renewal*, pp. 206–7.
4. Muzafer Sherif and Carolyn W. Sherif, *Reference Groups*, p. 292.
5. Saul D. Alinsky, *Reveille For Radicals*.
6. Marshal B. Clinard, *Slums and Community Development*.

## The Interpersonal Orientation

The main purpose of the interpersonal orientation is to initiate a set of attitudes and activities by which members or representatives of a local community seek to identify, and to take action to solve, community problems—not, as in the change orientation, to take action to secure particular reforms or achieve organizational power.

### Establishing Relationships

A fundamental ingredient of organizing is establishing relationships with many different persons and representatives of groups who are concerned with a problem like delinquency. The enabler is likely to give special attention to meeting representatives of the formal structure—probation officer, youth worker, teacher, and minister; the developer, representatives of indigenous groups—block club leader, head of the ladies' auxiliary of the church, and especially parents of delinquent youths.

The worker uses every opportunity and device possible to elicit interest and draw people together to do something about a serious problem. He must be articulate and persuasive.

> I first went to the churches and talked to the ministers. If any were interested, I asked him to set up a meeting with members of his congregation. I would talk with these people about different possibilities and usually suggest that all these little groups get together to really do something about the problem.
> Often it was one key person from a group who was especially interested, who might have had previous organizational experience, and whom I could count on to bring people down to the next meeting.

The professional enabler systematically approaches the establishing of community relationships.

> The first thing I do is talk to the heads of the various agencies, especially the schools, the churches, and the police

department. I also go to some of the storekeepers, and the places where kids hang out. I make contact as well with the organizations that seem to play an important role in the lives of adults, Kiwanis, or the Lions' Club. The people who are most helpful to me are often the school personnel and the police. I find out what the main problems of the kids are, what the schools are doing about them. I find out who the main people in the community are, who are the most active. Then, I talk with them and get their ideas and feelings. I begin to probe the agencies as to what they see as the direction of their programs and how they plan to meet the problem. I get a line on people who should be invited to a first meeting to consider the particular delinquency problem. This is my first step.

## Communication

The process of communication is extremely important in any effort to organize individual groups and agencies. The enabler must state his purpose with clarity and conviction as he makes his contacts. In low-income areas, failures in communication may constitute a major barrier to any community problem-solving endeavor. Indeed, the problem of communication itself may need to be solved before any others are attempted. For example, one grass-roots organization gave first priority to its communication problem:

1. To assist our probation department in communications with our delinquent youth.
2. To aid and assist our delinquent brothers and sisters in their communication problems with various probation and law enforcement officers.
3. To aid and assist store and property owners and their communication with people of the community.
4. To aid and assist our teachers in their communication problems with delinquent students.
5. To seek a line of communication with various departments of public service. . . .

There are two key aspects to the worker's job of communication: he must facilitate the flow of information about community problems to the community group, and he must make certain that the role of the group is understood by other significant sectors of the community. The community group may need to discuss various aspects of the problem. They have to understand what their objective should or can be, and whether and how they can manage the resources to carry out a proposed plan. This internal group discussion phase serves to involve people in giving opinions, making decisions, and developing relationships with each other, and it may take a great deal of time. But preliminary discussion of the problem must at some point come to an end and a plan of action finally set and carried out.

The solution of any given problem, however, is never in the hands of the community group itself, not at least in the complex urban areas. Support for the purpose and program of the community group must be enlisted. "Selling" key groups in the community on the value of a particular project depends on communicating how the solution will directly affect the contributors.

> After four years, the committee people are beginning to sell the little businessmen such as the grocers, the pharmacist, the cleaning establishment on the idea of a recreation center so the kids won't be on the streets and in their stores causing them all kinds of headaches.

The scope of community concern about a problem is widened through an active process of communication. Communication is thus both an important prelude to, and a critical means of action for, solving a community problem.

## Enlarging the Scope of Concern

Getting people to a meeting may be fairly simple, but involving them in a series of constructive actions toward solving a problem is very difficult. One of the first things to be done is to enlarge the scope of people's concern about a given problem—no small task when their resources of hope, aspiration, experience, and educational background are limited.

> These people are looking for some way of expressing their interests in young people and doing . . . something in a direct and immediate way about them. You can hardly blame

them for picking up the first likely thing that comes along. Now, for example, it is quite characteristic, you know, that they say it's a law enforcement problem. Where the heck are the police, they say. They start hollering that they need more police protection.

• The task of the worker is to help the group engage in a problem-coping experience that has meaningful scope and depth. The problem needs to be examined within the limits of the understanding and resources of the participants. The emphasis may be on the development of new ideas and possibilities for action.

Maybe the answer is not alone increased police protection and recreation, but getting teachers to be innovative of school programs and to accept lower-class kids better. The problem may be how to influence key people in the school system to do any number of feasible things for which they have not taken enough responsibility, such as counseling, remedial help, job referral.

### Focusing, Partializing, and Progressing

Members of community groups in lower-income areas may have special difficulty in determining precisely how to achieve their objectives. They may, after considerable discussion, know what they want but not how to get it. The objectives, which may have seemed fairly clear at first, have become complex and elusive. The members seem suddenly to lack focus—they tend to confuse means and ends. The larger picture may be clear, but its comprising elements are hard to see. The worker may need to propose alternative actions and to assist the group in detailing particular tasks. Certain data may be needed. Membership responsibilities may have to be assigned. Subsequent activities may need to be anticipated.

The entire organizing process must be progressive in its stages. Limited goals must be set and relatively smaller efforts undertaken before larger goals and major projects are attempted.

This is the whole idea of the smaller projects. When I first met with these people they wanted a mammoth recreation center for their kids. They had been after this center for fifteen years. The group met sporadically every few months, but there was no real organization or build-up and preparation for this major and expensive undertaking. The people would get together and call four or five meetings in succession, but the project idea would fall by the wayside.

What I did when I came to the group was to get them to focus on the things that they could do fairly quickly and which would pay off with success. It was extremely important that they meet regularly, develop a sense of involvement and organization, and, of course, develop skill in organizational matters. We had projects on clean-up and fix-up of streets and houses. Then we invited speakers on health and sanitation. We set up a cooperative baby sitting service. From there we moved to sponsoring a project of day care services for working mothers. We may not get to the recreation center thing until next year or the year after, when the situation is ripe for it. Meanwhile, we're also planning a teenage beauty pageant and an adult fashion show.

All these things will provide useful organizational experiences. Success will build on success and we will tackle only the problems we can handle at any given time. My job is to keep these people involved and carrying out more and more important tasks.

## Providing Support

Grass-roots persons and agencies may be uncertain and ambivalent about their participation in problem-solving activities. They may develop resistance because they lack confidence about the value of their contributions. In such circumstances, a great deal of support is required, especially by persons of limited education and organizational experience.

> They will say they don't know anything and I'll say, "You can describe the problem as you see it. You have ideas as to what should be done."
> Then they'll say, "But suppose we decide to do something I can't do. Suppose we decide to talk to the principal or the police captain."
> Then I'll say, if it's a woman, "You know how to talk to

your child. You can tell your husband what to do. The school belongs to all the people. You have a right to talk to persons who are doing the job of education for you."

Then they have this pitch, "You're getting paid to bring us together. It's your job. You do it."

Agencies will give you basically the same pitch. Their representatives will come to one or two meetings just to see what's happening. But they say they are too busy with their own programs. I tell them, "Your recreation and casework programs aren't going to be worth a damn. They're too little and too distant from the problem. You got to hit the problem more directly, maybe in the schools or the homes. It takes extra effort, but it makes their programs more meaningful."

Such supportive comments help encourage and stimulate people to participate, to take the first steps toward organized involvement in community problem solving. Emphasis must be on their ability to solve the problem as well as on the serious nature of the problem itself.

The interpersonal approach to organizing assumes that people must first meet their own personal needs before they can solve the problems of others and of the community. Community activity may serve primarily as a means for certain low-income persons to project their own personal anxieties, hostilities, and distorted perceptions and to interfere with the realistic solution of social problems. Such problem-ridden individuals must therefore be helped themselves before—or even as—they attempt to assist others. Social, educational, and cultural enrichment services may be needed to widen their horizons and to develop their self-confidence.

A service program tied in with community action assumes that there are persons who want to receive personal gratification as well as give energy and time to other people's problems. People expect a *quid pro quo,* one way or the other, for efforts expended. The return to the low-income person is personal and social development.

We consider delinquency prevention and neighborhood improvement as part of the same process. We try to get people naturally involved in issues that are coming up. Now this is a nonpolitical and nondenominational approach. We don't as a rule have politicians coming down to sway our people or take over our meetings. We encourage our people to read and to become involved in every way they want.

We have adult education classes. Speakers come down to discuss general subjects. There are also classes of specific interest, for example, to parents about raising their kids. We have had psychiatrists, heads of social agencies. We had some one come down to speak on Social Security. The public aid commissioner of the county discussed the kinds of problems his agency faces.

We also have a crafts and recreational program for adults and their children as well. All these things are kind of interrelated. For example, we had one woman who came down for a lecture on child care. The concern and the enthusiasm that was generated resulted in organizing a tot lot. Some of the men in our classes go to court to represent our organization's interest in kids who appear before the judge.

Youth programs are often leverage points for developing contacts with parents and others who may themselves be recruited into both recreation program and community solving projects.

We have a game room and the adolescents come down two or three nights a week. We have a weekly dance. Adults in the community do most of the supervision and teaching of the kids. When a kid gets into trouble in the program, that gives us an opportunity to go to his home and meet his parents or go to his school. You get to know what's going on with the youngsters and what the problems in the community are. You begin to involve teachers and parents in the organization's larger concern about poor housing, poor facilities, poor curricula. We can then call a meeting of all these people and develop some kind of joint project to see what we can do to solve not just the one youngster's problem, but the problem of a lot of kids.

Finally, the worker may be in a position to supply a supportive service to another agency, usually less well developed in its problem-solving skills. The worker may provide experience, facilities, or simply stimulation to another group to initiate a program or do a better job with a problematic sector of the youth population.

The Sisters of St. Mary were wondering about setting up a program serving delinquent girls in the community. We consulted with them and urged them to go ahead. They had obtained a group of volunteer young women from the local colleges to assist in the program, but they needed help in orienting these volunteers to serve the needs of the girls and in recruiting the delinquent girls.

The community worker was assigned to meet with the group of volunteer college students. At the first meeting general information about the community and the needs of delinquent girls was given. The community worker arranged for a female detached worker to lead a discussion about the dynamics of girl street gangs. At another meeting, the volunteers discussed the forthcoming program. They decided they wanted to work with the girls in the area of music, art, homemaking, physical education, and beauty culture. It was very successful. In a short time, by virtue of additional word of mouth contacts, 72 girls were registered in the program.

## Developing Group and Individual Competence

Organizing the community at the local level is fundamentally a group process. The community group or organization represents —or *is*—the community to all intents and purposes for the worker. As an enabler or developer, his primary job is not to get this group to solve particular community problems, but to learn to use an appropriate interactional process for attacking these problems. The sense of community and the success of the organization depends chiefly on the quality and quantity of interaction of the members among themselves and with others.

Unlike the development worker, the enabler, especially if he is a professional, tends to give very careful attention to recruiting those persons and representatives of local agencies who are leaders, have influence, and can make a significant contribution to community problem solving. Depending on the purpose and structure of his sponsoring organization, he will attempt to involve mainly key people in the initial meeting of the community group. (This does not deny the responsibility of the worker to assist a great variety of persons, with and without leadership qualifications, to participate in the group once it is under way.)

Community groups appear to go through a life cycle. The members may have difficulty in forming at the beginning, and their membership may be quite passive, inept, and fearful. Then suddenly a few of the members seem to take over and provide drive and energy for the entire group, and a superabundance of energy may be released. In low-income communities this may be an over-reaction to past inertia; the group moves from being highly dependent on the ideas and direction of the worker to a kind of rebellious independence. It is only at a later stage that consistent, substantive, and steady movement is made by the group with decreasing assistance from the worker. However, with elections and the departure of key members, with unanticipated failures in group projects, the community group may have to form again and the cycle begin anew. An organization may be fixated or set at any one of these stages for an indefinite period of time. Then, too, many local community groups are paper organizations. A handful of people meet irregularly to conduct business and plan events of limited problem-solving utility. The organizational process here may be highly ritualistic.

One of the early pitfalls the worker has to avoid is over-structuring or over-formalizing the group before it develops the sense that it is a group. Low-income groups tend to move too rapidly into a formal organizational phase, for example, election of officers, drawing up a constitution or bylaws, and dues collection. The group needs to have the experience of interaction and shared experience in limited problem solving before it is really a functioning organism and is aware of its own potential.

> Some people think they have an organization when they really don't have one. A couple of people with grandiose ideas go off and work on an idea of their own. It is only when you have a series of activities in which a fairly large number of people are participating that the idea of organization begins to develop.
>
> If you have, for example, six consecutive meetings, fifteen to thirty people meeting once a week, you begin to have an organization. People begin to want to come to meetings and

feel part of it. Habits begin to form. If you start collecting dues and formalizing the structure too soon, then it's somebody else's organization, and they don't really identify with it.

Of paramount importance, especially to the social-work trained staff, is the meaning and quality of involvement of individual participants in the community program. The worker should be highly sensitive to the need for as many selected individuals as possible to participate in making decisions and implementing them. He may devote an inordinate amount of time in discussions with people outside of meetings to support their participation in meetings and projects. He tries to tailor jobs to meet specific interests. He is constantly aware of blocks in communication and relationship among members, and if he can't solve them, he will try to work around them. For example, two ladies on a committee may be constantly at each other's throats, vying for leadership. The decision for the worker may have to be support of a third person for a particular office or responsibility, but at the same time, he will attempt to keep the other two ladies as much involved as possible, taking time, if necessary even during the meetings, to smooth ruffled feelings.

This trained sensitivity to the interacting process is the mark of the professional social worker. He may even decide to sacrifice a program in order to preserve harmony among group members, since the capacity of the group and its individual members to develop and keep functioning is his major objective. Consequently, the organization's task objective in terms of solving a particular community problem may in the short run take on secondary importance.

There is a tendency in local neighborhood organizations to focus too highly on particular needs of individuals and indeed indiscriminately to select service problems which are readily available. Funds to send individual youths to college may be raised, special training and work experiences for a few promising youths may be developed—and the notion of a planned approach to a major problem of educational reform or job development is easily subverted. More concrete and immediate service types of programs tend to be given preference. Also, programs which have less immediate payoff require a delay in organizational gratification of which the membership may not be readily capable. The worker needs to steer carefully between the Scylla of social and personal development programming and the Charybdis of more significant but difficult community problem solving. The group may founder either in its development toward a social club orientation or in trying to solve a problem for which sufficient resources of interest, concern, expertise, and time are not available.

### Developing Leadership

Leadership development, or more precisely the guidance of the process of leadership development, is of extreme importance in organizing the community group. The life style, the mission, and the accomplishment of the organization hinge largely on the type of leadership it develops. It is assumed that every organizational and group situation serves to develop certain opportunities for leadership. The worker, particularly the enabler, tends to exercise a great deal of influence over the leader selection process.

> The staff has to exercise a certain amount of control over the selection of leadership. It sounds like a very undemocratic thing, but the fact is, in many situations, the prospect of getting erratic leadership is very great. This is not so great a problem at higher echelons of organization, because the competitive process tends to weed out poor leadership, but the possibilities at the local level are considerable.

Frequently in grass-roots organizations, individuals who have great personality needs for domination, attention, and status but who are without demonstrated competence—in areas of living such as family, job, peer group—assume leadership roles. Such persons may be highly conscientious and invest a great deal of time, effort, and even their own limited funds in the organization, but—unfortunately—their leadership may be manipulative, erratic, authoritarian, or paternalistic and their participation may short-circuit the interactive process. Weak or obviously incompetent leadership can also be a problem, but it may in some respects be easier to solve than domineering leadership because the group is more likely to express its dissatisfactions openly and to accept the need for change.

Both domineering and weak leadership tend to retard the development of the community group, and particularly to thwart the objective of shared leadership. Various devices need to be employed by the worker to guide the leadership process. Facilitation of the group process encourages democratic decision making in the group, is a major warranty against poor individual leadership, and creates opportunities for new leaders to arise.

> Right away when a group meets for the first time they want to elect leaders. I prevent this as best I can. Sometimes we compromise with the election or appointment of a short-term chairman or president. It's important that people really get to know each other and especially what each can do in the organization. In fact, I try to delay the election process as long as possible. Meanwhile, we get a number of projects going. Each project will have its own chairman; this gives a number of people a chance to demonstrate and develop leadership capacities. Then later, say six months to a year after the first meeting, if they want to elect officers they can do it. By that time, though, they really don't have to elect because they know who the real leader or leaders are, and who is constructively putting out for the organization.

The worker must be ever alert to evidence of leadership ability as it arises in the course of ongoing organizational affairs or business. For the development worker, it is generally less important to select persons who have relatively high formal status in the community—such as a doctor, lawyer, or businessman—than to encourage the selection of persons who are motivated to work for the good of the organization, are fairly articulate, have community contacts, and can use these contacts appropriately.

In attempting to encourage the development of leadership, the enabler or the developer may take over the leadership role himself, at least temporarily. While the worker attempts generally to assist others to exercise critical decision-making power and seeks continually to help the group become self-sustaining and independent, there are times when he must step in and exercise clear and forceful leadership. The worker, particularly the developer, may allow himself to be elected to a position such as secretary or vice president for a limited period of time. More likely, if he is a professional social worker, he will provide advice and consultation which affect the direction the organization takes. The danger here, of course, is that freedom for new leadership to arise may be hindered.

The worker, however, cannot avoid influencing the development of leadership, and he therefore needs to know why, when, and how to provide support, how to make clear whose point of view or position he supports and whose he does not. He can, for example, focus the group's attention on the utility of an idea or suggestion by a group member, thereby enhancing that person's status and providing an opportunity for that person to exercise additional initiative and leadership. The worker may also be drawn into a political game of aiding this or that organizational faction. If he is, he must decide deliberately which subgroup or leader he will aid and what the consequences for his own relationship and the development of the organization will be as a result of his action. Ideally, the growing strength of the organization and the development of competent leadership will permit gradual but steady withdrawal of the worker's influence.

## Exercising Control

The community worker, regardless of type or organization out of which he operates, must pay at least some attention to the control function. The process of community problem solving requires the constant delineation of purpose, scope, and action. A major difference between those workers oriented to social maintenance and those oriented to significant environmental change is the emphasis given to the issue of control. For the enabler and the developer, control and limitations are a basic goal or function of almost all activities. For the advocate and the militant organizer, the imposition of controls is secondary; their goal is the release of energies; they hope to encourage fragmentation or rearrangement of existing patterns. A basic objective, indeed, is de-control, at least from established institutional influences.

### Typical Use of Control

The control objective of developmental- and maintenance-oriented organizations might best be illustrated by quoting the statement of purpose of a block association: ". . . . to improve the moral and living standards of the community it will be necessary for every person living in this block to observe law and order and maintain the property and welfare of the block." The observance of acceptable standards of behavior by members of the community is a key control function of the neighborhood organization. But though control over deviant families may be of great concern to certain grass-roots organizations, it is best exercised with considerable compassion.

This was a family everybody in the neighborhood organization was worried about. Here was an ADC mother with eleven children and no father. Two of the girls, thirteen and fifteen years, had babies. Another girl, age fourteen, was in the state correctional institution. Three boys had already been to the boys' reformatory. The kids in this family were a constant annoyance to people in the community. They would break windows, trample gardens, steal from backyards, apartments, stores.

At first, members of the organization, individually, bawled the kids out or complained to the mother. They even called a big meeting and were ready to sign petitions to get her and the kids out of the community. Now I was at the meeting and they asked me what I thought. I told them that "Each of you is representing yourself when you talk to the kids or the mother. Why don't three or four of you get together and make up a committee representing the organization. Also when you talk with her, treat her as a human being. Try to show her that you want to be helpful."

So they did this. They went and talked with her, and she cried like a baby. She said that was the first time anybody had ever approached her like that. She told them from now on they had her full cooperation and she'd see that the kids don't break windows or get into any trouble. They put pressure on her, but they also included her in. They just didn't ostracize or condemn her as they had done before. Now it was the whole community that wanted her in but on their terms.

Well, this woman started to come to meetings. The kids began, strangely enough, to go out of their way to protect the neighbors' property. Some of the younger ones turned out real nice, graduating from high school. A couple are in the military service.

Control may be the underlying rather than the manifest function of the agency. For example, the identification of delinquents and their problems may fulfill a control rather than a service function. The needs of the community for stability and protection rather than rehabilitation and treatment of delinquents may be the real aim of organization.

For agencies with a stability orientation, almost any supportive service may have a control function. Counseling and therapy also in part serve the ends of control.

Oh, no, we don't carry on a recreational program. We have plenty of parks and social clubs. We are mainly concerned with therapy. We have many young men and women who are school dropouts. They can't get jobs. They feel hopeless, after going downtown and getting turned away time and again. What we do is call them in and talk to them so they can cope with their feelings of discouragement. We want to give them hope so they can still keep trying. We keep them in counseling sessions and try to find available training opportunities for them. We believe this approach does more to reduce delinquency than anything else. Our workers are also in the streets on a regular basis providing spot counseling. With the situation so tense over Vietnam and civil rights, anything is liable to happen. We're there to help these kids keep out of trouble and protect the community as well.

Control may be a deliberate objective and directly built into the service aspects of the community work program. Neighborhood organizations may use drum and bugle corps, paramilitary, recreational, or other service activities to instill a "respect for discipline" in delinquent youths. The indigenous organization may be more direct than the professionally oriented social agency in revealing its control purpose.

The past year we have engaged 1500 of the area's youth in our military program. Our prime concern is military discipline. Discipline means respect for authority, whether it be for parents, law enforcement agency or any person with authorized authority.

There are some one hundred tough teenagers involved in various cleanup or recreational programs. The kids who do well in the program get higher rank and become supervisors, i.e., lieutenants or captains. Finally, they can even become coordinators and get paid for keeping other kids out of trouble and involved in constructive activities.

### Countering the Influence of Social-Change Organizations

In periods of rapid social change and community crisis, social-maintenance organizations may be seriously threatened. Their membership begins to dissipate. Even more critical is the fundamental challenge to the very basis for the organization's existence. The perspective of the militant organizer may be totally alien to that of the enabler or development worker, at times utterly incomprehensible to him.

I know these civil rights boys. I'm friends with them, but they're wrong. I believe in explaining and protecting the situation. This is the meaning of organization. I'm not for causing combustion and taking advantage of people, especially kids who don't know what it's all about, and involving them in protest marches.

We can't have these kids, for example, picketing and staying home from school. It sets a bad example. They are told they can violate the law because it's a bad law. This opens the door for mob action and for disregard of all rules and regulations.

The maintenance-oriented worker develops a series of specific tactics to counter the influence of militant groups. He may persuade membership to avoid participation in protest activities. He stresses his faith that patience and hard work will bring each person his just reward in a society which is basically democratic and still produces adequate opportunities. He emphasizes the importance of self-help. He encourages youngsters or adults to organize and express themselves through established organizations such as the churches. He points out the consequences of participation in demonstrations—"You are certainly going to get yourself arrested and you could also get killed."

The worker encourages people to see that they are being used as pawns in a game from which they will derive little direct benefit.

> The protest march is for middle-class open housing in the suburbs. I told them they would get little out of the demonstration. They couldn't possibly afford housing in the suburbs.

Various forms of coercive power may be employed, directly or indirectly, to counter the efforts of social change organizations.

> Mr. G. said the young adult group almost affiliated with a confederation of young adult clubs in the neighborhood to protest police brutality, but he informed the group he would have to withdraw all facilities, equipment, and organizational service, if they did so.

> Larry said they enlisted the support of all the Parent Teacher Association groups in the community to counter the agitation of the militant groups. The parents were trying to keep their youths close to home and would not permit them to participate in any demonstrations.

> There was evidence that a number of gang kids were contacted by adults who represented Muslim and Black Power type groups. They wanted the youngsters to participate in various militant demonstrations, including disruption of the Independence Day parade. Our gang worker alerted the police and other agencies. The police were given leads on the rabble-rousing adults. They were arrested and charged with conspiracy. Needless to say, none of our young people participated in the demonstration—which did not take place.

## Preventing and Delimiting Riot Situations

Delinquent adolescents appear to be among the elements involved in fomenting or sustaining a riot. A variety of tactics have been developed by maintenance-oriented organizations to reduce pressures for rioting. They include positive worker relationship, pinpointing explosive situations, providing appropriate services, correcting communication, substituting equivalent activities and facilitating intervention by indigenous leadership.

### Positive Relationship

The worker uses the friendly contacts that he has in the community, particularly with grass-roots leadership and influential young adults and gang leaders, to control the situation. In times of crisis he may "go the rounds" of street corner hangouts, parks, playgrounds, and even the local schools to urge coolness in the behavior of young people in the community.

> Almost all the high school students in the area know me by now. They call me the Peace Man. I just show up in the area and the kids seem to relax. I kid around with them, shoot the breeze, assess the situation and caution them to play it cool or freeze, baby.

### Pinpointing Explosive Situations

The worker may take the lead in calling representative community groups and organizations, including the police, together to periodically and systematically review specific problem situations, troublesome youth and adults, planned demonstrations, and the changing climate or mood of the population. Arrangements for continued surveillance, special programming, and follow-up are usually made. The accurate identification of explosive situations may require long and arduous field duty by the worker and the suspension of almost all other community problem-solving activities.

### Providing Appropriate Services

In times of crisis, the community worker may engage in continuing discussions with members of his organization and other community groups generally to provide emotional release. Verbalization or "lifting the lid" on problems serves as an expedient means of moving aggression from the acting-out to the vocalization stage, especially if it is done in a skillful manner. Follow-up of these discussion sessions, at which many specific grievances may be raised, with casework, group work, and other services, is an important aspect of the community worker's contribution to the control of riots or near-riot situations.

### Correcting Communication

Corrective communication is probably the single most essential device which the community worker can employ in the prevention of a riot. Significant community persons and organizations must become aware of what is happening and what might happen. The basis for any emergent situation needs to be fully explored, rumors quashed, and distortions of fact corrected. This may involve an aggressive stance on the part of the worker. His own approach and value system and the position of his agency or organization must be clearly impressed on the target groups.

Corrective communication may require the worker and his organization to take a position in direct opposition to another organization in the community. The timing of such efforts may be of key significance. For example, a worker was assigned as an observer at a community meeting called by a black nationalist organization to protest a variety of issues. A near riot had broken out several days earlier a block from where the meeting—attended mainly by older teenagers—was held. The worker reports:

> The main speaker began his speech by criticizing the local school board for not having an adequate Negro history program. He then gave a brief résumé of his version of Negro history slanting his facts along racist lines, with liberal insertions of present-day corner jargon and heavy emphasis on past injustices. Then he swiftly moved into the present-day unjust treatment of Negroes. Then he presented some questionable statistics on jobs, draft, education, Vietnam, Negro-white death ratios, etc.
>
> He ended his hate-filled ramblings by urging the boys to tear up their draft cards and to "ignore any draft notices," and he implored them to "pass this along to all the young men you know and who might be subject to the military draft." He suggested they join some of the more aggressively militant organizations such as SNCC or CORE as an alternative to going into the service.
>
> He said that if he could just get youth gangs from fifty corners to band together, he could take over the city. He said that such action here could trigger similar action in all the

large cities of the United States. One of the young men of draft age asked the speaker what would happen, "If we followed your advice and didn't go to the military service?" His answer was, "Nothing, if you could get five hundred of your black brethren to do the same."

I had been instructed not to get involved, but when I became aware that I was apparently the only one present not in accord with the views of the speaker, I demanded the right to be heard. I was allowed to do so because they thought I was in sympathy with what was being said. I explained that the boys present were being misled by a lot of half-truths, emotional pleas, and half-witted suggestions. I pointed out the legal, patriotic, and moral responsibilities of all citizens of this country, and that the whole character of the meeting was in direct violation of laws governing peaceful assembly. They were gathered to plot overthrow of the government or its programs, that the boys were, in fact, being induced to commit subversive acts of violence against their fellow Negroes and white countrymen.

Over loud protestation from the speaker, the chairman of the proceedings, as well as a number of others present, I went on to correct some of his statistics on the Vietnam death ratios and categorically pointed out the flaws in the statements made in his speech. I ended my dissertation by identifying myself as a community worker with the Northside Community Agency.

There were attempts to respond to my comments but squabbling, boos and hisses, mixed with applause, broke out. The main speaker now could only stammer outworn, antiwhite slogans, but with all the fire and exuberance gone.

I glanced at my watch. It was 11:00 P.M. Slowly and deliberately, I gathered my belongings, got up and looked at the main speaker, who was still leaning on the lectern, and smiled at him. Then I turned my back and slowly walked out with two teenage girls following me, shouting, "Black coward!"

A high quality of moral courage and perceptive intelligence must be possessed by the worker who would seriously counter a highly explosive situation of the type described. He must be able to run against the tide of group opinion and he needs great faith in his own sense of reality and traditional norms and values.

### Substituting Equivalent Activity

Another device which may serve to nip riots in the bud, particularly among gang and conflict-prone youths, is the use of a substitutive activity such as a peaceful protest, vigil, demonstration, well planned to support law and order. One such technique, "Peace Squad," has been adopted by the Youth For Service Agency in San Francisco.

> It actually originated among the teenagers themselves when on their own, way back in 1960, some delinquents beat up a Chinese storekeeper. Members of a gang served by Youth for Service were upset by this, decided to post a vigil in front of the Chinese man's store. This was for the purpose of demonstrating that they were not involved and also to indicate that they were against actions of this sort. They marched around with signs saying, "Down with hate." The agency picked up on this technique and has been using it with success ever since.

### Facililating Intervention by Indigenous Leadership

The community worker needs to tap indigenous leadership, especially older teenagers or young adults, prior to or during a riot. Ex-youth–gang leaders, even petty criminals with influence, status, or "rep" in the community may well be among the few sources of leadership which are effective during times of extreme crisis.

> Last summer, during our riot and the other near-riot situations, we organized fifty young adults. Call them pimps, punks, and hoodlums if you want. We gave them special identification cards and emblems. We paid them to go into the streets to avert another Watts. We figured by the end of the summer, they had averted eighty incidents. Some of these young people even assisted the police in making arrests. They worked long hours, well above the number for which they were paid. They stopped fights, looting, property damage.

They continued to work even when we told them to go home. It makes you think twice before labeling anybody a delinquent or criminal.

Ultimate responsibility for the control of a riot once it has broken out, of course, rests primarily with the police and other law-enforcement agencies. The community worker can at such times, work only in some secondary and cooperative capacity with law-enforcement officers.

Finally, the organizing job of the community worker as enabler or developer, obviously has wide scope and requires extraordinary talent and skill if a majority of the challenges and contingencies which he encounters in the slum are to be handled successfully. Considerable attention has been directed to the important control function of the worker. Stability is an essential attribute of any viable community or society. The enabler and developer clearly make a major contribution toward this end as well as to the stimulation of organization of people and agencies for self-help and the more efficient balancing of human needs and social resources. They do not, however, seek to change basic organizational arrangements, nor do they significantly add to the supply of opportunities available to delinquent youths in the slum.

# 5

# Organizing the Local Community

## *The Social-Change Approach*

There is an unpredictable and inchoate quality about the social-change approach. The methodologies of the advocate and—particularly—the militant organizer at the grass-roots level almost by definition, reflect a tenuous, labile, and relatively unsystematic process, one that tends to create its own dynamic. The community worker, as well as the community participants and institutional structures he is trying to influence, may become creatures of swiftly moving events, and under such circumstances the distinction between worker and constituent, leader and follower, actor and person or institution acted upon may become difficult to make. Social change, then, is a far more elusive concept than social maintenance. We know what we have and what we probably can continue to have with minor, incremental, or natural growth changes; we are not clear what we will actually obtain with radical or major change. (Furthermore, how to bring about major change is far from clear.) [1] At the same time, however, although the way significant change occurs is difficult to plot, the change approach tends, at least ostensibly, to be more task-centered or instrumental in purpose than a stability or process approach; that is, specific issues and policies seem more often to be addressed.

1. Robert A. Dahl and Charles E. Lindblom, *Politics, Economics, and Welfare*, pp. 3–54, 369–526.

## Youth Involvement—Instrumental Orientation

In this chapter we shall focus on the efforts of the advocate and the militant organizer, particularly in relation to the youth community organization. The clientele or the members of such organizations are youths—often delinquents—in the ghetto, and the assumption of a youth community organization is that the essence of specific change efforts in relation to the problem of delinquency requires the significant involvement of delinquents or vulnerable youth themselves in leadership roles.

The community worker committed to social stability views the problem of delinquency as residing within delinquent youths, and requires the intervention of parents, neighborhood groups, and social agencies in control efforts and programs of service enhancement. The change-oriented worker views a series of problems as residing within the institutional and organizational structure of the community, and requires the efforts of youths themselves to change the system. Nevertheless, the advocate and the militant organizer will differ on the degrees of freedom of self-determination permitted youths to engage in such community change efforts.

Delinquent youth in the slums of our large urban centers are doubly and trebly disengaged from the norms, values, and opportunities of the larger culture and society. They are often poor, they are alienated by definition of their adolescence, and they are deviant by their condition of serious conflict with the expectations of dominant persons in their neighborhood and larger society. Yet with rising aspirations, with increased relative numbers of youth, and with the emergence of adolescent subcultures, the influence of youth as an organized force has and will continue to grow, especially perhaps in the ghettoes of our cities, where median age often ranges from 13 to 19 years.

> The adolescent may well determine the direction, form and rate of success of this developmental process of modernization and the concomitant epigenesis of new social and political and economic forms. The implication is clear: in the rapidly changing "emergent" nation, huge proportions of the

population *are* adolescents, and it is the adolescents who will determine the maintenance of cultural continuity or be the innovators of discontinuity and social change.[2]

At the same time in our society a traditional and somewhat primitive way of dealing with adolescents, particularly delinquents, remains. We do not provide them with the "status affirmation and group acceptance afforded youth in the past." [3] Youths are nurtured, more or less well, but in a dependent position. Adults plan and legislate for them. At best, youths are forced into the role of recipients of "benevolence" and protection. The problem in part is the enforced submission of youths to the dictates of adults—and the severe reactions of rebellion, conflict and delinquency which may result.

Demonstration programs in this country significantly involving youth in key decision-making roles are of recent origin and are mainly due to the interest and support of the President's Committee on Juvenile Delinquency and Youth Development, The Office of Economic Opportunity, the civil rights movement, and the militant organizational efforts of Saul Alinsky. Most of the youth community organizations these efforts have generated or supported are committed to a change approach, and it is from the brief history of these programs that principles and procedures will be extracted to form a model of practice.

The elements of youth organizing for social change (and in most respects they approximate the tactics required for organizing adults to achieve significant change) are the following: establishing commitment, developing leadership, articulating issues, educating and developing political power, and exercising control. These elements or techniques are interactional and interdependent, and we may consider them as developing within a partial time sequence. For example, a community organization is ordinarily not expected to develop into a political force before it has established some sense of commitment, clarity about issues, and an effective leadership structure.

The community worker, whether advocate or militant organizer,

2. David Gottlieb, Jon Reeves, and Warren D. Ten Houten, *The Emergence of Youth Societies*, pp. 27–28.
3. S. R. Slavson, *Reclaiming the Delinquent*, pp. 8–9.

employs these elements in the achievement of his objectives, particularly at the local community or grass-roots level. While we will focus on the elements common to the approach of both roles, we will emphasize the role of the organizer. The advocate is more often a professional operating under more institutional constraints than the militant organizer, and is more likely to limit the freedom of youth leadership; he prefers to use techniques of education and persuasion, not protest—though he is surely as concerned with the elements of commitment, issue creation, and political development as is the militant organizer.

### Establishing Commitment

The notion of commitment is inherent in the purpose and particularly in the implementation of a youth community action project.

> The primary purpose is to shift the apathy, hurt, deflected anger of low-income minority group adolescents into action for social change. We plan to organize the teenage community to collectively contest the injustice and deprivations within their social environment. Implied are bold, active, adolescent-styled social action projects in such areas as racial discrimination, barriers to employment, housing violations, etc.

The change-oriented organization, then, is built on "realistic" negativism or dissatisfaction with particular as well as general problems. The more closely related the problems are to the interests and needs of the adolescent population, the stronger the potential for youth commitment to the program.

> The agencies are lousy. . . . Recreational facilities are much too small to serve the population. The equipment is no good and the staff is lousy. We really don't have any place to go. . . . As for jobs, it looks like we just don't qualify. As for police, . . . they just don't dig us or they don't want to.

Coupled with intense dissatisfaction with social conditions, there must be a desire for change in community agencies and programs. This desire is expressed in terms of change "now," not gradually over time. The nature of the change, initially, tends to be in global, visionary, utopian or messianic terms, but at this stage the content of change is not so important as the sheer desire and need for it.

Fundamental to commitment is faith in the potential of members of the organization to bring about change. Commitment projects a sense of almost unlimited promise in the efforts to be undertaken so long as these efforts are essentially self-determinative, that is, so long as they originate, are developed, and carried out by the members of the organization—with the aid of a broad cross section of the slum community.

The notion of commitment also requires a willingness to be tested, that is, a willingness by members to demonstrate that they will not flinch nor will the organization dissolve under opposition and attack. And it requires an investment of time and energy on the part of its youth staff participants that transcends the idea of paid employment or traditional volunteer service.

> They said that they would continue to work for the organization and its program even if they weren't paid. Some of them had worked three months or more on a volunteer basis. One of the boys said he had quit a job in order to take this one. They were committed to this particular cause.

The origin of the commitment is often difficult to determine, but it is encouraged by promises of support from federal programs, local militant neighborhood associations, or the civil rights movement. More immediately, it may be stimulated by particular staff members (fired by idealism, zeal, and militant fervor) who are sometimes in leadership positions in local agencies. These persons are the adult staff advocates and organizers, the focal points for organizational efforts. It is their drive and commitment which is communicated to youth leadership, diffused to others, and ultimately incorporated into available change-oriented structures which become part of, separate from, or affiliated with the initiating or parent organization.

## Developing Leadership

### Recruitment

Depending on a number of factors, including the degree of control to be exercised by the parent organization, the worker may earlier or later engage in bringing in youth leader candidates. The advocate will tend to initiate this process only after a period of careful planning and due consideration of implications and risks to the existing programs of his parent organization, while the organizer will tend to recruit more quickly, since usually a well-established youth program does not already exist in his agency and there are fewer risks entailed in building such an organization.

The recruiting process, particularly for the organizer, takes advantage of social situations which fortuitously arise, but the process requires attention to interpersonal relationship building as well as the task of "selling" the idea of youth organization and its general potentials. The unemployed or dropout youth may need to be clear about the relationship of his investment in the organization to his long-range career goals. Youth leadership in the organization may bring with it the assurance of a job, income, and status, but they are time limited. The youth ultimately will have to return to school and obtain a job with long-run potential for advancement. The limits of youth leadership positions need to be clearly specified from the very start.

Various criteria for leadership and membership in the youth organization are developed. The contest-oriented organization is likely to recruit the more stable youths in the community in the initial organizing phase, only later include delinquents.

> Mr. Lorenz, the worker, said that in the beginning about two years ago they recruited and selected the cream of the youth in the area. These were mobile-upward kids. These were not street kids, let alone delinquents. About a year ago, they initiated an effort to bring in street kids, including some delinquents.

Alternately, a cross-section of youths may be sought by the advocate, including delinquents and non-delinquents, representing the various ethnic groups in the population. Recruitment, however, may be directed primarily to delinquent youth, particularly if the agency is highly committed to the problems of deviant youth population or views these youths as the best potential available for participation in militant activities.

Recruitment and selection criteria, however, are applied regardless of the type of sponsorship of the youth organization. Drug users and addicts, extremely criminalistic and violent youths, young people already committed to an alternate radical program are generally not desired, nor are they usually susceptible to recruitment efforts. Also, youths who are selected may be required to continue or re-enroll in school. The time-limited character of the youth organizer's job may be stressed, and a one- or two-year limit on assignment may be established. This provides for some circulation or change in the leadership cadre over time.

### Orientation

As part of the recruitment and selection process, but also on an ongoing orientation and training basis, the worker needs to convince the potential youth leaders that they can do an effective job and can make some impact on the community. Such stimulation of confidence must be based not only on commitment to a course of action but also on understanding of the nature of community problems and how specifically something can be done about them. The community worker may need to structure a series of training or orientation sessions.

Group cohesion should develop rapidly in these early meetings, particularly as the initial leadership group know or get to know each other. Often a special event serves to create a sense of solidarity and the beginnings of effective organization.

> We went to Green Valley for the weekend where the structure was developed and the constitution evolved. Officers and committees were formed. This weekend event took place about two or three months after we began to invest in these kids.

> Specifically, I don't remember what program came out of that weekend, but I do remember we initiated an action phase shortly thereafter. We went to Washington, D.C., in support of the Youth Employment Bill and also got petitions signed to present to the state legislature on a pressing issue.

It should be noted that in the change-oriented approach the quality of leadership is especially important in determining the group's effective evolution. While first leaders may be readily selected, the development of ultimate leaders is more uncertain and depends in the final analysis on actual performance in relation to particular projects.

> The gang leader may turn out to be inarticulate and scared to death in dealing with the local alderman. The college kid really isn't as bright as his credentials make him out to be.

The girl who was good at sounding off to the head of the recreation department may be good for nothing else. And the freedom fighters who spent two weeks in Mississippi may look like egomaniacs living off deeds done long ago.

In the beginning stages of development, then, the group structure needs to be kept relatively loose. Those youths who are highly focused on the achievement of particular project ends appear to provide the most promise for successful leadership, possibly because these persons are acting less out of personal needs than out of response to group or organizational purpose. In the initial action phase, special care should be taken to engage youths at relatively low levels of responsibility and in actions where "success" is easily assured. An attempt to solve a particularly difficult problem, such as change in police arrest procedures or civil service qualifications, may lead to failure and serve to disintegrate the group.

## Articulating Issues

The focal concerns of the youth community organization must be articulated as issues. Specific problem areas are selected for attention and discussion, because ultimately positions need to be established to guide the organization in the development of its tactics. By issue articulation, therefore, we are referring to a process of identifying a problem area of concern to the group, understanding its dimensions, and creating a position by which a program of action can be outlined. Thus, problems such as discrimination, slum housing, and police brutality are specified respectively as discrimination in youth employment, housing violations, and police mistreatment of youths. Positions may be further particularized, for example, as equal opportunity for Negro youth, regardless of arrest background; strict code enforcement in regard to six-flat apartments; or protection of the human rights and civil liberties of juveniles suspected of a crime. A strategy of contest requires the selection of relevant tactics—participation by the youth group or its representatives in various publicity campaigns, meetings with key administrative officials, initiation of legal proceedings—while a conflict strategy may call forth such tactics as employer investigation squads, rent strikes, or demands for removal of the police captain or police commissioner.

The articulation of issues, furthermore, implies the creation or solidification of a group structure, and provides a further opportunity for orientation and education of youth leaders. Outside speakers may be brought in to present information and points of view about a problem. A considerable amount of dialogue must take place among the youth leaders and other interested persons before a specific position is created.

The extent of community worker predetermination of the issues, strategy, and actions of the youth organization will depend partly on the readiness of group members to see an individual problem as a collective problem. The community worker encourages a certain perspective. He may deliberately urge youngsters to "become angry at the system."

> I told these kids they should no longer look at their school failure as something for which they alone were responsible. The reason they failed was part of a complex process—curriculum was poor, teachers were not very good, and they were not really provided with opportunity to learn and master school content. They had to believe that a school failure or a dropout was a result of a system which has to be changed. They had to define the problem as out there in the system and not inside them.

The worker must be aware that certain issues are more feasible than others, and he may need to assist in the selection of those limited problems and issues which can be successfully managed and resolved through actions of the youth organization. It may well be that the issue of police brutality in a given police district of the city is more readily capable of solution by a youth organization than the issue of discrimination in employment by the civil service commission.

## Educating and Persuading

The community worker is required to engage in a continual program of education and persuasion of leadership and constituent members of the youth organization, particularly in the early period of its life. He must not only provide information about community problems and organizational patterns, but he must persuade the members that these problems and patterns can be changed. Attention by the worker must be directed to the development of communication which effectively educates and persuades, rather than neutrally conveys information. Word-of-mouth, personal contact, and a "street style" of exercising influence tend to be selected, since the written word and literate communication are devices of limited usefulness in attempts to persuade a generally non-literate youth population.

The major obstacles in obtaining grass-roots youth support are lack of interest, inertia, and apathy. A youth organizer describes the response to his efforts at building and "selling" the concept of youth organization as follows:

> Well, first the response was—"Aw man, you're crazy. You don't know what you're talking about. I'm out here. What do I care?" So I started pressing these kids from two points: their sisters' and brothers' future as well as their own. That's where I got them because I think that anybody who really loves their family don't want to see their sisters and brothers come up the same way they did. And they know for a fact that in this environment their sisters and brothers were following in the same footsteps. By just hitting at that point it started working on their minds—"Do you want to be like that old junky or wino down the street or do you want to make something of yourself. But you can't do something for yourself until you change the situation. You got to fight for changes!"
>
> It was hard at first, but I was constantly talking to them. Everywhere I'd go, I'd talk with them. They'd think about it and think. At first I wasn't sure they'd accept it. Then one day they came up to me and said, "We're ready to go." I said, Okay, so I brought the guys to Sam's office.
>
> There were nine of us that wrote the first constitution of the organization. Then we really went to work. The membership rose to 115, then to 300. We were all out on the streets constantly, getting kids to join our program. We got over 500 kids now.

Attention must also be paid to persuasion of the representatives of established organizations, especially those which represent authority and power, as to the legitimacy of the organization and its program. Overcoming the resistance of the police department to the idea of a youth community organization may be no easy matter, particularly if the youth organization formerly was a youth gang. Persuasion needs to be resourceful and even manipulative to achieve acceptance or at least neutralization of opposition.

> They made contact with the precinct commander, but at first he wouldn't listen to them. Then they tried to get the commander at least to recognize the fact they had a legal and legitimate right to engage in community organization activities. The police in the area stopped, frisked, and abused them, as if they were still members of a delinquent gang. The leaders of the organization wanted the commander merely to introduce and identify them to members of the force so that they would not be harassed on the streets.
>
> Still, the commander didn't listen. Then the youths made contact downtown and got the chief inspector to put pressure on the commander. In the past week, introductions between all the youth organizers and all the local precinct police officers have been made.

The essence of the youth organization's effectiveness is its ability to reach quickly and deeply into the heart of the community in relation to a given issue. Parents and neighbors as well as other youths are the most immediate targets of the youth organizers to obtain support for their organization and to begin to implement its objectives. If, for example, housing is high on the agenda, youths, as paid organizers, volunteers, or assistants, may fan out to persuade the local community to support this concern.

> The organization recently decided that housing had to be improved in the area. The youth aides went out into the community and got other youths and their parents on the various blocks alerted to the problem, to their potential for getting landlords to make repairs, to filling out forms complaining to the housing department. The focus of the efforts of the youth aides, however, was to get other kids to stimulate the adults in the community. Each aide was also given a list of block clubs and organizations in the area and told to talk with key officers explaining the housing campaign. In

some cases, they attended meetings of the groups and informed adults publicly of their rights and obligations.

Finally, it should be emphasized that the process of persuasion is an ongoing internal, as well as external, tactic for achieving organizational goals and objectives. The worker must constantly educate and persuade members of the youth organization, especially its leadership, to new knowledge, perspectives, and interpretations of community problems and situations. One worker terms this the technique of "seeding."

> If there was a good idea, and I thought I could make some headway on the idea with the kids, I would begin to seed it. I would say, "Joe, what do you think about this?" Then I would outline the idea partially and let the rest come from him, or the group, if it was a staff meeting of youth leaders. The idea gets picked up, if it seems right to them. It's important that the youths participate in the process of developing the idea of the plan. This way they'll think it's theirs, which indeed it is as they develop it. This kind of participation at the beginning means they will become dedicated to the idea. They'll spread the idea and implement the action that derives from it.

The advocate or the organizer, usually with and through the youth organizers, must cast a wide communications net. He must know the key persons in agencies and at the grass-roots level. He must know especially who the influentials and the power people are and make concerted efforts to educate and persuade them to support the youth organization. Forthright advocacy of certain positions is essential, although when reasonable persuasion and education fail other techniques are called for.

## Protest

The distinctive character of the change organization is to be found in its use of protest, generally disciplined, but nevertheless coercive. Protest should be a device of conscious selection, and preferably of last resort, with full awareness of the risks involved. The picket, the strike, the boycott, the vigil, the sit-in, or any other protest activity are not actions to be employed without due consideration or exploration of alternative tactics which might produce more efficient and effective results. The tactic of persuasion is ordinarily employed, for example, before resort to a picket is made.

> Jackson said they did not just automatically go out and picket. They liked to figure things out to discover what the trouble was and reach some of the big people in the agencies, like the recreation or police department. Then, if things did not work out, they would start working on their picket signs and begin to plan the specifics of the demonstration.

There is a force operating—with youth as much as with adults —which impels community organizations over time to become cautious and conservative. Ordinarily, the longer the youth organization is in operation, and is successful, the more reluctant it is to engage in militant activity. In part, this is a result of learning that each situation is highly complex and requires adequate investigation before appropriate tactics of action can be selected.

> Our kids have learned there are two basic ways to get something. The first is to sit down with the opposition and try to discuss what it is you want. If this doesn't work out, then to move into militant action.

It is not merely that groups become more conservative over time; they also become more sophisticated, and more resources become available to them. Influential contacts have been made, channels of communication opened. It may not be necessary to openly protest when pressure can be applied indirectly and with less risk.

Protest in the final analysis must be regarded as a quasi-legitimate, high-risk means of exercising influence. It is an expression of direct conflict. It alienates middle-class and establishment sensibilities. It polarizes positions, attitudes, and feelings. Short-run victories, furthermore, may result in long-term defeats if basic trust and working relationships are destroyed in the process of ongoing conflict.

What is clearly of paramount importance in a decision to protest or not is that the basis of action should not be a moral one alone. To warrant militant action, the injustice of a given situation must be joined with a reasoned calculation of the feasibility or likelihood of immediate and long-range gains.

There are certain essential conditions for the development of protest activity. First, there must appear to be fairly broad, if latent, community support for the position of the organization. Second, there should be elements within the opposition which are wavering and which seem to support the organization's point of view. Third, the position itself should be seen as compatible with the opposition's own long-range purposes or goals. Finally, the issues should be fairly clear and simple, at least on the surface, and capable of relatively quick resolution, one way or the other.

Certain internal organization needs must also be satisfied by the militant action. The action should serve to build the ego image of individual participants and particularly that of the organization as a whole. The militant action must be seen as a means to cohere, not fragment, the organization. There should be faith in the idea that a strike, a boycott, any militant action, even if unsuccessful in the short run, may have long-range positive value—that is, ideally, an enhanced public image and increased organizational strength should result from the action.

The protest itself must be well planned and coordinated. Its visibility should be high and capable of rapid communication to the community at large. Above all, its meaning needs to be sharp and dramatic. The conditions for successful protest activity are met in the following illustration:

> A couple of years ago when our youth organization was just getting underway, the issue of lack of toilet facilities in the local park arose. This was a large park serving a population of 50,000 people. On a Sunday as many as 5,000 persons would be engaged in various recreational activities. There had been a park house with facilities, but it burned down and the park department apparently was not rushing to rebuild it. People had to use the facilities of stores, restaurants, and homes adjoining the park.
>
> We discussed this problem with the youths. Indeed the idea for doing something about the situation came first from the kids. The decision was made to send letters and telegrams to the officials concerned. The youngsters got in touch with

various local politicians. They even tried to contact the mayor, but he was too busy to see them. They picketed briefly in front of the park department office downtown. But all to no avail. Finally, the action which seemed to spell out and dramatize the lack of toilet facilities was when the older youths, particularly those with street leadership, got a hundred youngsters, ages eight and nine years, together in a circle on the spot in the park where there used to be a toilet. This was on a Sunday when the park was filled to capacity. They invited representatives from the newspapers, TV, and radio to come down. When all were present, on a prearranged signal, they had the youngsters urinate. There was a minor furor in the park. Most of the people present understood what the objective was.

The incident was not reported in the mass media, but the message got through loud and clear to the park department. In a very short time, thereafter, it began construction of a new park house.

Protest action may have limited scope and consequence, especially if it is related only to a particular event. If another situation arises, a similar sequence of influence efforts may be required. There are times, however, depending on the particular community and political factors, when a protest action may lead to broader consequences than anticipated. This occurs when the youth organization deliberately or accidentally touches on a basic current issue which the larger community has not adequately resolved for itself. The protest actions of the youth organization can then be a focal point for a coalition of interests, and a trigger for major, complex and extraordinarily rapid change in a community.

The following conflict, precipitated by a youth organization in a large midwestern city, had important social and political ramifications for the city and the state as a whole. While the role of the community worker (in this case a priest) is not clear, decision-making and planning were apparently a function of a collective leadership shared by both priest and the youth leaders.

The Ravens Club in X city is the second largest private club in the country, enjoying a membership of over 5,000. Its members consist of the political elite of the community. Its roster goes something like this, ten of 24 county supervisors; three top elected county officials; five top city officials, such as the city attorney, city treasurer, and city clerk; plus a state representative. The club serves as the "gathering place and clearing house for politicians. It is a must for political aspirants."

The youth council, locally affiliated with the NAACP, comprised middle- and lower-class Negro youths in their late teens. Many of the middle-class youths had participated in civil rights activities during the previous summer in the south, and they had organized to express concern about the situation in X city. Lower-class youths had been deliberately recruited into the organization, but represented only a minority voice. Father Gentile, a White Catholic priest, had assumed major responsibility, on his own, for energizing the group during its initial organizational phase.

The decision to embarrass the Ravens Club had been made after the parent NAACP organization had publicly voiced opposition to the club's discriminatory membership policy. The youth council selected four liberal judges who were members of the Ravens and requested that they take some action in relation to this policy. One judge agreed not to reinstate his membership when it lapsed. Two judges failed to respond, and the fourth, Judge Raymond, had no comment. Unofficially, however, he was annoyed at receiving the letter, and gave a long lecture over the phone to a youth council caller on all he had done for Negroes.

At a subsequent meeting, the group decided to picket Judge Raymond's home in the suburbs, their overriding reason being a wish to make an example of a prominent white man whom they felt would be vulnerable to adverse publicity. The youth council also wanted to convey the impression that their power was not only within the Negro ghetto but that it could reach out and hit white suburbs that were otherwise largely undisturbed by Negro agitation in the inner city.

The action started on a warm Saturday night in the summer of 1966 when 28 pickets showed up in front of Judge Raymond's home carrying posters, singing songs, and attracting a crowd of about 40 spectators. Judge Raymond was not at home. The pickets continued their demonstrations on consecutive evenings, drawing larger and larger crowds. By this time there was ample newspaper publicity, and polarization of community attitudes began to take place. On the fourth night, several robed Ku Klux Klan members showed up along with counter-pickets and about 250 spectators appeared. The police had all they could do that evening to keep order.

The community began to become apprehensive when the KKK leadership indicated that if the picketing continued they would come back in force. The newspapers reported that this action put the white community in a dilemma, since it didn't wish to become associated with actions of the KKK. The police chief of the suburb as well as the chief of police of X city made appeals to the youth council to halt the picketing, since they were afraid the presence of extremist groups, such as the KKK, would lead to open violence. The pickets refused and privately acknowledged that it was gratifying to know that they could demand and get police protection under the law, especially at increased expense to the city (police action was costing the suburban town over $1,000 a day). The group was also gratified that this time the police would be protecting instead of harassing Negroes.

As the picketing progressed, it appeared that Judge Raymond's membership in the Ravens was no longer the major issue. As a conciliatory gesture, Judge Raymond offered to work against the Ravens' discriminatory policy, if the youth council would halt its picketing. The council refused. The issue now seemed to be one of rubbing it in according to one council spokesman, "for all the hurt we have suffered in the past."

In preparation for more picketing, the police reinforced their numbers and began to set up barricades. They were equipped with riot helmets and clubs. This time the pickets, for their own protection, came in a bus from St. Cecilia's Parish where Father Gentile was assistant pastor. The use of the St. Cecilia bus created many interesting sidelights, with the church being severely criticized by the white power structure for not keeping Father Gentile in line, and even more for letting him use the parish bus. On the seventh night, the spectators had increased to about 700, with quite a few counter-pickets heckling and jeering the demonstrators. The pickets had now grown to about 80 in number. They were also joined briefly by a Negro assemblyman and other prominent Negroes. The tension began to mount and there were instances of fighting, hurling rocks, insults, and damage to property near Judge Raymond's home. The increased size of the crowd, plus the presence of some of the NAACP elders, served to legitimize the picketing, and the youth council was determined to see it through.

There seemed to be no advance planning by the youth council during this time except that which took place on an hour-by-hour basis. The only cohesive force seemed to be Father Gentile who was beginning to weaken after continuous sleepless nights of meetings and trying to control the enthusiasm of the youth council members. Flushed with the sense of their own power, the group wanted to picket at other places in the city to drive home the fact that they were a powerful group that had to be recognized. After night-long debates, the group was persuaded to return to its focus on the issue of Judge Raymond's membership in the Ravens.

As the picketing continued and the situation became even more intense, a plea for help was made by the city officials to the governor. Noteworthy was the fact that the suburban community could not move quickly to pass restrictive ordinances forbidding marches at night or on weekends so that the picketing and growing disorders would be kept under control. The town council of the suburban community was polarized in its attitudes so that no effective ordinance could be legislated. Several of the suburban politicians who had been in opposition to the dominant political clique took advantage of the situation to get good press coverage by publicly castigating these officials for allowing something like this to happen.

Under considerable pressure from the local community, the governor finally ordered the National Guard out for the coming weekend. He also offered the services of the State Industrial Commission to intervene and end the demonstrations. Over the weekend the situation got ugly and reached its peak with the crowds swelling to over 4,000. Many counter-pickets appeared and the National Guardsmen had to protect the demonstrators with fixed bayonets. Violence erupted at several places and tension was spreading beyond the suburban area, with threats of bombing the Negro ghetto in the city and the Negro community preparing for an attack by the whites.

The governor personally intervened with the youth council over the weekend and tried to get them to stop the demonstrations. They reminded him, however, that they were picketing peacefully and legally, and it was the white community that was precipitating the disorder. The governor, however, dropped the strong hint that if they didn't stop their demonstrations, he would ask the attorney general to issue an injunction enjoining them from picketing altogether.

Although the youth council did not entirely go along with the plea of the governor, they did agree to slow down the picketing and to a temporary truce in view of the fact that a fact-finding committee had been appointed by the governor to investigate discriminatory policies by private clubs.

In addition, a group of about 50 clergymen, Catholic, Protestant and Jewish, met with youth council representatives and Father Gentile and decided on these four actions:

1. A statement saying that they looked with disfavor upon public officials belonging to segregated clubs.

2. Appointment of a seven-member commission to meet with Judge Raymond and urge him to reconsider his decision not to resign from the Ravens.

3. Interviews by the committee with other judges and public officials who belonged to the Ravens to discuss the morality of belonging to clubs with discriminatory membership clauses.

4. Continuing efforts by clergymen to work on the issues and other civil rights matters with the youth council and the Greater "X" City Council on Religion and Race.

Although Judge Raymond turned down the clergymen's request, pressure against the Ravens' Club was mounting from many sides. The NAACP national chairman met with the governor to propose legislation forbidding public officials to belong to clubs with discriminatory membership policies. Two other civil rights groups announced they were sponsoring a "Quit the Ravens Day" march on a forthcoming Sunday. Members of that group picketed the Ravens Club and demonstrated before the courthouse, calling upon public officials to resign from the Ravens.

During the period of truce, much pressure was brought against the Ravens Club by the State Industrial Commission and other groups. Several prominent white religious leaders preached sermons to their congregation about the moral issues involved. The Governor's Commission on Human Relations issued a statement asking public officials to "consider in good conscience whether or not they can belong to an organization that discriminates on the ground of race and religion in its membership policies."

A few days later, one of the county judges resigned from the Ravens saying he did so on the basis of the statement by the Human Rights Commission. Other judges in the area also resigned from the Club as a matter of conscience but did not make their resignation public.

With the truce extending beyond Labor Day, the pickets went back to school, and the steam seemed to go out of the demonstrations. The press began to lose interest in the affair, but the youth council appeared to have precipitated a major change in community attitude, if not in practice.[4]

Despite the success of the militant action of the youth council, the dangers and risks inherent need to be emphasized. Conflict during the height of the demonstrations did get out of hand and damage to property, but not to persons, did occur. Conflict appeared to feed on itself. The notion of power for its own sake, rather than to achieve particular constructive objectives, began to develop. External forces, however, mainly through the governor's involvement and the clear support of other public officials and community groups, served to improve the bargaining position of the youth council, and ostensibly assured resolution of the conflict in its favor.

4. I am indebted to Alfred L. Kasprowicz for this example.

Bargaining

All community workers engage in a bargaining or exchange process. While maintenance-oriented workers tend to use normative resources, change-oriented workers tend more often to use coercive resources to achieve interorganizational accords. Maintenance-oriented workers seek to reestablish consensus mainly through exchange of good will, respect, approbation, and "reasonable" expectations. These resources derive from traditional program structure, legal sanction, and established community status of the organization. The change-oriented worker, because of his organization's lack of resources, especially economic and certain normative resources, must utilize measures such as embarrassment, annoyance, and threat of violence to achieve interorganizational agreement on objectives. In either case, the disequilibrium or disagreement must be resolved through a redistribution of resources. Conflict is resolved or avoided as bargaining takes place. Only recently, however, have youths, whether as delinquent gangs or constructive youth organizations, consciously sought to employ this process in their dealings with adult organizations.

> In April, when the war between the Lords and the Nobles was at its hottest, a veritable multitude of official, unofficial, political, and religious groups came courting. The Nobles group received most of the attention. SCLC sought to enlist the Nobles' leaders as special aides in the civil rights marches being planned. Gang leaders would be accorded special status and prestige in this process. But they would have to cease their violent activity. A West End Citizens group sought to furnish a recreation center for the Nobles. The YMCA hired a skilled street worker for the Nobles.

In the process of bargaining, the community worker's role is to support the demands of the youth organization, but it may be also to establish contact and communication between the antagonists or participants in the situation. His objective may be to clarify and highlight points at issue. His major contribution may simply be to identify the particular resources which can be exchanged to serve the benefits of the youth organization and the community it represents. In a youth organization committed to self-determination, the youth leaders themselves will need to make final determination of the items to be exchanged in order for an accord to be reached.

The worker explained that the youth group was now negotiating with an adult community group composed of agency representatives and business people. The adult group had agreed to push efforts to get a library built and a high school expanded. The adult group was already putting pressure on the mayor's office to get a public swimming pool into the neighborhood. The youths had declared that in return for these things they were going around preventing kids from engaging in vandalism, gang fighting, robbing stores, and attacking white people.

The worker said the kids had openly threatened that if some of these things were not forthcoming soon, they would resort to specific other actions, such as boycott and picket, which they had done earlier against a plant in the area which had discriminated against Negro youths.

Bargaining may fail for a variety of reasons. The issues may not have been clearly defined and the participants to the agreement may not have really reached an accord based on common understanding, or one or both participants may not have the power to produce or exchange the resources desired by the other, or one of the participants may have second thoughts after the agreement is reached and renege because the price paid for the other's resource is too high.

Coercive resources are extremely tenuous and ephemeral. The resource of threat may dissolve as soon as its possessors sit down at a bargaining table. Further, the conditional capacity to use these resources is of great importance in bargaining. Youth are particularly handicapped by lack of experience, the skills of articulate persuasion, and self-discipline to sustain influence effectiveness. The absence of economic resources is also a special obstacle once bargaining has begun.

After the Judge Raymond picket, the youth council seemed to lose ground. They became involved in many meetings and negotiations with the State Industrial Commission and the Ravens Club itself. In these meetings the youth council leaders often had difficulty restraining themselves, and their inappropriate behavior embarrassed and put them at a disadvantage in the community. Heretofore, they had many community leaders speak out in their behalf. Now the Ravens Club mounted a massive community education program on radio and TV that highlighted their benevolent and philanthropic works. Some people who had considered dropping membership in the Ravens now proclaimed their allegiance to the organization. The community reaction seemed to be that while the pickets had a moral point, so did Judge Raymond in not having his privacy invaded. Thus the moral issue shifted to one of invasion of privacy with a great many people now praising Judge Raymond's actions.

### Providing Support

The change-oriented organization does not avoid recognition and responsibility for social deficiencies and problems which reside in individual persons. The worker and youth leadership assume that social deprivations have incapacitated its membership and the low-income community at large. These deficiencies must be dealt with on their own terms, but never without relation to the social context in which they originated. Treatment, rehabilitation, and services of any kind must be developed in such a way that major attention is not distracted from primary influence efforts directed to the social environment. Indeed, the assumption is that participation itself in social change serves to enhance feelings of adequacy and provides learning of a positive educational and social nature.[5]

The priority assigned by the change-oriented approach to supportive services is lower than that by the maintenance-oriented approach and is often made a function of the direct environmental change program. Further, the style of support tends to be deprofessionalized. Members of the organization themselves are viewed as possessing capacity to help each other with individual problems. The character of service is highly informal, and bureaucratic procedures and limitations are kept to a minimum.

> Youngsters would come in almost any time of the day to participate in some kind of special program. For example, if

5. See Frank Reissman, "The 'Helper' Therapy Principle," pp. 27–32.

they were interested in typing they could come in late in the evening, almost till midnight and have some instructor available to work with them.

Probably the greatest asset that youth organizers have is their wide range of contacts and the positive, easy communication they have with other youths in the community. They are thus ideally suited to provide a referral service for other youths, even though they may not be able to offer qualitative or specialized services. The success of referral, however, depends on the client's readiness to make use of the resources of the agency ready to accept him. Training and educational programs are the obvious objectives for most referral efforts, but a fairly skilled job of counseling is required.

At first these youngsters want to be doctors and lawyers. But this is an impossibility for most of them. Many have already dropped out of school. The youth organizers try to encourage them to get down to reality and become involved in training programs that are available. This does not mean that the youth organizer doesn't at the same time orientate the kid also to system problems.

The youth organizer also attempts to assist various organizations —such as the school and social agencies—to help meet the needs of street youngsters. He may assist agencies to admit or readmit youngsters. He plays the role of communicator to the school or agency of those particular community and family problems which are relevant to the youth's difficulties. He may be an advocate on behalf of individual students, or if a school procedure or approach prevents a great many youths from taking full advantage of educational opportunities, may seek a change to benefit all.

The service component of the youth organizer's job, then, is closely related to strategies of change in the target system itself. That is, social services must never become an end in themselves. The assumption is that if opportunities are fully provided, they will be adequately utilized, with little need for additional supportive or mediating service.

## Facilitating Self-Determination

At least three distinct perspectives may be used in the resolution of a social problem such as delinquency. The problem can be viewed as a defect of individual human capacity and socialization, with efforts made mainly through services—whether social, psychological, or educational—and law enforcement to correct the deficiency; or the problem may be viewed as a defect of the social structure, particularly its failure to provide sufficient qualitative resources to all people to enable them to strive for success on equal terms. In this second instance, a variety of special educational, training, job-development, work-career, and income-maintenance programs may be provided for purposes of correction. A third perspective is that a social problem such as delinquency is essentially a political problem, that is, that people are socially incapacitated because they do not have the corporate power to remedy their situation. It is this latter view which more or less guides the strategy and tactics of the change-oriented worker, particularly the organizer.

While the advocate is probably more interested in modifications in the social structure and its opportunity-delivery system, the organizer is concerned essentially with the political development of people so that they can themselves change the structure of agencies and the community to better meet common human needs. The concept of corporate self-determination may, therefore, be critical in the development of a change-oriented youth organization, and for the change-oriented worker such self-determination is a guide to daily practice. (For the community worker oriented to social stability, corporate self-determination is treated more as a long-range objective.) But for the advocate, the concept of self-determination presents fundamental difficulties. While he seeks to invigorate and make effective the youth organization as part of the structure of a democratic society, he is constrained by his professional and sponsoring agency commitment to do this within limits which will not lead to a fundamental change of power positions in the community; the organizer is not bound by such constraints.

The development of the youth organization is guided by a certain political rationale: The delinquents must be engaged in significant community decision-making which affects their own lives and the positive development of the community. Probably no group in our society feels a keener sense of alienation than youths, particularly delinquent youths, in the low-income community. Youth are highly impatient and frustrated with their lack of involvement in community decisions and programs which affect them; further, it is assumed that lack of such involvement is a direct cause of delinquent behavior. In other words, a basic goal of the youth organization is the reduction of delinquent acts through the involvement of vulnerable youth in significant community decision-making processes and consequent development of community and organizational change activity which will flow from such decisions.

A basic function of any youth community group, then, is to constitute itself a corporate body representing the needs, interests, and concerns of youths in the community. Its objectives are to deliberate on issues in the community affecting the welfare of youth, to take positions and recommend action on these issues, and to exercise direct decision-making power on the programs established or to be established. Ideally, the structure of a youth organization assumes that each youth participant will have one vote equal to that of any other youth or adult participant. In most communities, this ideal structure has yet to be seen. Instead, the members of the board are self-selected or -appointed, sometimes by the sponsoring agency. Members of the board also frequently operate as staff, and opportunities for cooptation of the board by the sponsoring agency exist through formal and informal advisory mechanisms and especially by virtue of the fact that the sponsoring organization ordinarily serves as the fiscal agent.

Nevertheless, the intent of the structure is that it be representative of the youth sector of the community, however broadly or narrowly defined, and a key source of organizational power resides in the youths' initial right to select key staff and facilities, and subsequently to structure their own action and service programs:

> Well, when we first started, all teenagers came over and the building didn't look anything like this. We tore down defective partitions and scraped the walls, and did everything with just a little advice from Mr. Taylor, the director, and Mr. Graham, the assistant director. We picked the colors for the walls and all the furniture that's in the building. We hired everybody who is on the staff now, including Mr. Taylor and Mr. Graham. We hired them even before we knew for sure we were going to get funded.
>
> Like we had a meeting and nominations were set for

director and assistant director. In just about everything we do, there's a vote and Mr. Taylor and Mr. Graham don't have anything to do with the vote. They don't have anything to do with the meeting, either, because a youth is chairman of the board. You know, you just have your say, so if they don't like it, they just have to take it.

To what extent, however, skilled adult staff do guide or manipulate youths in the process of decision-making is an open question. Some of the evidence suggests that youths once sensitized to their responsibility for making decisions can and do exercise such responsibility. On the other hand, a critical ongoing problem may be, not that youths are prevented from or "manipulated" in the determination of organizational policy, but that they are indifferent, apathetic, lack confidence, and possess insufficient organizational skill. Staff may need constantly to encourage and support youth in taking responsibility for decisions and train them to implement decisions. In fact, two worker styles have arisen for educating and involving youths to their decision responsibilities. One style calls for provision of considerable freedom to youths to make decisions, with adult responsibility for setting appropriate limits. The other style calls for collective responsibility by the youths and the worker in decision-making and setting appropriate limits. The distinction is essentially one of a teacher-student relationship versus a more egalitarian relationship in which the worker is a leader among equals in making important decisions—essentially a paternalistic versus a democratic approach.

The paternalistic style, and it is as much a function of individual worker temperament as it is of parent organizational structure, recognizes that adolescents are being dealt with, and that adolescents will act like adults only part of the time. They will "mess up, get drunk and disorderly," at times; they will be their age in a lower-class community. At the same time, they have a contribution to make and the worker is there to help them. They need to be given freedom to have their thoughts and ideas accepted, yet they do need advice, guidance, and clear limitations.

The democratic style, and it is a radical approach, assumes that youths need a helping hand, but perhaps, in the past, "they have been given too much of a guiding or driving hand." This approach assumes that the adult, despite his experience, may not know more or know better what to do than the youths are capable of developing on their own.

You've got to come to meetings with these kids, with an open mind. They have to find the answers to community problems as they discover them. You can't pick their brains and say, "Uh, huh, this is how it is, so we will apply the remedy." They have to work with the problem and discover for themselves what the answers are.

In the beginning our meetings were extremely open-ended. The kids would say, "Gee, here we are, and there's the problem, and what do we do?" Sometimes they would look to me for the answer, as much as to say that I am an old pro, and I should know. And so, I would say, "Yeah, what do you do?" Then they would start kicking it around. After they got going, I would participate. They would shout me down, and I would shout them down. Pretty soon we were really working on an equal basis. I would make suggestions, never directions.

The democratic approach, furthermore, assumes the development of a strong group normative framework. Thus, youngsters who step out of line, who "goof on the job," who violate trust, or who work against the policy of the organization are chastised by the organization itself, rather than by the worker.

In general, we may observe that the limits to self-determination are more narrowly set by the advocate than the militant organizer. The advocate generally has a plan or some set of issues or concerns, often a function of parent agency goals and objectives, which he will encourage the youth organization directly or indirectly to support. He may not go all the way with youth decision-making.

The contest-oriented organization is committed to professional standards. Among other things this means that certain types of workers are likely to be selected to guide or staff the youth community organization. Such staff are often white and middle class; in other words, of a background and orientation quite dissimilar to that of lower-class delinquent ghetto youth. A serious cultural, class, and ethnic gap may develop.

We preached self-determination, yet our staff was three-quarters white. Our workers were mainly middle-class, young

Jewish intellectuals who basically could not establish a relationship with these kids who were from the streets and, in turn, could not understand half the time what the workers were driving at. Staff would use one kind of language with each other, and speak a different one to these kids. It was a subtle thing, but the kids sensed they were being basically talked down to, and even manipulated.

The militant organizer is more likely to have been recruited from the community, or from a population directly representative of the constituency of the youth organization. Theoretically he may not be so constrained by organizational pressures to move the youth organization in one direction, rather than another. He may provide wider latitude of decision-making by constituent, indigenous members of the community. A serious problem may arise, however, if the staff member has strong need for personal status and career advancement at the expense of the members of the youth organization. The organizer, while he may be less constrained by professional commitment and organizational standards, is also thereby freer to utilize situations for his own personal aggrandizement. There may be a credibility gap between what these workers say they do and what they actually do.

Mr. Jackson said the program belongs to the kids. They do whatever they want to, whenever and however they want to. He said there was something wrong with the existing social agencies. They are too middle class in their way of doing things. The kids have got to really run the organization.

Mr. Jackson spoke of the campaign against police brutality they were mounting. He was currently negotiating with Captain Longstreet of the local precinct on the issue. I asked if the kids themselves were involved in developing the demands made of the Captain. Mr. Jackson said the kids were not ready for this yet. It was also too complicated for them to handle specific things such as the negotiations he was carrying on with the probation department or the businessmen in the area. He said that he knows how to holler better than the kids. He has the political contacts to apply pressure. The kids don't have the knowledge or ability yet. Later, once basic patterns are set, they would be involved.

It is obvious that, in practice, the concept of corporate self-determination is interpreted differently by staff from different community organizations. There are apparently limits to the idea of self-determination. The limits tend to be more structural in the case of the advocate, and more personal in the instance of the militant organizer. We shall return to this matter later in our discussion of organizational control.

## Developing Political Power

It is a short hop, skip, and jump from the idea of self-determination to the concept of political power. The youth organization in its truly militant form seeks to recast the community and, indeed, the entire society in an image where justice, equality, and goodness prevail. It seeks, however, not only to direct its energies to achieving the ideal community but also to actualizing and enforcing its organizational power over as wide a scope of community activity as possible. The youth organization seeks to represent all youth in its community in a broad range of decisions. Operationally, this means that youth organizations with change orientations sooner or later may attempt to control the appointment or actions of those who manage the affairs of other organizations and of the community itself.

Control of organizations in the community, particularly those which implement important policy, such as social agencies, anti-poverty councils, and the police department, is a major political objective. The principal means available to the youth organization to achieve political objectives is coercion or, more accurately, the threat of violence, but it may also develop power through use of normative and economic resources. It is entirely possible, for example, that good relations may have been established between the local police and the youth organization. Various cooperative arrangements may have developed, perhaps subsequent to successful protest actions.

> The worker said that the youth group now had access to the police hierarchy. They could get on the phone, many of them individually, and call the local captain and inspectors downtown to talk to them about various problems. The police respect the youngsters and work out special arrange-

ments with them. For example, sometimes these youngsters got picked up for some minor infraction and the police called on the youth organization to square things before the youngsters were referred to the court. These were usually instances of minor nature, such as disorderly conduct. Indeed, this process had developed to such a point that the probation department was making use of members of the youth organization to sponsor various youth offenders, or act as assistant probation officers.

The youth organization may engage in a community political process through voter registration drives, or it may sponsor special meetings to inform adults of the issues at stake and what the particular candidates stand for. The candidates themselves may be invited to engage in debate with each other, or even with the more articulate members of the youth organization. While members of the youth organization are careful not to participate in partisan politics, the positions of approved candidates, as well as those of disapproved candidates, may be communicated widely in oral and printed form to the community, and it becomes obvious which way the youths would prefer the adults to vote.

For a few of the youth leaders, such experiences may serve as a training ground for future political careers. Youths are educated to the importance of participation in the political process, and their perspectives about community problems and affairs and about their own organizational responsibilities are politicized. But political development and sophistication of youth organizations are still in their beginning stages. For a youth organization to play an even limited political role, certain conditions apparently have to exist. The financial support of such an organization probably has to be derived from non-public sources, which is generally not the case at the present time. The community, itself, may need to be highly active politically, and a condition of fragmentation and weakness of community organizations and political groups in the community probably has to exist, permitting the youth organization to form coalitions and act as a balance of power. Further, effective means of communication in the community must be available to the youth organization.

The political power of any organization is half reality and half myth, particularly when that power is not tested through a public election process. In the following instance, a deliberate campaign to increase the political bargaining power of a youth organization —the Nobles—was attempted by its parent organization, in this case a Presbyterian church, through a "black paper."

> The enormous power of the Nobles exists because of the numerical strength of the whole nation, and because of its history of violence—a history not as violent, by the way, as the mythology invented by the police and the press has pictured it. The staff believes that the power of this group will not be diminished by lessening the force and incidence of violence. The power of this group is its numbers and its point of view regarding self-determination.

It is obvious that here at least a partial effort is being made to frighten the community and, in this instance, bargaining verges on blackmail, since the primary base for power is violence. But of course the youth organization whose membership is largely delinquent youths cannot be expected to adopt middle-class norms or base its political ideology on a traditional Christian ethic. The youth gang is the essence of militancy, although undeniably for largely inappropriate and destructive purposes, and should it adopt a political character, its illegitimate base may not be quickly transformed. The weltanschauung of the leaders may be, to say the least, exploitive, if not criminalistic. Thus, great care needs to be exercised by parent organizations, not so much in sponsoring politically oriented youth organizations, but in making certain that the groups supported are clearly committed to positive social change. A danger arises when a militant organization has not established a difference between legitimate and illegitimate objectives and legal and illegal means. On the other hand, the potential political power of the youth organization may not be realized, if its major resource—coercive violence or its threat—is too quickly surrendered.

### Exercising Control

Control of a youth organization emanates from at least four sources: the community structure, the parent organization, adult staff of the youth organization, and the youth organization itself.

No worker, not even the most militant, can operate without some attention to the constraints, both internal and external, on the organization which are necessary to the achievement of the youth organization's change goals. The organizer seeks not a community without rules or controls, but rather a system in which the existing rules are modified or replaced. The worker, while he may seek not to abide by one set of controls sanctioned by the established community, must project and adhere, then, to an alternate set.

A fundamental constraint on the worker, and one he must be clearly aware of, is the nature of the community context in which the youth organization operates. A youth organization established in an arch-conservative community, where political, economic, and social power are highly concentrated, cannot realistically set itself the same objectives as the youth organization in a liberal community, where power is diffused or located in multiple centers. Another constraint is related to traditional adult doubt about the capacity of adolescents generally and delinquents in particular. Another is that the youth organization may be viewed as a competitor for public funds and therefore as threatening to other organizations and community groups.

> We run into a lot of people and organizations that think the concept of youth organization is silly. They don't believe that young people can sit down and discuss social problems, and do anything constructive. They think we're wasting money that might better go to established programs, particularly their own.

Most community groups believe that a major function of any organization dealing with youth, even a youth community organization, should be controlling or policing the actions of youth.

> Frankie, a youth organizer, spoke of some of the community's unreasonable expectations. Whenever anything goes wrong, and any kids, for example, throw rocks, or there is vandalism or disorderly conduct anywhere in the community, they expect us to come running and put it down. This is impossible. We don't have the energy, and we have other programs as important. We do as much as we can, and I think too much. One of the things we're watching right now is not to get too involved in sponsoring kids from court.

Before you know it, all our time will be taken up as assistant probation officers.

In essence, the general community and most of its organizations are unwilling to accept the youth organization on its own terms. Continuing, and sometimes massive, attempts at coopting or derogation are made, and while these pressures can serve to cohere the organization, and sometimes to enhance its status and prestige, they also distract it from its major change mission. Inevitably, the youth organization is forced into a series of compromises in order to survive.

The formal origin and ongoing sustenance of a youth organization lies with its initiating adult organization, and informal but powerful advisement and consultation functions continue to be exercised by the parent organization, often through staff who formerly were employed by it. At worst, the youth organization may be little more than a creature of its founding agency; at best, a tension develops between the two organizations in relation to the freedom and integrity of decision-making to be exercised by the youth organization.

The worker plays a key role as a mediator or intermediary between external groups and the parent organization and the youth group. More importantly, he serves to bridge the norms and values of the adolescent, which still are sometimes delinquent, and those of the adult, which are not always legitimate. The manner in which he does this is essentially an extremely difficult art of supporting freedom of decision-making for youth while exercising responsible adult organizational control.

The community worker, even the militant organizer, must engage youth leadership at various levels of responsibility; for example, at the individual interpersonal or socialization level, and he needs to be both idealistic and realistic. The reality is that delinquent youths are not angels and do not become conforming youths overnight. Program inefficiency may develop, for example, if youths are not held accountable for putting in a full and good day's work as organizers. Clear specification of responsibilities for youth leaders is important. Further, delinquents may be manipulative and come to regard their positions as personal sinecures. Also, a climate of corruption may pervade the youth organization unless its members and workers clearly accept objectives and particular tasks required to make the organization morally viable.

Youths, delinquent youths in particular, are prone to impulsive or hurried action without due consideration of possible outcomes. The worker must try to act as a balance wheel. On the other hand, the exercise of too tight a control may have adverse consequences.

> The youth organization decided to picket the daily newspaper for its editorials against low-income housing. The newspaper also currently was attacking the parent organization for its administrative inefficiency in using antipoverty funds. While these two issues were not related in the minds of the youths, they were in the staff's. The parent organization threatened to withdraw funds and staff, if the youth organization picketed. The youths backed down.
>
> There was a marked decline in activity and vitality of the group after this incident. In fact, the group, for all intents and purposes, ceased to exist by the end of the year. It had to be reconstituted with an almost entirely new membership.

In this situation, more adequate communication and genuine collaborative decision-making might have prevented the crisis and ultimate demise of the group. The complexity of community situations and the volatility of youth organizations create operational hazards which cannot always be surmounted, however. Great presence of mind is required by the worker to blend appropriate portions of freedom or self-determination by youths with organizational control.

The skill of the worker is nowhere better tested than during a potential riot situation.

> We had one thing happen—we almost had a riot. One of the youth organizers was arrested at a block party. I was there and the kids were absolutely furious about it all. They suddenly stopped functioning as a staff, although they were on duty. They began functioning as young people who resented the police. They screamed and raved and threatened to do something about the situation. So it was building up, and I was worried that two police officers who were present might be attacked, and we would have a riot. So I went from one of the youth organizers to the other, and said, "Come on

now, let's do something about it, and make it count." Most of them I didn't get through to at first. They were too excited to listen. Then some of them agreed with me and said, "Let's go down to the police station." I said, "Great, I'll take some of the people in the car."

The other staff members and several of the youth organizers proceeded with most of the remainder of the crowd to the settlement house, a block away to wait the outcome of our meeting with the police.

Ultimately the youth organization must be responsible for developing its own controls. It must be clear about its goals and objectives and the means by which it can achieve them. Relevant organizational goals and norms must be internalized, and this will occur only as individual members develop a sense of corporate responsibility for each other's actions.

Key leaders of the youth organization have a major responsibility for developing organizational norms and controls. One youth organizer responded to the question about the major danger he saw in the development of the organization as follows:

A group can go wrong, if it loses the purpose for which it is formed. We must say that we'll do so and so, and then do it. It's true we can do the wrong thing. We can also sit still and do nothing, especially since some of the guys think they've got soft jobs as youth organizers.

This happened in my program, and the way I handled it was to tell the guys, "O.K., let's take the money away, so where are you going to be?" They know that the only way to keep getting the money is to work hard. You got to back up the threat from time to time and take jobs and money away from some of these guys.

The group itself must sooner or later develop its own rules for appropriate behavior and organizational action. The deviancy of individual members can best be controlled through group pressure, and continuing resort to group discussion and group action is essential. One community worker notes that he prefers group to individual activities for members of the youth organization:

For example, when I place a group of these youths on a tutoring project, as instructors in one of the schools, I get much better results than when I spread them out in many schools, placing one in each. The members of the organization goof, get lost, or somehow never do a very good job.

There are typical problems in developing the kind of group cohesion suggested: Groups may be too heterogeneous; the interests of members may diverge over time; one subgroup may become more interested in recreational activities, another in more militant action; differences in class or ethnic background may split the group, causing intraorganizational conflict and failures to adhere to appropriate organizational norms. Finally, there appears to be a tolerance point beyond which divergence of member characteristics may serve to disintegrate the group. Common interest or concern in relation to some set of issues would appear to be a major condition to maintaining group cohesiveness and permitting the exercise of effective controls.

A test of a youth organization's self-discipline and its ability to contribute to the community's welfare is its performance during a community crisis. If the organization acts with due regard for preservation of basic law and order and the legitimacy of key democratic processes, we may say it has arrived as a self-determining and responsible organization.

During the riots on the West Side, contrary to the fears of many agencies, the Nobles Youth Organization developed and carried out, with great effectiveness, a riot control program among the youths of the community. The following program evolved in close conjunction with the police, several churches, and parent organization: (1) The leadership of the Nobles manned a 24-hour phone service during the three days of tension and riot in the city. The Nobles called on the police and other agency workers every time there was even a slight possibility of disturbance. Members of the youth organization usually accompanied the police to the site of a potential youth disturbance and aided in dispersing any crowds that were developing. (2) The leadership of the organization was alert to any effort on the part of youths or adults to incite or plan a riot. They were prepared to report all such efforts to the police. None occurred, apparently. (3) Every night of the riot a dance was held by the Nobles and their members were compelled to attend. The dances lasted until curfew, and the curfew was enforced by leadership.

Certain people in the community assessed that the most important reason that riots did not occur in the community was the preventive action of the Nobles.

Thus, though the youth organization is a difficult social device to manage by the parent agency or other organizations in the community, it may well represent an evolving institution that presents extraordinary opportunity to solve simultaneously a variety of adolescent status problems, including delinquency. It may also be that the choice of acceptance or rejection of the idea of the youth organization is no longer open to the adult community. A lower-class youth population sensitized to the problems of the ghetto may demand corporate responsibility. It may no longer be content to accept passively the conditions imposed upon it by the dominant adult society. At the same time, unless basic social needs and aspirations are met within the framework of an affluent and egalitarian society, youth organizations can become instruments for riot, insurrection, and revolution.

# 6

# Interorganizing: Cooptation

We may view interorganizing as a process of purposeful impact on another organization, the consequences of which are of value to a particular agency or a constellation of agencies and community groups. The nature of the influence, furthermore, may be systematic or ad hoc. We may classify interorganizing efforts along two dimensions: purpose or intention, and character or degree of development. Four patterns of interorganizing are identified: (1) cooptation, (2) cooperation, (3) coordination, and (4) planning (Table 1). We may also view these types of interorganizing as overlapping phases, moving spirally from simple, situational, and individualistic efforts to complex, systematically designed, and mutually interrelated attempts to achieve organizational and, indeed, community goals.

TABLE 1

TYPES OF INTERORGANIZATIONAL ADAPTATION

| CHARACTER OF EFFORT (DEGREE OF DEVELOPMENT) | ORGANIZATIONAL INTENTION (PURPOSE) | |
|---|---|---|
| | Individualistic | Communalistic |
| Ad hoc | cooptation | cooperation |
| Systematic | coordination | planning |

Cooptation is a bargaining mechanism,[1] sporadically used, by which one organization, through effective influence or power, causes another organization directly or indirectly to maintain or change its objectives, with limited reciprocal effect. The coopted organization adapts to the pressure of the initiating organization which is in a position to enforce its demands. The organization thus coopted "enhances its chances for survival by accommodating to existing centers of interest and power within its area of operation."[2] The coopted organization, as well as the organization initiating the interorganizational effort, may emerge from a community situation with more, rather than less, power than it had before, or the coopted organization may find itself in a weaker position after subjection to the influence of another organization. It is possible also for a small, weak organization, depending on the situation, to coopt a large, strong organization.

The concept of cooptation is not used here in its formal sense as a process "by which new elements are absorbed into the leadership of an organization as a means of averting outside threats."[3] It is employed in its informal, reciprocal, and wider sense of control of another organization's program decisions. Cooptation limits the opportunity of another organization to choose its goals. At the same time, it reduces the possibilities of antithetical actions by all the organizations concerned.[4]

The important considerations are that the organization initiates and develops influence efforts toward other organizations, presumably to achieve its own organizational goals and program enhancement. Whether the organization receiving or responding to influence actions derives significant gains is of secondary importance to the initiating organization. These interorganizational efforts, furthermore, arise, depending on the needs and interests of the coopting organization, situation by situation. Cooptation may be regarded as the principal form of interorganizing existent in the community at the present time, since organizational interests tend more often to be competitive rather than cooperative.

1. Philip Selznick, *TVA and the Grass Roots,* pp. 14–16, 217.
2. *Ibid.,* p. 217.
3. Peter M. Blau and W. Richard Scott, *Formal Organizations: A Comparative Approach,* pp. 196–97.
4. James D. Thompson and William J. McEwen, "Organizational Goals and Environment: Goal-Setting as an Interaction Process," p. 143.

The cooperative but ad hoc pattern of interorganizing arises when organizations are mutually or collectively concerned about a problem and act to achieve a common goal. An organization agrees, usually on a short-term and limited basis, to seek jointly the achievement of an objective with another organization. Cooperative endeavor in this sense tends to occur mainly during times of crisis or when there is a sudden reallocation of resources such that a joint effort results in greater gain than individual organizational endeavor.

Coordination, for our purposes, refers to a deliberate and systematic effort, usually over a substantial period of time, by which organizations seek their respective objectives in a manner which does no harm to, and, indeed, often enhances, each other's program. This form of interorganizing is essentially a more systematic type of cooptation, although it may also have cooperative elements. It is a deliberate system of relationships between or among organizations in which domains of influence are pursued by particular organizations with minimum interference from other organizations. It is not usually a truly cooperative system in the sense that organizations share significant common objectives. Shared objectives are either of minor or *pro forma* value, with insufficient authoritative input.

The coalition of agencies to achieve particular program objectives may be viewed as a form of coordination which verges on planning. Coalition formation is a process by which organizations become formally committed to a limited range of significant objectives and participate in joint or cooperative decision-making in relation to them.

Planning is the most sophisticated form of interorganizing and provides for systematic collaboration by organizations to achieve long-run common ends. It differs from coordination in its emphasis on meaningful as well as collectively determined goals, and on rationality of interorganizational endeavors. The notion of coordination in its truly meaningful and cooperative sense is incorporated and further developed by planning. This kind of coordination may be viewed as part of a planning process directed to the systematic achievement of significant and common ends. In its successful form, planning tends to be centralized, official, and contains a large authoritative input.

These various forms of interorganizing may be regarded as a series of stages, each partially incorporating elements of a previous stage. They characterize the community as it develops from the inauthentic and incompetent to the authentic and competent community. Thus, cooperation includes some cooptative elements; coordination embraces elements of cooptation and cooperation; planning includes elements of coordination and cooptation. In the light of the relatively free and competitive nature of interorganizational relations which prevails in urban communities today, however, it is likely that cooptation and coordination are the more common forms of interorganizing.

Interorganizing, like organizing, is characterized by two general orientations, social change and social stability. The stability-oriented worker is more likely to develop interorganizational relationships in terms of some widely shared interest, preference, or objective. The change-oriented worker is more likely to approach interorganizing through an intensity of commitment to a specific interest, preference, or object, which may not be widely shared. The resources of influence of the stability- and change-oriented workers will vary in relation to the interorganizing process. The resources of the enabler and the developer will continue to be normative and economic, and those of the advocate and organizer, in addition, may emphasize coercion. As the form of organizing moves from cooptation to planning, there tends generally to be a decreasing emphasis on use of coercive resources of influence. Indeed, the concept of interorganizing in this progression suggests a condition of increasing adjustment or adaptation which tends to reduce the viability of a social-change orientation, if by change we are referring to significant institutional reorganization as enforced by one of the participants to an interorganizational relationship. Interorganizing, particularly cooperation, coordination, and planning, presents a built-in bias toward social stability.

## The Social-Stability Approach

The cooptive tactics or subprocesses employed by the stability-oriented social worker are: informal relationship, resource exchange, interpretation, complementation, and mediation.

### Informal Relationship

By and large, there exist relatively few formal or official patterns of relationship between agencies or organizations in the community. Yet, it is obvious that one organization cannot usually accomplish its goals and objectives without some kind of relationship with another group. At the same time, no group or organization, at least not at the local community level, is sanctioned to interfere or influence the objectives, structure, or programs of another organization whose operations are defined as legitimate. Consequently, various patterns of informal and in time traditional relationship arise between organizations.

We should note, furthermore, that patterns of informal relation between police or law enforcement agencies and social welfare organizations have traditionally been poor, particularly where there is a polarization or clash of ideologies.[5] The clash, theoretically, is between an authoritarian-punitive orientation towards clients, and one of humanitarianism-welfare. In reality, however, certain police departments, or segments of a police force, particularly the juvenile division, move toward a welfare function, while certain social agencies and community organizations are highly committed to the control of deviant or delinquent behavior.

The power of the community worker to influence members of other organizations where no formal set of interorganizational policies and procedures has been established and, indeed, where ideological differences exist, depends on the positive evaluations he can communicate to and receive from the other organization. The personal character of the relationship established between the community worker and the representative of the other organization is, therefore, often the critical means by which influence is directed and objectives achieved. For example, whether the police will move quickly and efficiently in the control of a delinquency situation, potential or actual, may depend significantly on the quality of informal relationship the community worker has established with the local police commandant. Even more important, whether the police will temper their interpretation of what is delinquent, or

5. John P. Clark and Edward W. Haurek, "A Preliminary Investigation of the Integration of the Social Control System," pp. 9–11.

even overlook certain infractions, may depend on the influence the community worker can exert through his informal relationship with police officers. Particular relationships, if they are positive, serve to counter mind-sets or stereotyped patterns of behavior built up by the police with respect to low-income ghetto youths. These positive informal relations may take time to establish, however.

> The police used to be looking to arrest our youth aides and even some of our adult community workers. The older teen-agers, now working for the agency, were especially vulnerable. But the fact that Perry Gordon, one of the adult community workers, was around so often and got to know many of the police officers seemed to make a major difference. He would always stop to talk with them, and took great pains to explain what they were trying to do with various gang kids in the neighborhood. He even involved several of the policemen in off-duty volunteer coaching jobs for the kids.

The informal and positive character of the relation which the community worker develops with representatives of other organizations, whether the police, school, or social agency, permits him to modify attitudes and behaviors which are antithetical to the interests and objectives of his own organization. Face-to-face contact in a series of non-threatening situations appears to stimulate perception and understanding of each participant as capable of performing some legitimate role. The police, prone to regard themselves as members of a beleaguered minority, may perceive that others positively accept them in their role as "public servants." Such informal relationships tend to lower barriers to changed expectations of what other individuals and groups will do, and anticipation of negative or hostile stimulus and response is thus reduced.

## Resource Exchange

Resources such as information and services may be exchanged between the community worker and representatives of other organizations. The exchange may be initiated by one organization and serve its purpose more than that of the other organization, but in general these exchanges assist each of the organizations to better fulfill their respective objectives. For example, when both the community worker and the police officer or teacher are concerned —even if for different reasons—with the conduct of members of a delinquent gang, opportunities for cooptation arise.

> Well, it's a two-way contact. I know the neighborhood better than the new juvenile officers who are supposed to cover the whole south side of the city. I know when things are happening or going to happen in the community. This is the kind of information the police want, in order to be on top of every situation. So I feed them information, but just enough so they can do the kind of job we think is effective.
> · They can stop things from happening and prevent trouble. If they break up a fight, based on information we give them, we can take some of the credit; and we let the community know.

### Interpretation

The community worker may also influence other organizational representatives through the skillful use of communications media. He is constantly interpreting and seeking to persuade others of the value of his organization's policies and objectives. The following is an interpretation and set of recommendations developed by a community worker at the close of a conference on ghetto youth. He had arranged the conference in such a way as to involve police officers as well as members of youth gangs, its chief purpose being to modify the structure and operations of the police department. The proceedings of the conference were published and widely distributed in the community. The following is a summary statement at the end of the published report:

> The basic question to ask, in our view, is "Where does it all begin?" There is no doubt that these teenagers are sometimes in the wrong. But there also seems little doubt that some teenagers are suspect in the eyes of authorities, not for anything they may have done, but because of who they are—their past, their associates, their style of dress and language, and so forth. Arbitrariness by law enforcement agencies only reinforces the teenage view that it doesn't matter what you do, you're going to get it anyway.
> There are immediate steps that can be taken to improve

the situation. One of them has already been taken by the Police Department. It is the Police Community Relations Division. This unit should be strengthened in the Police Department, and it should involve the people who are the real indigenous leaders of the communities with high crime rates and delinquency problems. A second step would be an intensive program of education of the policemen on the beat.

The effect of the cooptive technique of interpretation and the use of mass media may come very slowly or, on the other hand, the response may come quickly, positively, and with little resistance. A maintenance-oriented worker reports:

> I had a long conversation with Captain Chester about the state of police-Puerto Rican relations. He said he was just becoming aware of how deep hostilities ran. He expressed appreciation of the time and effort I had put out, particularly in keeping him abreast of matters occurring in the community. He agreed with my suggestion that he publish a weekly column in a local paper on issues relevant to police-Puerto Rican relations. He was ready to implement these suggestions right away.

Effective communication is an extremely important lever in almost any effort at behavioral change. It is required, not only in the initial phase of the change process, but later in the stabilization of desired organizational behavior. Public communication, or a consensual display of support for the coopted organization, serves to reinforce positive behavior.

> The youth workers have informed us that the behavior of uniformed policemen toward the Puerto Rican groups has changed drastically. Although they continue to do their job of policing, they approach it with more of a professional attitude and, certainly, with courtesy. The youth worker indicated, further, that the Latin Angels, a youth gang in the area, were very happy with this turn of events, and are showing a willingness to cooperate and help the police in some cases. As a result of this change, our community organization is calling a special public meeting of the major Puerto Rican groups in the community, to which the commander

will be invited. The purpose of the meeting will be to indicate appreciation for the change in relations brought about.

## Complementation

The worker may influence the decisions and programs of another organization through a process of complementation, or providing complementary services, assisting the target organization to more efficiently carry out its objectives, his purpose being to make certain that the other organization's program meets community expectations, or at least the expectations of the community worker's organization. For example, for a variety of reasons an organization may be held responsible for an area of service but will not have the personnel or expertise to adequately render the service. The community worker may either secure such resources and make them available to the organization or, through some other arrangement, assure that the area of service is adequately fulfilled. In the following example, a worker from a neighborhood organization is able to develop a citizen's project to deal with a truancy problem which the local public schools are unable to handle.

> We are in a district which has the poorest attendance rate in the city. A public school principal asked me to suggest what might be done. I consulted with the people in the neighborhood association, and we came up with a plan which the district superintendent and the general superintendent of schools agreed to.
>
> We have given the project the name "Committee of Friends." This committee is a group of parents who will work on the truancy problem. We all know that truancy is usually a first step toward delinquency. Four pilot elementary schools will be used to begin with. Parents from the committee will be on the streets and available in the neighborhood from nine o'clock to twelve noon and from one o'clock to three o'clock. Any youngster of elementary school age whom a parent sees will be stopped and questioned as to why he is not in school. If the parent knows the child, there'll be no difficulty in stopping him. If the parent doesn't know the child, she'll watch to see where the child goes. A telephone call will be made to our office, identifying the child and the

place he goes to. We will then contact the appropriate school attendance officer. If the attendance officer is out in the field, the principal will be contacted. If the principal feels that it is an emergency, the youth bureau of the police department will be contacted.

Regardless of how it gets worked out, every child not in school, and not accounted for as being excused, will be checked out. We expect to cut the truancy rates drastically.

## Mediation

The primary means at the disposal of the maintenance-oriented worker for influencing another organization is mediation. The community worker uses this process when he adjusts the relationship of two organizations or groups to each other. Generally, one of the organizations is an authoritative agency, such as the police, the school, or sometimes a youth-serving agency, and the other is a community group, or some section of the client population which is dissatisfied or concerned with the performance of the authoritative agency. In a sense, the worker plays an ombudsman function. Only it is more than this, inasmuch as the worker may seek to change the perspectives and actions of both parties engaged in a disagreement or dispute. In this instance, the community worker is fulfilling his function as a stabilizing force in the community.

Informal relationship and interpretation are attendant processes often employed in carrying out the role of intermediary. The worker may attempt to bring parties in a dispute together. Each side will tell its story or air grievances. Greater understanding of respective role expectations and reduction of tension are sought, permitting smoother relationship between organizations and more effective delivery of services, as it meets the standards of the mediating agency.

For various reasons, a community group, such as a group of parents, may have difficulty in gaining access to an official in a school system. However, by virtue of the multiple positive connections the community worker has with the school hierarchy and the parents' group, both organizations may be brought together by him to resolve the interorganizational difficulty.

There was a terrible relationship between the parents and the teachers of the local schools. Indeed, there were physical clashes between teachers and parents. Some of the parents would go to the schools and fight with the teachers right in front of the children.

Our organization decided that I should write directly to the president of the board of education to see if something could be done to work out the problem. We didn't expect to get an answer back, at least not so quickly. Right away we got invitations from several principals to bring the respective parent groups in for discussions.

The problem was, in large measure, that Spanish-speaking parents did not understand the program of the school. So, in these meetings, and some involving teachers, we told them it was important to take extra pains to communicate, so that the parents understood what the schools were trying to do. Also, the teachers had to be more tolerant of the kids.

Also, we tried to help the parents get after their kids so that they would be able to do the extra work needed to keep them at grade level. In one case, the parents were very impressed with a tour of the classrooms and facilities and really got an appreciation of how hard the teachers and principal were working to give their youngsters a good education.

Our organization's main purpose here was to reduce community pressures on these kids, pressures which might contribute to delinquency.

Sometimes two sections of the population may be at loggerheads and the authoritative agency is brought to the support of one or the other by the worker. A youth commission reports the following incident:

The Hilltown Chamber of Commerce alleged that, as a result of a teenage dance hall, property damage, arson, and thefts had increased in the community. Our organization called these allegations to the attention of the Tenth Ward Alderman, the Hilltown Community Council, and the Fourth District Police Commander.

We investigated the dance hall program under private management. A carefully supervised program had been worked out and involved the use of two off-duty police officers. Regulations and standards of dress and behavior were apparently fully complied with. We checked with other organizations, talked with the kids, and finally spoke with the Fourth District Police Commander. At first, he reacted negatively to the program, obviously because of pressure he was getting from some of the businessmen and residents in the area. I asked specifically how valid the complaints were. He said that he had checked them all out and found they were not true. The commander mentioned there had been a rise in arson in the area, but this was attributed to a couple of youths who lived in another part of the community and had no connection with the dance hall program.

Meanwhile I encouraged several of the parents and the alderman to visit the dance hall when teenagers were present. I also discovered that a regular meeting of the Hilltown Community Council was to be held in a week's time. I contacted the director of the Council and got him to include an agenda item on the dance program and to invite down all the concerned participants, including representatives from the Chamber of Commerce, the alderman, the police commander, and the parents.

There was heated debate about the dance hall program until the police commander spoke. He went through each complaint he had received about the program and showed that each one was unfounded.

The alderman could not be present, but his secretary had visited the program and said she was impressed by the supervision and conduct of the youth. Some of the parents who let their children go to the program spoke in favor of it and encouraged other parents to send their children.

All the organization present agreed to the motion that the issue be terminated and support was voted for the dance hall program. It was recommended as a good resource for youth in the community, based on the evidence presented.

The intermediary role of the community worker may be difficult and unrewarding, since a great deal of projected or transferred hostility and anger may be directed against him. Clarity about his objective and care not to become unrealistically identified with one side or the other are essential requirements. Further, some situations are not always effectively resolved, even with the best intentions and skill of the worker.

In the stability-oriented approach, interorganizing by either the enabler or the developer differs only in degree. It is likely that the development worker makes greater use of the informal relationship process and the enabler greater use of the interpretation and mediation process. The strength of the developer lies in his greater access to informal channels of communication and authority in the community. The enabler, who more often tends to be a professional, has greater command of skills of interpretation and more acceptable status and entrée with authoritative organizations in the community. Both the enabler and the development worker, however, are highly committed to the maintenance and enhancement of existing institutional arrangements between organizations.

## The Social-Change Approach

Interorganizing at the level of cooptation, as indicated already, is concerned with the influence of decisions and programs of other organizations, primarily to meet the objectives of the community worker's organization. For the stability-oriented worker the central purpose is enhancement of services and effective control of a community problem. For the change-oriented worker, the central purpose is significant change in institutional patterns. There is a built-in dynamic in interorganizational processes, however, which requires the change-oriented worker to limit his objectives so that they are at least minimally feasible by the standards of the other organization.

We have identified at least four major cooptive processes characteristically used by the change-oriented worker: coercion, service replacement, support for innovation, and mediation. The advocate will more frequently make use of processes of support for innovation and mediation; the militant organizer, the processes of coercion and service replacement. Our illustrations again will be drawn largely from the area of community worker-police relations, but the objective here of course is to significantly modify program and tactics rather than to support or make them more effective.

## Coercion

In its extreme coercive form, cooptation is synonymous with conflict and seeks ostensibly to impair the decision-making capacity of the adversary. The change-oriented organizer and his group may launch immediately into attack against the other organization. Provocation by the organizer's group, however, tends to beget counter-provocation and abuse. There is no communication or interchange between the two organizations other than through the mass media or some intermediary.

> Reverend Jones contended via the newspapers that the raid was "police harassment." Captain Smith said in reply to Reverend Jones' charges, "That is the most asinine statement I have ever heard." According to Reverend Jones, the police go beyond their legal rights. They subject people, especially youths in the church program, to abusive language and may even interrogate youths at gun point. "The police act like twelve year olds."
>
> Reverend Jones said his church is preparing a suit against the police for false arrest and criminal damage to church property, on behalf of the people of the community.

If a direct meeting or confrontation between the militant organizer and the police occurs, it is short-lived and characterized by extreme aggressiveness, usually initiated by the organizer and his group. The militant organizer does not make requests of the police —he demands.

> At this time the youngster from the youth action group spoke up at the police meeting with the police; adults representing various organizations were present. The three youths were sitting in back of the crowded room. The chief spokesman for the youths said he had three demands to make of the police. First, that a local civilian review board be established; second, that all police be given psychological tests to screen out unfit officers; and third, that all local police be selected from people living in the immediate neighborhood.
>
> A little later in the meeting, another one of the youths got up and spoke of the unfriendliness of local police officers. The captain was a little hot under the collar by this time, but

still managed to answer the young people in a reasonable fashion. It was apparent to the observer that the youths were trying to egg the policemen on. The third member of the youth contingent finally got up toward the close of the meeting and said there had been no purpose to the meeting. They had accomplished nothing. One of his colleagues interrupted him and said the police could show their good faith, if they simply stayed out of the community during the summer coming up.

The adults at the meeting became extremely restive. Several began to shout at the youths, claiming the need was for more, not fewer, police. The youngsters got up and paraded out of the meeting room.

The coercive tactic, especially for the advocate, may be the outgrowth of a long series of unsuccessful meetings and confrontations by community groups with a particularly authoritarian and resistive organization. Use of coercion may follow failures in communication, but it may also itself cause further blockage in communication. The value of a coercive effort in the short run appears to be that it highlights a series of unsolved problems. Its success depends on the readiness of the target organization to accept at least minimally some of the objectives of the community worker and his group. The success of a picket or any demonstration therefore ultimately lies in the significance of the moral imperatives of the worker and his group. The worker must depend on the activation of supportive sentiments from key elements in the general community or even the particular target organization against the resistive organization, or more often subgroups within it.

The police took a totally aggressive and resistive position with the youngsters. Finally, one of the fellows said to the Police Captain, "You know the real problem is that you never listen. You are always telling us what a citizen's responsibility is. We want you to listen to what we are complaining about." The two sessions with the police ended in shouting and angry exchanges, with the youths feeling more frustrated than before. Out of these frustrations came the decision to picket the local police on a police brutality issue.

An interesting thing occurred during the picketing. The

police captain and his men were standing outside laughing at and castigating the pickets. The police were counter-provoking the kids and in some ways were inflaming the crowd which surrounded the pickets. A local woman, known in the community as extremely ill mentally, reached over the police barrier and yanked one of the pickets by her hair and dragged her over the barrier. At which point, the worker with the youth organization indicated that this woman should be arrested for molesting a picket. But nothing was done.

Luckily, a chief inspector of police had just arrived on the scene and was told of the incident. He immediately discussed this with the captain.

We don't know what the cause-and-effect sequence was, but a week later there was a new captain at the precinct and relations with the community and our youth group have begun to improve.

The coercive tactic is a drastic, sometimes last resort to bring about change in an organization's pattern of doing things. Interorganizing and organizing at the level of coercion are quite similar. The key resource of influence is essentially the power of people marshaled to express indignation and hostility. It is an instrument of great force whose consequences cannot always be anticipated.

## Service Replacement

This tactical process is based primarily on the notion that many key community services ordinarily offered by the professional can be better provided by relatively untrained persons from the immediate community itself. The change-oriented worker may accept the notion that the professional, whether as policeman, social worker, councilor, or teacher can do a good job, or even a better job than the non-professional, indigenous person. But for a variety of organizational and professional reasons, the professional may not be able to perform an adequate service in a particular community at a given time; that is, the interests and concerns of the ghetto population are not met by the existing system of services. Under these circumstances, the community worker and his group may insist that a replacement service be instituted.

For example, the police may be accused of causing the very trouble which they are expected to prevent. If the existing police service is not effective, then it needs to be replaced. The community work organization may believe it is capable of engineering and managing such a replacement service.

Mr. S. indicated that much of the problem which arose during the time of the riot was because of police action. He said that the police could have controlled the situation but were pigheaded and rushed in with billy clubs and dogs. Mr. S. insisted that people in the community can impose their own controls.

He pointed to the recent summer festival that was arranged in such a way that the police did not move into the area, but were on the periphery and mainly checked with the patrols organized by the group. These volunteers actively policed the area, and there were no problems.

The replacement threat is usually limited, its major purpose being to obtain modification in the target organization's strategy and program, though it may also be used to persuade the target organization to experiment with non-professionals in a variety of fields or client-contact positions. The replacement tactic, further, may evolve into a complementation tactic in which the change organization works cooperatively with the established or authoritative organization to manage crises in the community; for example, the change organization may volunteer or expect to be called on by the police to prevent disorders or assist with riot control.

Another variation of the replacement tactic is the provision of a direct staff service, such as training, by the change-oriented organization to the authoritative organization, for example, the police department. A variety of community groups may claim that the police do not understand the problems of low-income, minority-group members, and need special training in community relations, the assumption being that the police are not capable of providing this training function. In one large urban community, the local bar association requested and received permission to provide training in human relations to police officers stationed in slum areas of the city.

## Support for Innovation

The change-oriented worker, more often the advocate than the militant organizer, may develop a rationale for thorough overhaul of a major institution in the community, with proposals for significant change in purpose, structure, and program coming from closely allied professional organizations or special task forces. The progressive elements within a particular field such as law enforcement, education, employment counseling, or social work may encourage those structural rearrangements which bring the organization into closer relationship with the needs of the community, particularly those of the low-income ghetto residents. Change in establishment organizations may thus come through the careful articulation of new rationales, ideas, and insights about organizational service, usually by respected colleagues or experts in the particular or an adjoining professional field. (Because of the advocate's professional base, his influence is stronger in this interorganizational context than that of the militant organizer.)

The late Dean Lohman of the School of Criminology at the University of California, Berkeley, California, speaking before a Senate committee in 1959, encouraged a major shift in emphasis and role of the juvenile division of the police department from a punitive and restraining to a case-finding and referral function:

> The juvenile police officer's role as a professional is to be reconstructed so that he functions as a catalytic agent, through whom the resources, services, and institutions of the community can be activated in behalf of the needs of problem children. Hence, the target is no longer the act, nor its perpetrator, but "the condition of the child." The answer is no longer a single type of agency solution but those aspects of the community's total resources which relate to a particular child's needs.
>
> In short, we should increase the capacity of the community to serve the needs of its problem children by increasing the capacity of the police to draw upon the totality of the community's resources.[6]

Lohman added that the reconstruction of the police officer's role does not mean making social workers of policemen, but rather connecting these two professions. The police have partial responsibility for this.

6. Joseph D. Lohman (Statement), Subcommittee to Investigate Juvenile Delinquency, of the Committee on the Judiciary, U. S. Senate, 86th Cong., 1st sess., S. res., pt. 2, *Juvenile Delinquency*, pp. 116–17.

I want to say parenthetically immediately someone will say, "Do you want to make police officers into social workers?" Categorically not. Social work is a profession and ought to be performed by people trained for that profession, but social work cannot be effectively related to police action unless the policemen as law enforcement officers see in that function something that stands in relation to the job they do, and regard it as something that they will employ in discharging their obligation as law enforcement officers.[7]

While many, if not most, large city police departments would disagree with Lohman's model of police function, a police chief here and there may begin to experiment with the notion that the policeman cannot be an effective law enforcement officer unless he is also a community problem solver. The rationale and program of the community relations unit of the San Francisco Police Department stems from ideas similar to Lohman's and those of other leading professionals and experts in the law enforcement field. Chief Thomas J. Cahill of the San Francisco Police Department apparently agrees with the importance of a broad community orientation by police officers.

A police-community relations program affords opportunities to the police to become engaged in positive activity on behalf of the community. We also have learned that a police-community relations program invariably results in police involvement and discussion of such matters as education, employment, and housing. With regard to the last observation, there are those who believe that the police should not become involved in matters not germane to police work per se, the argument being that such matters are the concern of the social worker. While there are those who may argue this point with some validity, the experience in San Francisco indicates otherwise. The attention to, and the handling of, some matters not essentially police in nature has demonstrated to the people that the police are concerned and do care about their problems.[8]

7. *Ibid.*
8. Thomas J. Cahill, "The Police and Community Tensions," *Police Community Relations*, p. 3.

The notion that the police can be and should be helpful to youth, as well as controlling them, has taken the form of referral of youths for jobs, and interpreting and "squaring" arrest records of youths to employers. In one city, the local antipoverty agency persuaded the police department to station community relations officers in its Economic Opportunity Centers to deal with employment and arrest problems.

> Officer J. recalled one case in which a youngster had two charges of robbery against him. The employer refused to hire the youngster. The officer checked the record and found that the youngster had been booked twice in a southern town on suspicion of robbery. But on neither occasion had anything been proved against him. The police officer was able to get the employer to change his mind and hire the youngster.

Such institutional changes reflect fundamental reorientation to goals, structures, and procedures of operation, but they probably depend on and are more a response to changing ideas developed within a field than to pressures from opposition groups outside of it. Interorganizing for change here is a matter of a respected authority within a given field, or closely allied to it, exerting significant influence, direct and indirect, on it. It tends to be part of a process of change characteristic of every vital profession.

The community worker can usually play only a limited role in this process: He can support and work through the progressive forces within a profession for those organizational changes desirable to his own group.

## Mediation

On occasion, the change-oriented worker—especially the advocate—may, like the enabler, play an intermediary role, seeking to influence the expectations of organizations in conflict (usually an authoritative agency and a client group). The advocate may seek to bring contending parties together in order to open channels of communication, exchange views, and obtain some agreement or redefinition of respective roles. He plays more of a change-oriented role, however.

Our worker persuaded the program director of the YMCA, a priest of St. George's Catholic Church, and the police to meet with members of the young Kings.

As a result of the discussion of their grievances, the young Kings began to realize that their antisocial behavior only served to aggravate strong and perhaps excessive police measures. The police sergeant, on the other hand, promised to check on "harassment" complaints, especially if they were made promptly and accurately.

It is fair to suggest that the youngsters participated in this meeting, because they understood and trusted the role of the Community Action Committee to really obtain important changes in the community, especially concessions from the police.

There may be difficulties when an advocate plays the role of the intermediary, however, especially if he is also committed to the use of coercive tactics.

People might say there are contradictions in the community work of the agency. Here we are bringing together kids and agencies trying to work for compromise and agreement around police problems. Yet at the same time we have a worker assisting a youth group to picket the police.

This presents inevitable strains for an agency. But we will have to live with the strains. The staff feels it has to walk a very thin line, and it is confusing sometimes whether we should attack or go slow in helping these other organizations to change.

## Conclusion

The community worker, regardless of orientation, cannot push or pressure beyond the capacity and willingness of the target organization to respond affirmatively. What this capacity is at any given time and place is not always clear. Undoubtedly it is related to the readiness of the larger community to commit itself to support of organizational change. It is this important public commitment which the change-oriented worker seeks to stimulate and develop by his attacks on recalcitrant or slow-moving organizations. The stability-oriented worker more often depends on the normative resources available to him in his own institutional system to influence other organizations. He is much less willing to seek open support from the community at large or to provoke a crisis.

In either case, the process of cooptation is dependent on the commitment of the worker to achieve the objectives of his own organization. Benefits which are yielded to the target organization are of secondary consideration. The worker operates on the basis of his own organization's distinctive analysis of what serves the needs of the community best in the solution of a given problem, and without equivalent regard for the interests of the other organization.

# 7

# Coordination

Coordination emphasizes the systematic adjustment of organizations to each other's interests. It is concerned mainly with the regularized and the reciprocal character of communication and action of organizations to meet individualistic organizational objectives.

We shall speak of two kinds or levels of coordination: elementary and sophisticated. Elementary coordination refers mainly to a condition of reciprocal communication of decisions; this is the most common form of coordination among independent agencies and groups in the community. The sophisticated form stresses common objectives and interrelated decision-making in limited areas of organizational operations. This kind of coordination is typical of relations among departments or sections of large organizations, and among coalitions of agencies. Coordination in its sophisticated form may be viewed as an integral aspect of planning. In its elementary and prevalent form in our communities, it serves not so much to bring about program cooperation among agencies as to clearly demarcate and protect sovereign areas of agency operation. Coordination at this level deals essentially with the exchange and concert of expectations about organizational objectives and programs.[1] The sophisticated variety of coordination is not commonly found in community organization.

> We may note that it is extraordinarily difficult for a sophisticated form of coordination to exist in American communities, because of a lack of dominant social goals. There is no single set of consistent, acceptable, overall community goals to which organizations can relate their respective plans and programs. In a democratic society, the divergence of organizational goals, itself, may be regarded as a value to be protected. Freedom of organizations "to go their own ways up to some point which cannot be identified by any system of equations is even considered conducive to long run effectiveness by encouraging experimentation and innovation." But to the extent that divergence of objectives is sharp enough to lead to a stalemate among agencies or to greatly reduce effectiveness in the provision of services, it is a loss without adequate offset.[2]

Coordination in its prevalent and elementary or "market" form is powered by "diverse self-interests." It assumes that organizations can be efficiently related to each other without resort to the imposition of external controls, "without a dominant common purpose, and without rules that fully prescribe their relations to each other." [3] But in the extreme competitive, market sense, coordination tends to break down.

The techniques of effective communication at the level of elementary coordination are obvious and simple, yet even here difficult to implement; they include: developing commitment, facilitation of interaction, building on crisis, and improving interprofessional communication.

## Communication Processes

Organizations do not exist in a vacuum. Not only must they relate to clientele or constituents, but also to other organizations in

1. Thomas C. Schelling, *The Strategy of Conflict*, pp. 57–58.
2. Herbert A. Simon, Donald W. Smithburg, and Victor A. Thompson, *Public Administration*, p. 435.
3. Charles E. Lindblom, *The Intelligence of Democracy*, p. 3.

the community which may be attempting to serve or organize the same populations for the same—or for different—purposes. It is, therefore, essential for each organization to know as systematically as possible what the other agency, its competitor, actual or potential, is doing. And each organization must define its intentions and arena of operations as publicly as possible.

## Developing Commitment

The simple matter of commitment to the value of meeting with other organizations in order to learn what is going on is a first step in any systematic interorganizational communications process. The very act of meeting regularly seems to produce some valuable results, whether in terms of exchange of information or feelings of "togetherness," and in turn reinforces such commitment.

> This is a group called the Youth Service Coordinating Committee which meets once a month. Representatives of various agencies, particularly youth-serving agencies, and key community lay leaders sit on the committee.
>
> The committee has been very worthwhile because it breaks down a vacuum between agencies. At the last meeting we had representatives from the county board of public aid, the juvenile police, the department of housing, and various neighborhood groups. All of us feel we can share ideas about problems in the community and what we are doing, respectively, about them. The meetings have become a regular pattern and we look forward to them.

While community-work and direct-service organizations are aware of the importance of coordination, however, they apparently often do not have sufficient resources to support the commitment. Nevertheless, some organizations make special effort to facilitate communications, even within the limits of available means.

> The important thing is that you know what other organizations are doing and tell them what you are doing. This can be done at various levels—the executive or the line level. This means that certain staff simply make time to carry out this responsibility.

### Facilitation of Interaction

Formal meetings with representatives of other organizations or groups serve a function beyond that of simply exchanging information about respective programs. They serve to develop sensitivity to the program needs and interests of other organizations. Interaction may even contribute to common objectives in certain areas of operation, especially if organizations do not pose a threat to each other's significant interests.

> I think the coordinating committee has worked—and this is a pet theory of mine, because we don't have a power structure and no one runs the show. We have rotating chairmen. We don't have funds to be raised. The only purpose is getting together. We want the interplay of ideas and even recommendations about what each of us should be doing.

Interorganizing may lead to the development of a short-run coalition of agencies with common objectives and indeed to stimulating or organizing for general community interest and action. Further, coordination may lead to cooptation. Workers interact and get to know each other. There is sharing of information about programs and individual clients and a basis for the exercise of influence by one organization on another.

> I got to know the youth patrolman and the prevention officer at these meetings. I feel free to consult these people about various kids who are in our program. We call on these fellows for any relevant information that they have about a kid or a community situation, and they help us as much as possible. I actually think, though, that these people call me more often than I contact them. If the youth patrolman picks up a kid and knows he's in our program or that a parent is on one of our committees, he calls us in and asks what should be done, especially if the offense isn't too serious. The youth patrolman and the probation officer usually make dispositions based on our recommendations. These regular meetings have helped us to carry out our agency purposes better, although this aspect of it wasn't clearly planned that way.

### Building on Crisis

Probably the most important circumstance contributing to coordination and even cooperative effort among organizations is a crisis in the community for which organizations may be held individually and collectively responsible. There is, first of all, a great willingness on the part of organizations to communicate with each other in the face of a crisis such as a riot or series of gang fights. The joint program easiest to carry out under such circumstances usually has a strong control character. For example, the threat of a gang fight not only improves communication among agencies but it makes it possible to develop at least a temporary interagency staffing pattern to control any outbreak which might occur.

> On the last day of school, the youth coordinating committee anticipated a series of fights among various gangs in the community. Formal concern was expressed at earlier meetings by the police, the probation department, the family court, as well as the youth-serving organizations, like the Boys' Club and the Y. The Boys' Club was able to get a large block of tickets to take groups of kids to an amusement park and a baseball game. The police were assigned to patrol particular parts of the neighborhood which might become hot spots. Two probation officers were asked to ride with police officers in squad cars. The family court worker was responsible for handling a central communications post. All the above personnel were also in on the complicated control plan which was developed.

In general, however, there is a dismaying lack of communication and cooperation among groups and organizations in the same local community. There may be even less coordination between independent organizations at different governmental or geographic levels, and at local, city, and state levels, in relation to a given problem.[4] Serious threat to the integrity of agencies is apparently infrequent enough so that a united front is seldom achieved, even in those situations where obvious benefit would accrue to all. Unrelenting competition among organizations for recognition, re-

4. See Roland L. Warren, *The Community in America.*

sources, and membership, as well as traditional barriers to communication, continue.

## Improving Interprofessional Communication

The competition for success status among organizations is further aggravated by differential professional ideologies. Problems arise particularly at points where one professional group attempts to change or expand its area of expertise or competence.

> The youth agency, whose staff are mainly social workers, want to begin working with youth groups on a recreation basis, and with adult groups in terms of social action. They want the park department workers who are dealing with gang members to deal with parents now. The park department, however, prefers to confine its efforts to youths and recreation and, in turn, questions the value of any recreational efforts by social workers.

Various professional groups, dealing with the same youths, may also operate with conflicting philosophies about how the problems of delinquency should be addressed; they thus frequently work "at cross-purposes to one another."

> The police are interested in apprehending offenders, the probation department in treating them, and the judge in adjudicating them.[5]

The clash of professional ideologies most frequently involves social worker and police officer.[6] The policeman may view the social worker as inordinately protective of his clients; the social worker may view the police officer as insensitive and brutal. The difference often is between professionals emphasizing protection of the community, on the one hand, and of the individual and his family, on the other. The social worker and the lawyer often find themselves protecting the rights of individuals, even if they are deviants; the policeman and the teacher may be far more concerned with the personal and property rights of the (dominant) community.

5. Joseph D. Lohman and James T. Carey, "Rehabilitation Programs for Deviant Youth," p. 377.
6. John P. Clark, and Edward W. Haurek, "A Preliminary Investigation of the Integration of the Social Control System," pp. 9–10.

It has been argued by some that agencies should have sufficient resources to permit operational effectiveness without dependence on other agencies; that, indeed, agencies operate with greater efficiency if staffs avoid interaction with personnel of other organizations. Differential perspectives and approaches may be so far apart that attempts at coordination or communication would serve only to bring about even greater animosity and conflict.[7] It would seem more reasonable, however, to anticipate great benefit in community problem solving from increased communication, while not denying that barriers to communication among certain professional groups are high.

> It took over a year before their relationships with each other could be discussed openly among practitioners. They were too "polite" to approach the subject. Meanwhile, delinquencies were not reported to the police because social workers feared indiscreet handling and the loss of their clients. The police, on the other hand, felt thwarted in doing a good preventive job by not knowing from the social workers about the many problems. The children seemed to be drifting into serious situations. The [coordinative staff] group created by the Delinquency Control Project finally made it possible to speak frankly about these problems. Two full meetings were used to frankly discuss not only grievances but the ethics of each professional group and this resulted in a better understanding of each other's practices.[8]

## Coordinative Devices

The coordinative or communications process must be structured or formalized for it to be effective. There are three traditional devices or mechanisms which have served coordinative purposes. The coordinating committee at the interagency program level and the case conference at the interagency case level have been em-

7. *Ibid.*, pp. 2–3.
8. Albert Morris, editor, "What's New in the Prevention of Youthful Offending?" pp. 54–55.

ployed to facilitate communication and (limited) cooperation. The referral procedure, both within and between agencies, has also been so used. Referral may be considered a cooptive mechanism, as indeed may the other two, on occasion. Referral is a means not only by which several organizations relate to a specific case—individual, family, or group. It is also a device by which one organization often takes the lead and influences the programs of several other organizations with limited reciprocal effect.

### Coordinating Committee

The coordinating committees, interagency youth committees, community councils—even youth commissions—created to promote communication and limited coordination among agencies concerned with delinquency control and prevention have usually consisted of representatives of various agencies and community groups (including law enforcement, mental health, family, child welfare, recreation agencies, civic, businessmen's fraternal groups, and churches). Sponsors of such coordinative mechanisms have been state, county, and city governments, universities, particular service or community-work organizations, public or voluntary in varying combinations.[9] In the main, however, they have tended to be local community mechanisms, comprising private and public agencies.

The coordinating committee is established ostensibly to arrive at solutions to delinquency problems on a joint rather than a competitive basis. However, the diffuse nature of the objectives and authority of such committees or councils—in addition to the self-protective character of individual agency participation—suggests that their results have been minor.[10] One writer notes they have probably had

> . . . their greatest success in relatively small communities. They are essentially representative of middle class interests among lay groups. . . . In California and Wisconsin the work of the councils has been given official encouragement by the participation of public agencies. In New York City,

9. U. S. Department of Health, Education and Welfare, Children's Bureau, *Juvenile Delinquency Prevention in the United States,* pp. 16–17.
10. Sophia M. Robison, *Juvenile Delinquency,* pp. 467, 474–75.

the development of the Community Council movement has been extensive, but rivalry between different vested interests has weakened many councils and led to their dissolution. A factor in this rivalry has been the tendency of different public agencies, such as education, parents, and police, to set up their own citizen groups.[11]

Coordinating councils, thus, have been coopted by individual organizations which use other community groups and agencies in support of particular programs rather than as a device for cooperative and reciprocal endeavor. They may degenerate into public-relations, self-justifying, and highly innocuous enterprises.

### Case Conference

The case conference or conference committee may be a substructure of the coordinating council or exist independently of it. A loosely knit confederation of representatives of various agencies may meet on a regular or ad hoc basis to provide for service integration and to facilitate case accountability, especially in relation to problem individuals or families.

Cases are carefully selected for discussion because they represent "multiproblem" situations, a number of agencies are involved and adequate progress has not been made. Agencies are represented by personnel on a supervisory and/or administrative level (augmented, perhaps, by the worker directly responsible for the case).

This form of case conference involves a sharing of information and evaluation, culminating in a new case diagnosis or evaluation, as well as in an action plan mutually arrived at. Professional confidentiality of material revealed in the conferences is ensured through agreement. Particularly crucial is the agreement generally made as to which agency is to "take the lead" with the family and how the others are to support the efforts (case integration). Furthermore, a "reporting back" date is set for a review of progress and the making of further plans (case accountability).[12]

11. Harry M. Shulman, *Juvenile Delinquency in American Society,* pp. 738–39.
12. Alfred J. Kahn, *Planning Community Services for Children in Trouble,* pp. 453–54.

The case conference has probably been most useful to voluntary agencies seeking to enlist the coercive power of law-enforcement agencies in keeping or "supporting" a client in existing treatment. Some of its drawbacks are that professional social workers are often reluctant to share information about clients with professionals from other disciplines and especially with lay persons who may be present at such conference meetings. (Such "confidential" information has, in fact, been misused.) There is also the underlying suspicion by some agency workers that little effective action can occur through use of the conference committee. What may actually occur is that instead of the development of a joint plan of action, there is a complicity of agency inaction. A further problem is the high turnover of staff attending many of the conference meetings and, thus, mutual trust among agencies—which takes a long time to develop—may not occur at all.

Recently, in a few communities, the concept of the case conference has been broadened so that clients themselves are involved in problem discussion and planning of action. The idea behind this innovation is that instead of "manipulating" clients, perhaps clients can be directly brought into the work of the conference and contribute to the determination of solutions of their own problems. The precise nature and development of this kind of case conference is not yet clear.

The conference committee—as any of these coordinative structures—may evolve into a mechanism for purpose of program development and ultimately cooptation.

> In our community, which is very conservative, the agency heads and the so-called lay leadership were not sufficiently interested at first in doing anything about the delinquency or poverty problems. The so-called community leaders, especially, did not want any federal money coming in. The professionals used the case conference committee as a place to plan Head Start, Neighborhood Youth Corps, and other special programs for youth. The professionals did the demonstration planning, wrote proposals, arranged for contacts with the federal representatives, and finally were successful in bringing new programs into the area and convincing the

powers that be that a change in the pattern of services to youths was essential.

## Referral

Referral is usually initiated by a particular agency worker to secure a new or additional client service which is not available at the originating agency. A function of referral is the ad hoc or preferably the systematic interrelationship or coordination of services on behalf of clients or constituents. In some cases it implies a follow-through to see that the client, whether individual or group, is connected and receives adequate initial and ongoing service. Referral responsibility on some occasions may extend to "picking up" on the client again when the referral service at the agency to which the client was sent is completed. On occasion, referral agreements and procedures for transferring cases may be worked out between agencies. More often, referral involves particular communications and agreements by individual workers about the nature of the client's problem and the kind of service he is to receive. The term may also be extended to procedures within a large, complex agency for transferring clients from one program or department to another.

A given agency, because of its commitment (and sometimes official mandate and sanction), may determine it has special responsibility to connect up individuals and families with other agency programs and to follow through to see that some improvement in the client's condition is obtained. Two key qualities of referral service which apparently need to be developed to maximize effectiveness are *accessibility* of the referral service itself (to the client), and aggressive *follow through,* especially to overcome the bureaucratic obstacles imposed by service organizations.

The referral worker may focus on the delinquent in a family of multiple problems and seek to relate the youth—and other members of the family as well—to appropriate services.

> We might have a family with a husband, a wife, and ten kids. Maybe the father is unemployed; the mother may be alcoholic; one of the kids is on probation but needs a job; another is having trouble in school, etc., etc. This involves

several agencies. Our case worker will be in contact with each of these agencies to provide the right service to each member of the family.

It's a big job. We are encouraging the family now to really work with other agencies. For example, we had a case where the youngster had to appear in court and the mother and father were very upset about this and felt that since the youngster had gotten into trouble that she had to handle this on her own. The girl was fifteen years old and the parents didn't want to go to court for her. We helped the parents to understand that they had to be present in court, share responsibility for planning on behalf of the child. We dealt with some of the problems the parents had in relation to the girl, but got the probation officer also to do part of this.

The referral process within the organization may involve the meshing of various programs such as family counseling, leisure time, group work, cultural enrichment, leadership training, and social action. The goal of the organization, for example, may be the development of a sufficient number of indigenous leaders who will be able to carry on the group-work and community-work components of the service under minimal professional supervision. Therefore, success "would be based on the expansion of indigenous aides in service positions. Casework would remain as a necessary supportive counseling service" [13] in the development of such leadership. Referral is integral to the meshing of client services and staff development processes.

Intraagency referral may not merely mean transferring a person from one part of the organization to another, but also changing the level at which a problem gets handled: from social service to community action and back to the service level, if necessary. These phases or programs may not be readily separable, although problems of focus do arise.

Surely, if you're going to establish yourself in the community organization role, you still can't turn down requests for service. At the same time, you're put in a dilemma. If you get

13. Catholic Welfare Bureau, *Imperial Courts Community Development Project,* p. 6.

involved in individual service too much, there's little time left for community action.

But you can't get away from service. You can't throw people out, when they come to you for counseling, legal, employment or other kinds of help. You pave the way for them to get help elsewhere, and in many cases, because of your relationship, you become the crucial agent in getting them this help. But this can be terribly time consuming. You don't have enough time for community organizing. This is terribly frustrating.

As with the coordinating committee and the case conference, serious questions have been raised about the utility of the referral process.

A group of agencies and agents are coordinated not through a plan or a central structure but through common commitment to a body of values, and consensus about appropriate activities for each agency and agent. . . . When a client or patient is injected into a pinball type of system, he approaches or is taken to the agency seen as relevant, and the boundary conditions surrounding that agency determine his rebound to the next port of call. . . .[14]

Another writer speaks of the referral process as "self-deception." Well-intentioned staff "arrange disposition of cases on the basis of need" of clients, relevant to the resources of organizations which are theoretically available. But in fact the resources do not exist— are not accessible—particularly to youth from lower-class areas. Further, there is a lack of data on the availability of resources of agency service at any given moment. It is true that people in need are easily found or contacted, but to get people with the specific problem into the right available resource may be difficult. Finally, the work of referral itself may not be skillfully handled.[15]

Breakdown of referral may occur because of the fragmentation of agency programs of service. To receive a complement of interrelated services—for example, training, job placement, health care,

14. Elaine Cumming, "Allocation of Care to the Mentally Ill," pp. 130–31.
15. Kahn, *Planning Community Services for Children in Trouble,* pp. 32, 57, 60.

family counseling, public assistance—an individual may have to go to half a dozen agencies. It is difficult to sustain people in the pursuit of services from such a variety of agencies.

One recent attempt to structure the referral process more efficiently, and consequently make the impact of service more effective, is the neighborhood service center. The center's purpose is to provide a "variety of needed services, particularly to newcomers of low income background or to multi-problem families who have not in the past been successfully reached by social agencies." [16] The approach requires that services and "help" programs needed by disadvantaged individuals and families be offered in one building or location in the low-income area. A central agency is established and may be designated to accept referrals from agencies such as the court, police, and schools. The neighborhood service center concept may involve the ceding of limited authority over agency intake and closing of cases.

> Participating agencies will be asked to give up their autonomy over their intake and closing of cases. They will be asked to accept a central agency's referrals and to remain in contact with their family until they have consulted with the central agency and reached an agreement about withdrawal.[17]

The implementation of such service center programs is apparently no simple matter. Individual agencies and their program may be established under one roof, but the problem of common procedures of intake, similar record keeping, and systematic follow-up remains. The ideologies of service intervention may be radically different among agencies, and it appears to be extraordinarily difficult to develop joint or shared approaches. Also, lines of authority of individual agencies tend to be vertical when, indeed, they need to be lateral. Communication and coordination barriers remain where the authority for overall program development is not clearly or fully established. This is not to deny that informal means for overcoming differential agency philosophies and program strategies may be possible on an ad hoc, worker-by-worker basis. But

16. U. S. Department of Health, Education, and Welfare, Children's Bureau, *Juvenile Delinquency Prevention in the United States*, p. 26.
17. Community Chest and Council of the Cincinnati Area, "Aid for Troubled Children under Twelve Years of Age," pp. 263–64.

the sheer contiguity of services and workers can only mitigate, not resolve, the referral or coordinative problem.

The problem of fragmentation of effort at the neighborhood service center may be alleviated by the use of the generalist worker to provide a broad range of "reaching out," supportive, protective, and rehabilitative services.[18] Consultation and specialist services may be provided to the generalist worker from units such as legal aid, employment counseling, public assistance, health care, etc. Yet we must observe that neighborhood social service centers are still in an experimental stage. Little evaluative material is available. The problem of systematically interrelating a variety of programs, public and private, of independent jurisdiction, with a variety of philosophies, policies, and procedures, is, to say the least, extremely difficult.

## The Underlying Political Problem

Coordination at the present time may be viewed as a relatively systematic adaptation of organizational programs to each other under market conditions. Its primary purpose is to meet individual organizational objectives rather than to solve community problems. There is a critical distinction here. Organizational decisions are made to achieve *particularistic* organizational interests, not to meet *collectively* the problems of a community, and only coordination of a relatively elementary or primitive character results under these conditions. Organizations develop and implement common objectives secondarily, and only as such action enhances particular organizational interests.

Each organization represents concepts and interests of particular groups or sectors of the population. In a sense, community-work and service organizations are politicized fragments of a hydra-headed community welfare system. Each agency or fragment of the system attempts to protect or enhance its program. Further, agencies do not always essentially represent the interests of the clientele they serve but sometimes mainly those of staff or board members.

Thus, each organization is designed to perform its special set of

18. Kahn, *Planning Community Services for Children in Trouble*, pp. 471–72.

activities without primary reference to other organizations.[19] Meanwhile, the community problem which the organization sets out to solve is not segmented, and the fragmentation of programs and services intensifies social ills. The dilemma is that no organization by itself possesses the resources to solve a community problem such as delinquency. In its attempts to, however, the agency must deflect its energies from a holistic and effective attack on the problem to a struggle for scarce resources with the very organizations with which it needs to cooperate. The struggle produces consequences which, although functional for agency purposes and sometimes for partial solution of community problems, is dysfunctional for genuine community problem solving.

The competition for scarce resources is evident in all sectors of the welfare system but is especially serious among voluntary agencies for the "private" dollar. Increasingly such agencies seek to cancel each other's programs out, particularly at decision-funding levels.

> The director of the Juvenile Protective League noted that he was encountering considerable resistance from the Community Fund in getting regular appropriations because the settlement representatives, who are on the Community Fund screening committee, were charging them with overlapping their own community organization function in the area of neighborhood control of delinquency. The League is now organizing community groups in the same area where the settlements are located. The Juvenile Protective League said it was doing this to support its newly decentralized counseling and recreational service programs.
>
> The director said there were many agencies now doing community work. He said the situation was like a jungle. Every agency is in there pitching for its own community organization operations.

Competition among producers in the welfare arena does not drive down the price of service or increase the availability of services, however. There may simply be excessive production of particular types of program or services without loss to the pro-

19. Richard A. Cloward, *The Administration of Services to Children and Youth*, p. 21.

ducers, but with loss to the community and its consumers. Fragmentation of programs leads to duplication of services. While it may be argued that overlapping or duplicated programs make possible alternate choices of obtaining particular, needed services, in effect scarce resources are wasted. Certain important or alternate programs are thus not available because resources have already been spent.

Scarce resources may be squandered not only through duplication of effects, but also through contradictory purpose and impact of similar programs.

> In a large Eastern city one family agency encouraged delinquent and truant youths to stay in school and get the most of their educational opportunities. At the same time, another family counseling program sponsored by the local antipoverty council was encouraging the same youths to believe that schools were "big and bad" and that policemen were "against" them. Each of these organizations had contact with the same families. Agency cross purposes were serving to tear the families apart.

Sometimes, too, organizations, in their efforts to obtain community support, oversell, misrepresent, or misdirect their programs. They make exaggerated or false claims of service, or secure funds to do one kind of program but end up providing another. Community organization itself may be a device for avoiding solution of a direct service problem. In some communities, the key problem should be assessed as, not lack of coordinative efforts, but lack of services. An agency may develop a sophisticated rationalization for an unnecessary community worker program and avoid provision of a necessary service.

> I'd say one major complaint that agencies have against us is that we don't do anything. We keep giving them the problems, and they say, "Why the hell don't you do the service?" For example, we come to them with a group of gang kids and say, "Look, these kids need service and we'd like you to do it." They answer, "But we don't have enough space or staff."
>
> The reason we can't do it ourselves is very simple. You know, we would dissipate staff. In about two months we

would be committed up to our ears in direct services. Then where would we be in regard to providing community organization programs? Although it is true most of our community organization is related to the coordination of agency efforts on behalf of delinquent youths which really don't adequately exist.

Coordination, if it is to be carried out effectively, implies some kind of legitimate control over other organizational programs. The control may be very minimal, especially in relation to elementary coordination. It may indicate merely that one organization can communicate with another or can refer clientele for services. This kind of minimal coordinative control may be used or misused by agency executives, and especially by aspiring politicians, to develop personal power.

> Mr. Serrat is a new assistant district attorney, but is bucking for higher office. He has become especially interested in the problem of delinquency and has been advertising himself in the community as someone who can make services available because of his contacts. In effect, when any organization or person calls his office for help with a problem, he refers them immediately to the Youth Referral Bureau, which has official responsibility for the actual referral. But he goes around making speeches, quoting the number of people that his office has helped get services. This keeps him constantly in the public eye.

It may well be that the causes of faction among organizations in a democratic society are unavoidable. James Madison commented on the problem of political faction in a way which is relevant for an understanding of the shortcomings of coordination of welfare organizations:

> We see them everywhere brought into different degrees of activity, according to the different circumstances of civil society. A zeal for different opinions concerning religion, concerning governments, and among other points, as well of speculation as of practice; an attachment to different leaders ambitiously contending for preeminence and power . . . have in turn divided mankind into patterns, inflamed them

with mutual animosity, and rendered them much more disposed to vex and oppress each other than to cooperate for their common good. So strong is this propensity of mankind to fall into mutual animosities that where no substantial occasion presents itself, the most frivolous and fanciful distinctions have been sufficient to kindle their unfriendly passions and excite their most violent conflicts.[20]

Madison noted there are two methods of curing the mischiefs of faction:

There are again two methods of removing the causes of faction. The one by destroying the liberty that is essential to its existence; the other, by giving to every citizen the same opinions, the same passions, and the same interests.

If it could never be more truly said of the first remedy that it was worse than the disease . . . the second expedient is as impracticable as the first would be unwise.[21]

The conclusion to which we are brought is that the causes of faction or fragmentation among organizational programs, cannot be removed, and that "relief is only to be sought in the means of controlling its effects."

The principal, albeit partial solution, to the political problems of failure of coordination is the imposition of control over agency programs through some external authority, usually possessing funding or legal power. This may be done directly or indirectly. For example, an organization, preferably a public agency, may be assigned the power of coordination of other agencies engaged in prevention of gang fighting. The public agency enforces its authority through the funding of a part or the whole of such programs, so long as they meet certain criteria. All gang fights or threats of fights are required to be reported to a central source. Assignment of workers during emergencies, regardless of agency sponsor, is to be made through the central authority, and critical performance standards are set by the central authority. An alternate pattern here might involve the contracting of coordination to a voluntary agency. In either case, the sanction for effective coordination is

20. James Madison, "The Inevitability of Faction," pp. 480–82.
21. *Ibid.*

legal or financial, or both. Failure by organizations to participate adequately in such coordinative arrangements might mean termination of funds or, in extreme cases, even suit for violation of an ordinance or law.

Finally, coordination may be encouraged on a more indirect basis using mainly financial persuasion. Grants by organizations to agencies concerned with the problem of delinquency may be provided only on condition that they coalesce or systematically interrelate their purposes and activities. In essence what occurs here is that two or more organizations are induced to form a coalition to achieve a common purpose. Coalition may involve joint action in only a limited aspect of the agency's overall program, but it does require the commitment of each organizational member for a specific period of time or even indefinitely, although the ultimate power of withdrawal from the coordinative arrangement is still retained by the member organizations. There is evidence which suggests that the coalition form of organization will be increasingly used to pursue goals calling for more support or resources than any single organization is able to marshall unaided.[22] This assumes, of course, that funding sources, mainly public, will insist on a strong coordination component in agency plans to deal with delinquency.

22. James D. Thompson and William J. McEwen, "Organizational Goals and Environment: Goal Setting as an Interaction Process," p. 413.

# 8

# Planning

Planning for interorganizing incorporates elements of cooptation, cooperation, and coordination to achieve meshing of organizational purposes and actions in the solution of community problems. Planning is a rational means of dealing with problems and is inherent in most human interactions and organizational endeavors. The process is essential to the efforts of any specific agency seeking to achieve its goals and objectives, whether they are of an environmental change or service nature, or both. In this chapter, the central question addressed is not how organizations, individually or independently, plan and develop programs, but how they collectively become interorganized to solve the problem of delinquency. There are almost no tested guidelines for effective community planning in this interorganizational sense, yet the growing severity and complexity of certain urban problems require that a community planning process be undertaken.

## The Problematic Context

The fundamental problem is that organizations usually operate without adequate empirical reference to the complex nature of a

233

social problem and the interdependent needs of people in the community. They tend to plan and execute their programs in relative isolation from each other. There is "minimal utilization of interagency resources through mutual collaboration." [1]

Specific planning efforts in the area of delinquency prevention, control, and treatment have foundered for at least four reasons. First, they have generally ignored the fact that community conditions and organizational arrangements significantly contribute to and differentiate who is to be or not to be a delinquent. Second, they have been built on the assumption that the label "delinquency" denotes a population to be dealt with as though "all their members were relatively similar." [2] Third, and most important, communities have been too willing to accept the individual agency and institution as the planning unit. Fourth, communities have reacted spasmodically and irrationally to delinquency, mainly in punitive terms, instead of in rehabilitative and preventive terms.

A few of the specific characteristics of the condition created by lack of adequate community planning are that agency administrative function precedes service to people according to need; the wrong clients are served by the wrong programs; insufficient resources are expended for the right programs,[3] and excessive resources for the wrong ones; and personnel are inappropriately trained, or their expertise is used for the wrong purpose.

Organizations, then, are self-binding and encapsulating; the concepts, definitions, and programs they create, indeed, may perpetuate the very conditions they were intended to alleviate. They emphasize issues central to the achievement of organizational purposes, but peripheral to the solution of community problems. They may fail to concentrate on the most important targets affecting the public interest and concern.

There are dozens of organizations, public and voluntary, which carry "pieces" of responsibility for the delinquency problem in almost any urban community, each with its particular perspective and criteria for effective service.

1. Herbert Sigurdson, "The Community—The Locus for Delinquency Prevention," p. 18.
2. Alfred J. Kahn, *Planning Community Services for Children in Trouble,* p. ix.
3. Lyle C. Fitch, "Social Planning in the Urban Cosmos," p. 340.

At the top level of city government, there is no authority for overall planning and coordination. Authority is diffused among many individuals and groups, including the two deputy mayors, the director of the budget, the mayor's aides, and a variety of interagency coordinating devices . . . The tendency has been to create new interagency devices to meet each new crisis, whether it is gang violence, drug addiction, or unemployment.[4]

At the state level, interorganizational planning also is largely nonexistent "either in the field of juvenile delinquency or in the broader field of social welfare." [5] Sieder, in her study of state level planning in Rhode Island, Pennsylvania, and Kansas, found that "not only was there no single organization in any one state responsible for comprehensive planning, but neither was there a system of planning organizations which together might constitute a comprehensive approach to planning in this field." [6] Responsibility for planning was not vested in any particular agency of state government; there were competing approaches to the problem of delinquency, representing different value orientations—a "corrections camp" and a "child welfare camp." [7]

State-level planning organizations seemed not able to withstand pressures, either from within their own governmental or even the voluntary structure.

Voluntary organizations, such as the National Council on Crime and Delinquency, often threaten the domain of a state level planning body by insisting that a state level affiliate (of its own organization) be established to undertake juvenile delinquency planning.[8]

What seems apparent is that not only are organizations of a service or community action character unable to mount interorganizational planning programs, but that organizations specifically set up to plan are unable to do it either. The existence of multiple

4. Richard A. Cloward, *The Administration of Services to Children and Youth*, pp. 2–3.
5. Violet M. Sieder, *An Exploratory Study of State Level Planning for Prevention and Control of Juvenile Delinquency*, p. 6.
6. *Ibid.*, pp. 11–12.     7. *Ibid.*, pp. 13–16.     8. *Ibid.*, p. 16.

planning structures creates, at the interagency planning level, what already exists at the organizational service and action level—a competitive market situation. Planning structures which were established to rationalize and coordinate diverse organizational programs, themselves become independent operations, competing like all the rest for scarce community resources.

## The Nature of Planning

Planning has been described as the systematic management of assets or resources.[9] In this fundamental economic sense, there can be no planning unless an organization has access to and control of resources. In other words, an organization cannot plan with another organization's resources, unless it can exercise some control over them.

Planning involves the identification of the goals or primary objectives in pursuit of which assets will be managed. These assets are limited and must be directed to the ends for which they are most desired. "The economic notion of opportunity cost enters here: the cost of using assets in one way, or for one objective *is* the other uses to which these assets might have been directed." [10]

Planning involves the integration of vertical and horizontal streams of decision about which assets are to be converted to the achievement of the objectives posed. General goals must be specified into the relevant policies and objectives, and priorities assigned to the use of resources.

Planning also involves a time perspective. Objectives and strategic decisions are not one-time matters but continue indefinitely through the life span of a problem, such as delinquency, which does not disappear, but which may assume a different or less virulent form. Resources, therefore, are managed not only in relation to a current delinquency problem, but in relation to a future problem and anticipated pressures and circumstances which affect the need to solve it.

9. Neil W. Chamberlain, *Private and Public Planning*, pp. 4–5.
10. *Ibid.*, p. 4.

There are three principal aspects of the planning process: ideological, technical, and political.[11] These aspects are interrelated. The ideological process requires the framing of objectives, both present and future, and the use of value systems to limit or prescribe appropriate devices, techniques, and programs for achieving these objectives. The technical process involves the selection and use of the most efficient means of achieving the objectives established. It requires, among other things, determination of appropriate relationship of organizational resources, such as program, personnel, facilities, and techniques of operation to types of delinquency problem over time. The planning process also requires the political manipulation and contrived coherence of the participants in the community system concerned with the problem, including both agency personnel, board members, and constituents or clients. This coherence does not arise naturally but must be managed with the use of such inducements—normative, economic, coercive, or conditional which the community system permits relevant to the problems of delinquency. It leads inexorably to a system of bargains at almost all levels of the planning process.

Planning thus is that activity which concerns itself with proposals for the future, with the evaluation of alternative purposes, and with the methods by which the proposals may be achieved.[12] It is rational, adaptive to the interests of the participants, and depends for its success ultimately on the control of resources it can bring to bear in the process. Furthermore, it assumes differential use of the changing resources in relation to changing problems of delinquency over time.

The features of a planning approach to a community problem, such as delinquency, require the following: (1) an examination of the key interests and sources of power at the community planning level which affect the development of the planning process in relation to the problem of delinquency; (2) a preliminary survey of the problem area to determine the scope of delinquency and criminogenic influences, including those which may arise from established agency service and operation patterns; (3) the canvassing of the community's constructive organizational resources and the

11. *Ibid.*, p. 9.
12. Herbert A. Simon, Donald W. Smithburg, and Victor A. Thompson, *Public Administration*, p. 423.

possibility of their more widespread and intensive deployment under central supervision or guidance, and determining the specific scope of existing relevant programs of education, training, employment, social and other services, especially the extent of cooperation, conflict and overlapping among them; (4) the application of a model of community action and service within the limits of power and resources available currently and in the future to the delinquency problem in its various forms and stages; (5) the development of an appropriate public or voluntary comprehensive planning or interorganizational structure with effective control function; (6) the staging of planned intervention at structural, program-development, and service levels, and specifying objectives at appropriate intervals; (7) the development of relevant processes and procedures of operational integration of the various programs; (8) the application of efficient management techniques for the implementation of planned interagency programs; (9) monitoring and evaluation of programs and procedures; (10) feedback to responsible administrators and public groups for redefinition of objectives, especially in the light of anticipated and unanticipated interactions with other planning programs, for example, those dealing with mental illness and poverty.[13]

## Values for Planning

If a community and its organizations are to transcend the isolation and fragmentation of its efforts, it must also overcome its traditional pattern of reactivity to a social problem. Its respect for social planning must derive not from attachment to some "abstract principle of bureaucratic centralism," [14] but from the basic interrelatedness of social behavior and the imperative need of intervention efforts to change it.

A sensitivity to wholeness, to totality, to the mutual effects of men's actions upon each other, moves a community to-

13. See Sheldon and Eleanor T. Glueck, "Paths to Prevention," p. 1,078.
14. Richard Lichtman, *Toward Community: A Criticism of Contemporary Capitalism,* p. 48.

ward the process of formal cooperation or planning. A community has outgrown the atomistic liberalism of the negative market and knows that even the great liberal concerns with self and privacy cannot be realized in a world in which men confront each other as alien or destructive forces in collision.[15]

We must be under no illusion: A planning structure must be the result of public policy decisions which determine which areas of human activity—in this case related to the problem of delinquency—are to be subject to collective or superordinate authority and organization.[16] How much integration of program and superordination is to be allowed depends on the institutional roles that are to survive and develop in the implementation of the planning structure. The decision as to the degree of control and the choice of appropriate planning and program structures are interdependent; further, the scope of social planning must be essentially subject to a value and political decision.

The community which operates with a short-term horizon or on an ad hoc reactive basis is committed to limiting the amount of change to a present pattern of activity and service. "It tends to keep on doing what it has been doing, without contemplating a major shift in its operations." [17] The community which seeks self-consciously to project itself into a farther future and to speculate about what other paths it might travel tends to think in terms of major changes and must necessarily invest more in advance preparations. In the first approach, the community builds on its present position and pattern of coping with the problem of delinquency, usually by small increments of activity. In the second approach, the community does not exclude, but neither is it confined to, such incremental activity.

It is distinguished by a determination to reach a future plotted position having no necessary relation to one's present and which for that reason requires the forging of a relationship through a series of programmed intermediate steps.[18]

---

15. *Ibid.*, p. 45.
16. James M. Buchanan, "An Individualistic Theory of Political Process," p. 36.
17. Chamberlain, *Private and Public Planning*, p. 29.
18. *Ibid.*, p. 29.

With advances in the social and behavioral sciences and technologies, we may anticipate that complex intervention processes will require longer lead time to bring program changes into fruition. If a community, for example, seeks to solve its problem of delinquency through development of "new careers" in the service field, it must begin laying plans for recruitment, selection, and training of delinquents and staff, and staged progression of delinquents through various levels of program,[19] utilizing a variety of resources not currently available or developed. Long-term commitments and major organizational rearrangements must be contemplated. The accelerated rate of change in a number of variables, including rising social aspirations, obliges a planning structure to look ahead for a period of years if its plans are not to be obsolescent before initial programs are even launched.

Social planning, however, is to some extent unlike economic or physical planning. Planning in relation to coping with a problem such as delinquency must be based on "probabilities, not certainties, with strategies to meet possible alternative developments, rather than with neatly constructed models based on known facts; and with continual rolling adjustments rather than with tidy consequences." [20]

## Conditions for Effective Planning

There are various kinds of interorganizational planning structures which may have some potential usefulness: interdepartmental committees, neighborhood or coordinating councils, citizen's committees, coalition of planning organizations, multi-function program agencies, task forces, etc. Their character may be relatively well developed and permanent, or ad hoc and transitory.

The rationale for any of these structures should be that planning can be effective only if there is some coalescence or centralization of power, usually within a formal framework of public sanction. Planning is worth nothing if the power to implement the plans is not available. The notion that planning "can be done without inter-

19. See Frank Reissman and Arthur Pearl, *New Careers for the Poor.*
20. Leo F. Schnore and Henry Fagin, editors, *Urban Research and Policy Planning, op. cit.,* p. 307.

fering with legitimate" agency prerogatives and without rigid controls must be questioned. This approach, still espoused by many, assumes most agencies left to their own devices can develop "a philosophy oriented to community strategy and integration of services." [21] The historical evidence clearly rejects the validity of this approach.

In part, the problem of planning is methodological and resides in the question of reconciliation of macro- and microsystem objectives.[22] The community's purposes are not necessarily the same as those of its agencies. It is the conflict or incompatibility component which must be reduced, the mutuality component expanded.

One way recommended for reconciling system and subsystem—that is, community and organizational—is to divide the objectives of the larger system into essential and optional objectives. The essential objectives are the community-oriented ones necessary to the solution of the social problem on its own rational terms. The optional objectives may represent simply an aggregate level of certain kinds of agency activity—from whatever source.

The planning structure (whether governmental or some combination of public organizations and voluntary associations) can give relatively free rein to the operations of certain sectors of public and, especially, private classes of activity. Organizations or the individual subunits may pursue these optional or secondary objectives vigorously and competitively without respect to the larger system. Collectively, their efforts, despite their lack of regulation, also help to achieve system goals under competitive market conditions. The freedom of private agencies, community groups, and certain governmental departments to innovate, experiment, and pursue a variety of delimited objectives provides a dynamic element which, over the long run, furthers rather than conflicts with larger or community-system objectives.

The planning structure might be either a central governmental authority or a combination of public departments and voluntary agencies under public supervision. The essential components must be public power supported by legal sanction and the availability of sufficient resources to implement objectives. The dominance of a

21. Kahn, *Planning Community Services for Children in Trouble,* pp. 68–69.
22. Chamberlain, *Private and Public Planning,* pp. 203–5.

public agency need not be a threat to the private agencies or community groups which are part of the community system concerned with delinquency. The planning structure can also function to expand the sphere of influence and discretion of the private organization, so long as it is relevant to the essential or primary system objectives. Indeed, the planning structure can encourage a degree of achievement by the private or public subunits which they could not manage on their own.

The ultimate political problem remains, however: selecting and balancing appropriate essential and optional objectives.

> The goals of system and subsystem are certain to be competitive in some respects, but they are mutually reinforcing in others. The real problem is one of balance between the public and private sectors or, even more appropriately, between the macro and micro sectors, since the latter include public as well as private units. But balance cannot be achieved by regulating system objectives to a secondary role.[23]

The logic of the argument of interorganizational planning conduces to ultimate responsibility for setting of standards of services and programs by the federal government, depending on the particular type of delinquency problem and the nature of the value—essential or optional—set on its solution.

> The central government could continue to collect and redistribute revenues and could specify minimum standards to be met in the provision of social services for which revenues were allocated. These would constitute the premise binding on local governments (and private agencies) and guaranteeing that the essential objectives of the community as a whole were reasonably met. But within these premises local government and agencies would be free to exercise their discretion to innovate and to experiment in line with local preferences.[24]

Under any democratic planning system, the possibility of divergence between private and public, larger system and subunit goals must be regarded as itself a value to be protected. Each group and

23. *Ibid.*, p. 13.    24. *Ibid.*, pp. 206–7.

organization concerned with the problem of delinquent youths will seek to gain resources and benefits from the planning unit—and as far as possible to displace the costs of program from themselves to others—but certain wider system interests should predominate. Certain independent organizational elements will undoubtedly have to be coopted by the planning structure, and there will be a price for this cooption. The price will be some adaptation by the larger system to the needs at least of some of the independent agencies and groups.

Planning and execution of a planned program may always be potentially negated by powerful interest groups. There is always the danger of unanticipated consequences when "positive social policy is coupled with a commitment to democratic procedure . . ." [25] Furthermore, the greater the number of objectives sought, the more difficult it becomes to design a course of action which will attain all of them.[26]

In other words, while the responsible planning structure is permitted considerable freedom and given certain powers to make significant decisions in relation to solving a problem in a comprehensive manner, it must still seek active participation and essential cooperation from many agencies and groups themselves.[27] It must be prepared for unanticipated consequences and particularly for compromises with powerful interests, especially those located in other planning systems concerned with related problems.

## The Role of the Planner

The perspective of the planner should be much like that in organizing as practiced particularly by the enabler or advocate. The planner, as enabler, should be oriented to enhancing the program potential (in this case of several organizations) through articulated program and service structures and procedures. His focus should be primarily adaptive to various problems that have

25. Philip Selznick, *TVA and the Grass Roots,* p. 16.
26. Martin Meyerson and Edward C. Banfield, *Policies, Planning and the Public Interest,* p. 320.
27. Selznick, *TVA and the Grass Roots,* pp. 28–29.

arisen or will arise. The planner as advocate should be committed to significant social change or innovation in multiple organizational programs and structures. While the focus of the maintenance-oriented planner should be more effective problem-solving capacity, especially in relation to rehabilitation and control, the emphasis for the change-oriented planner should be the prevention of the problem, at least, in its more serious forms. In reality, most planners at the present time perform a limited maintenance function, and possess limited political influence or technical competence. They

> do not so much make plans as reaffirm the norms, integrate, coordinate, and carry messages. They are domestic diplomats. They fill roles that have no core of technical expertise. . . . The planner has found a key function as a professional expediter of consensus in a complex pluralistic society. . . .[28]

Nevertheless, the role of the interorganizer as planner should be distinguished from the role of organizing by a greater emphasis on processes of goal formulation, technical development, and evaluation.

### Goal Formulation

Planning starts with a purpose or a goal, and goals possess an imperative quality; "they select one future state of affairs in preference to another and direct behavior toward a chosen alternative." [29] They have an *ethical* as well as a factual content: goals are guides for decision-making in relation to objectives and programs of service and community action. Until such goals are defined, "there can be no sense of direction, no standards for measuring the adequacy of effort or acceptability of results." [30]

Goals at this first general level have almost a metaphysical quality. They are essential because they give coherence to planning, without which purposeful organized effort might not be a consequence. Goal formulation "reflects the first series of choices on the long path of planning." [31]

Goals, nevertheless, must be developed into specific policies and

28. Elaine Cumming, "Allocation of Care to the Mentally Ill," p. 151.
29. Herbert A. Simon, *Administrative Behavior*, p. 46.
30. Chamberlain, *Private and Public Planning*, p. 17.
31. Robert Morris and Robert H. Binstock, *Feasible Planning for Social Change*, p. 27.

objectives. They must be "precisely defined, feasible, and generally acceptable" [32] to the constituency, the agencies, and the community groups over which they exercise influence and authority. At the same time, the more specific the objectives, the greater the potential conflict between micro- and macro-units. One method of reducing the conflict is by permitting those particular agencies specifically implementing the objectives to take significant but not total responsibility for their formulation.

There is often a tendency to make objectives ambiguous in order to avoid conflict between the larger system and its subunit.[33] However, if objectives are left vague and ambiguous, there may be unanticipated and costly consequences.

> The lack of more concrete goals [i.e., objectives] leaves the planner without a guide which can provide coherence and cohesion to his day-to-day actions. He lacks clarity about the ways in which single acts lead perceptibly to the resolution of preamble goals. He lacks a sense of direction about the progression from a small scale demonstration to massive programs. He has little indication of personnel and funds required and the social institutions which are involved at successive stages. . . . [He may] tend to view specific acts as guides to their overall effects. Sometimes actions, because of a faith that they are somehow appropriate, become the major focus of the planner's attention, regardless of their utility or relevance.[34]

Objectives and policy decisions may need full debate among all participating agencies and relevant community groups. Without such full expression, decisions may not be widely understood, and agency and community support and implementation may not be forthcoming. Given such widespread discussion, however, a core of consensus is usually created. Such consensus becomes a firmer basis for developing the strategies required to deal with the community problem.[35]

32. Lincoln Daniels, *A Look at Community Planning and Juvenile Delinquency,* p. 27.
33. Morris and Binstock, *Feasible Planning for Social Change,* p. 79.
34. *Ibid.,* p. 79.
35. Kahn, *Planning Community Services for Children in Trouble,* pp. 7–8.

Objectives and policies provide the framework for the development of specific program strategies and tactics, and priorities and critical issues are evolved in the process. They must be carefully specified not merely to include target conditions and populations, but also to clearly exclude those factors which dilute program impact and, indeed, serve to avoid dealing with the core of the problem itself. This has already become evident in some of the antipoverty programs based on the notion of expansion of legitimate opportunities. If programs are developed to encompass all youths, then the target delinquent youth group may be ignored or receive less attention and service than anticipated and desired.

> The charge has been made that the program has forgotten the delinquents and has departed from the objectives defined in the law establishing it. It is true that without built-in safeguards, the more rapid and visible rewards of vigorous programs for youth in general will lead to a slighting of arduous, slower, less visibly rewarding work with delinquents. . . .[36]

## Technical Development

The planner is responsible for the development of plans to fit departmental, agency, and community group activities into a comprehensive program towards solution of juvenile delinquency. These plans need to include, for example:

1. A statement of aims for services to children and youth, highlighting specific objectives to be achieved in the next year, as well as longer-range objectives.

2. General recommendations for eliminating, expanding, or adding programs, with rough estimates of costs for the next fiscal year.

3. An explicit schedule of priorities for action and for budget allocations.

4. An analysis of trends in appropriation and expenditures for services.

5. Results of program evaluation.

6. An assessment of the impact of departmental programs on individual neighborhoods.

36. Leonard S. Cottrell, Jr., "Social Planning, The Competent Community and Mental Health," p. 397.

To test the feasibility of objectives, it may be essential (as in economic planning) to use a technical model based on a theoretical formulation of causes and effects of the problem of delinquency. The planning model must also be developed in light of the availability of resources and competing objectives. The major value of such a technical model for performance is that it helps to

> establish the necessary relationship of the parts of the system to the overall performance. The functioning of any part is dependent on the performance of the other part—not only those to which it is directly related . . . but also to those to which it may be linked two or three or many removes. . . .[37]

The model requires the use of forecasts in relevant areas of activity. Obviously these forecasts can be made only as a series of successive approximations which may be somewhat circular in effect. Such a model, which possesses a normative aspect, would assure that "resources are directed into channels which, over time, are most likely to yield the system's objectives." [38]

The planner, then, must be thoroughly familiar with what is known and theoretically relevant about the cause and cure or control of various aspects of the delinquency problem toward which the community program is directed.[39] Despite inadequate knowledge of cause and effect relations, especially in the area of delinquency, planners do have some guides. There is evidence that certain programs and remedies have a positive effect, even though the relevance of particular programs for particular groups and the nature of the most fruitful priorities of alternate programs is still open to question. The planner's judgment, of course, weights the decisions which are made.

> What is troublesome is the lack of knowledge about which persons in any population benefit most from one approach as against another. Also, which of several remedies should take priority when they cannot be provided simultaneously? Given the present state of our knowledge as to the origin of social problems and ills, the planner relies, in the final analysis,

37. Chamberlain, *Private and Public Planning*, pp. 145–46.
38. *Ibid.*        39. *Ibid.*

upon his own axioms—his own mixture of professional training and experience, personal values, and beliefs—to choose
among the various opportunities which seem relevant for
solving the problem at hand.[40]

The initial task of transforming goals and objectives into plans is
to make data available in a single convenient source.[41] This requires the reporting of information by units of program, function,
geographic area, family types, etc. Automatic data processing is
highly useful, if not essential, for this effort. If, for example, a
central unit of analysis is the family and, more specifically, the
"hard core family," the following types of systematic procedures
may be required for program development:

a. Early identification of these families and continuous,
systematic rendering of data about them.

b. Integrated diagnosis for the total range of problems
which confront each family unit.

c. Classification of the rehabilitation potentials of families,
as well as of individuals in them.

What is recommended, then, is the establishment of a system of
social accounts relating various magnitudes of problematic characteristics associated with particular individuals and families to
human resource development. This assumes that accounts of types
of agency and community group problems and relevant agency
resource potentials will also be devised. Moreover, these various
systems of accounts need to be interrelated in light of the model of
cause and effect utilized.

The problem of the adequacy of data in relation to planning is
extremely important, not only during the initial phase, but also
later during ongoing operations of interrelated programs.

One of the most serious deficiencies, even at top-level
agency levels, regional, state, and local, is the lack of information and knowledge about other programs and agencies
which have responsibilities in the manpower field . . . and

40. Bradley Buell and Associates, *Community Planning for Human
Services,* 1952, pp. 420–21.
41. Morris and Binstock, *Feasible Planning for Social Change,* pp. 87–88.

this lack becomes far more serious as one moves down the organizational scale. When this lack of information is combined with a rather narrow and possessive view of one's own program, the effects . . . are not good.[42]

A series of questions must be raised during the technical planning phase: What is the problem in the particular neighborhood? Who are the youths in trouble and where do they come from—socially, economically, educationally, psychologically? What specific efforts are succeeding and failing in helping delinquents? Are sufficient effective efforts being focused on the adolescent delinquents who constitute the core of delinquency? What kind of resources are actually being made available to deal with the particular problem?

Specific analytic attention needs to be focused on agencies and community groups. For example, what is the real purpose or interest of the relevant community agencies and groups? What is the size of their active memberships? What is the nature of the types of programs developed with or on behalf of youth? What is the degree of access of members of the various organizations to centers of decision-making power affecting specific agency programs? In sum, what is the competence of specific organizations in actual operations? What is the degree of influence each organization could be expected to exercise, and actually is exercising, on objectives related to solving the delinquency problem?

At the same time as answers to such questions are being formulated, the articulation of specific planning variables and alternate strategies should begin to take shape. For example, in relation to a manpower development objective for delinquents sixteen to twenty-one years of age, we can make estimates of the number of people to be involved in the future. We can begin with the total number of youths classified as delinquent or potentially delinquent under the definition chosen, then we can determine which are problem youths in school and out of school. In relation to the various youth programs available, particularly in relation to jobs, we can estimate that a certain proportion of youths will be ineligible or uninterested. For example:

42. Donald Dodge, "Community Planning and Fact Vacuum," p. 34.

Many already have steady jobs, paying at least the legal minimum wage. And many, especially young mothers, have no desire to join the labor force.[43]

For these delinquents or potential delinquents out of the labor force, there may be data indicating whether they worked "more or less than forty weeks" in a given recent year. If a youth worked less than forty weeks, the assumption can be made that he will be interested in one of the available manpower programs. This analysis, adjusted to certain other factors, provides an estimate of all delinquents and potential delinquents in a community who are out of school and in need of manpower programs. Many of these youths will be ineligible for certain programs, eligible for others, and further adjustments in the estimate will have to be made to account for changes over time. The dropout rate may be dropping; housing changes suggest loss of population; age distribution (such as a burgeoning adolescent population) may indicate the need for increasing the estimates.

The next step is to decide what the various categories of individual need are. Also, categories of manpower development need to be identified; for example, job creating, skill training, literacy, personal or social development, health care, child care (for young unmarried women).

The succeeding questions will be what are the programs available to service the needs, and what is the extent to which these programs can cope with the needs effectively? Job Corps opportunities, local Neighborhood Youth Corps, special manpower development programs, business and industry, other organizations and programs provide relevant employment opportunities. Schools and a variety of agency and industrial training programs are available for literacy and skills training. Social service, counseling, and psychological service agencies provide programs for personal development. Various recreational and informal educational programs assist in further, usually secondary, kinds of social enhancement. Clinics, hospitals, and other agency programs afford primary health care. Social welfare agencies provide limited day care for families. Some of these programs are adequate; others are not.

43. Joseph A. Kershaw, "The Need for Better Planning and Coordination in Manpower," p. 18.

Other essential or important types of services, depending on assessment of need in relation to particular objectives, may not exist.

Next, to what extent are these programs and services dovetailed so that an individual who should be trained can go from one to another in terms of some meaningful, graded progression ultimately eventuating in a job with career potential? Further, different types of programs and sequences of progression should be available for different types or categories of delinquents.

Planning of programs and services relevant to the problem of delinquency within the community system also must take cognizance of influential factors originating outside the system. For example, in relation to manpower development, the state of the economy may be highly influential.

> Job creation is an important element of manpower policies whenever there is a deficiency of jobs, but as the labor market tightens up, the emphasis should shift from job creation to job training. This is never a black and white situation, and some job creation and some job training are probably always necessary. But certainly job creation is much more important, relatively, when unemployment rates are high and, conversely, training becomes more important as unemployment rates decline.[44]

Planning for the solution of an aspect of the delinquency problem such as manpower development requires consideration of a variety of relevant contributory or alternate problems. For example, in certain ghettos that are isolated and distant from centers of industrial and business activity, young people may drop out of job training programs not simply for lack of motivation but because there is insufficient money or time for commuting. Provisions for adequate means of transportation may, thus, be a critical element of manpower planning.

> Various trips were taken . . . and records kept of the time required and the costs of trips to hospitals, downtown, where jobs might be available. From one to two hours each way and a round trip cost of almost a dollar were common. In addition, there were usually three or four changes from one bus

44. *Ibid.,* p. 3.

line to another, with waiting time for each. Some places were not possible to reach by public transportation from Watts.[45]

Finally, it needs to be reemphasized that the heart of a planning apparatus in relation to the problem of delinquency must be an effective pattern of youth accounting procedures. This requires the early location of cases for services and the unbroken continuity of services during the delinquency risk period, usually to the age of at least eighteen years.[46] Key agencies in a system of early location should include the schools, welfare departments, police, courts, and the employment service, as well as neighborhood organizations. Ideally, the planning structure must take responsibility through and in collaboration with these agencies for location of problem children and their families, referral to appropriate places for diagnostic study, referral for services as well as maintenance of follow-up, systematic resumptions of authority to reassign individuals and families at the end of each phase of service, and closing of cases only when the youth and his family leave the community or the youth has made a relatively stable and successful adaptation, usually in the later teens.

Such an accounting system would develop information on all children at risk in the community as well as in conflict with the law. It would involve agreements on services for each individual and family by all related agencies; it would make possible evaluation of services of the community agencies in connection with various types of behavior.[47] It would involve the continuing "interplay of intention and action." [48] There would need to be built into its accounting procedures adjustment mechanisms for change of analysis of the problem and consequent change of strategies and services. The confidentiality and positive or appropriate use of this material from the point of view of individuals and families would need to be protected and perfected.

Finally, the planner must also pay attention to techniques for assuring the integration of service programs and for coordinating

45. *Ibid.*, p. 16.
46. Saul Bernstein, *Alternatives to Violence*, pp. 29–30.
47. Harry M. Shulman, *Juvenile Delinquency in American Society*, p. 730.
48. Sophia M. Robison, *Juvenile Delinquency*, pp. 46 ff.

agency and community group interest.[49] Appropriate policy, staff, and community committee structures must be established, especially to develop and monitor the connecting links of the programs of service to delinquents. Of extreme importance is continuing attention to the key objective of the "right" youth receiving the right services. There needs to be full awareness of the inherent tendency of organizations to divert attention and service from more difficult delinquent youths. In the last analysis, planning, like organizing, is an influence process and requires skill in the use of appropriate resources of power to achieve objectives. While particular kinds of normative, economic, and coercive tactics may need to be employed, in general the most useful measures will be rational persuasion, based on expertise—and control of funds.

49. Chamberlain, *Private and Public Planning,* p. 157.

# 9

# Intraorganizing

Internal resources and how they are used are a function of agency goals, policies, and objectives, and consequently are a product of forces which in large measure are external to the agency. Intraorganizing is thus highly interrelated with the processes of organizing and interorganizing. The administrative or the internal implementation aspects of goal achievement, however, will be the primary object of attention here, rather than the formulative or executive aspects of organizational leadership; although we shall also deal with the latter.

## The Administrative Role

Planning requires continuing clarification of organizational goals and policies, and specification of the effects desired of each particular program. It calls for identification of units and means of action to implement goals, and for identification of the alternatives of action and their projected consequences.[1] In addition, appropri-

1. David Street, Robert D. Vinter, and Charles Perrow, *Organization for Treatment,* p. 263.

ate organizational structures must be devised or utilized within a relevant framework of policy to achieve planned objectives,[2] and resources of staff, money and property must be secured and effectively used. The administrative role, finally, in the large, complex agency, requires access to specialized competence in personnel management, public relations, fund raising, management of financial and business affairs, and the use of research to measure the effectiveness of agency programs.[3]

The administrator, however, is not entirely a creature of the goals and policies which have been set for him, nor of the special expertise which he may have to use.[4] The very goals which constrain him, may also have been in part determined by him, usually through a political process inherent in his role. Intraorganizing, then, may be regarded as a struggle in which the administrator survives and augments his position—but only as he effectively uses the influence resources available to him, or which he can develop.

The administrator "is neither wholly free nor completely a prisoner," within the organization. "Tradition and the perspectives of the staff set limits," as do the expectations of clients or constituents, and the community in which the organization is embedded. Yet the administrator "may retain, discharge, or promote staff members; violate traditions or create new ones; alter intake criteria. . . ."[5]

The power of an administrator derives largely from the "uncertainties and contradictory pressures"[6] that play on his organization from within and—especially—from without. The multiplicity of both external and internal groups with differing expectations offers opportunities for administrative initiative and discretion. Moreover, vague and contradictory goals may sometimes—perhaps usually—have to be pursued at the same time.[7]

We have really four major goals—that is, the agency has. The first is supporting the institutional fabric of the commu-

2. Arthur H. Kruse, "The Management Function in Planning Human Care Services," p. 16.
3. *Ibid.*, p. 21.
4. Herbert A. Simon, Donald W. Smithburg, and Victor A. Thompson, *Public Administration*, pp. 539–40.
5. Street, Vinter, and Perrow, *Organization for Treatment*, p. 46.
6. *Ibid.*, p. 47.
7. Simon, Smithburg, and Thompson, *Public Administration*, p. 540.

nity; the second is increasing opportunities for youths; the third is building support for law and order; and the fourth is strengthening family life.

Actually, the way we work, the first goal on institutional support cuts through everything we attempt to do. Also, the number three goal—law and order—must be maintained in all our programs.

But note that the second goal—increasing opportunities for youths—may be contrary to the first—supporting the existing system of services. (In this instance, the administrator resolved the dilemma of contradictory goals by ignoring or lowering the priority of the social change goal, that of increasing opportunities.)

Street, Vinter, and Perrow in their study of youth correctional institutions, identified two approaches to administration—*resigned conservatism and dissatisfied innovation.*[8] The two approaches are similar, but not identical, to the two different organizational orientations of stability and social change. Conservative administrators are described as follows:

> [They] were largely satisfied with current levels of organizational attainment. Demands or expectations of others for higher achievement were regarded as inappropriate because of limitations set by resources and the intractability of inmates. These executives readily proposed concrete improvements which could be undertaken only if resources were increased. Typically, such improvements were additions to present services and contemplated no significant departures from current practices. In this view the executive's obligation was to define the needed resources.[9]

Administrators committed to change or innovation were described in the following terms:

> [They] were far less content with the current levels of organizational achievement and sought improvement in directions they already had charted. These executives also cited needs for new resources but did not believe that failure to secure them vitiated all possibilities for advance. They accepted

8. Street, Vinter, and Perrow, *Organization for Treatment,* p. 60.
9. *Ibid.*

responsibility for mobilizing as well as defining needed resources and contemplated somewhat greater innovation if
new resources were forthcoming. Within existing circumstances they found many opportunities to enhance operational patterns and they were interested in new informational
techniques.[10]

Opportunities for administrative freedom of action are particularly evident during times of crisis or rapid social change, when
even in the stability-oriented organization there may be alternatives open to the administrator, if he cares to use them, to modify
or, at least, to implement existing goals in such a manner as to
change the approach of his agency.

> When SCLC came to town, a number of civil rights people
> addressed our staff. We were dealing with gang kids mainly
> in terms of a traditional street worker approach, and the civil
> rights people wanted to use the kids for protest activity. We
> got concerned about our relationship to the civil rights move-
> ment. Some of our key staff thought that each worker, de-
> pending on his assessment of the situation and what it meant,
> both to the development of the kids and solving of various
> community problems, ought to cooperate or not cooperate
> with a particular civil rights group or activity. As executive
> director, I went out on a limb and agreed with them.
> We brought the idea to the board. The first reaction was
> completely negative. The chairman of the executive commit-
> tee rejected it, and the president of the board said he had
> certain reservations and wouldn't accept the idea. Well, we
> discussed the matter further. What stuck in the board's mind,
> however, was the notion of protecting the worker when he
> had to make a decision in an emergency. It had to be based
> strictly on his own professional knowledge and views. The
> board finally accepted this.

The effectiveness of the organization depends in large part on
the initiative of the administrator in setting objectives. This initiative in turn depends on the administrator's ability to communicate
or sell his ideas to the community and to members of his own

10. *Ibid.*

organization. His chief task within his own organization is to set up an operative staff and superimpose upon it a supervisory group capable of persuading it toward a particular type of coordinated and effective behavior.[11] He allocates authority; that is, he determines who in the organization is to have the power to make decisions for lower-level staff,[12] and he sets such limits as are needed to coordinate the activities of individuals in the organization.

The administrator must also set up a feedback system among his staff; that is, he must establish systematic lines of communication between representatives of different disciplines within the organization concerned with the same problem. Most important, he must make sure that there are provisions for follow-up among his staff in relation to the completion of an activity.

The administrator is particularly concerned with "intended and bounded rationality" [13] in the behavior of his staff. He determines particular policies or limits and objectives and then he seeks to ensure that his staff will carry them out in a problem-solving manner as satisfactorily as possible. Effective communication is perhaps the critical factor in this work process.

## Organizing the Board/Advisory Committee

Prescriptions for administrative performance with a board have been examined in detail in other places.[14] Some attention will be paid here, however, to the use of indigenous persons on board or advisory groups, particularly in relation to the social problem of delinquency.

A board of directors is ordinarily a goal-formulating and policy-making body, and ultimate authority for operation of the agency, as sanctioned by law or tradition, rests with it. An advisory group

11. Herbert A. Simon, *Administrative Behavior,* pp. 2–3.
12. *Ibid.,* pp. 8–9.      13. *Ibid.,* p. xxiv.
14. Ernest B. Harper, *Community Organization in Action;* Ernest B. Harper and Arthur Dunham, *Community Organization in Action;* Cyril O. Houle, *The Effective Board;* Roy Sorenson, *The Art of Board Membership;* Audrey R. and Harleigh B. Trecker, *Committee Common Sense.*

is usually a less authoritative body representing various interests and resources of the community; it can be—is intended to be— useful to the organization in achieving its purposes. Both types of structures seek to exercise varying degrees of control over the administrator in the development and extension of policy, and both have a special commitment to the organization, particularly in the area of supply of resources—normative, economic, and coercive. The administrator's problem is to maximize the positive contribution which board and committee members can make to the shaping of program, as he comes to view it, and at the same time to minimize (or negotiate) differences of view between them and himself.

Of special interest is the increasing use made by community problem-solving organizations of service recipients or constituents as members of their boards or committees. The inclusion of these individuals makes available additional sanction and information required for effective and intelligent planning, and it may be a means of reducing community resistance to the organization's program,[15] since by participating in some of the planning, members of such policymaking or advisory groups may become convinced of the need for the program. They will interpret or defend it to other community members, and may become, in effect, an aid in the administration's public relations activities. They are also in a position to interpret the community and the problems of delinquency to staff as well as to other board members. But thereby, of course, they bring pressure to bear, especially on the administrator to modify policies and practices—and thus may pose a problem themselves, particularly to the stability-oriented administration.

At the same time, the community worker in his role as administrator is under pressure to shape the organization's program "according to the exigencies of the moment"[16] and those exigencies have to do primarily with the requirements of administration, narrowly defined. As the needs of administration become dominant over time with the management of large, complex programs, the meaningfulness of involvement by representatives of the client or constituent population may decline. Further, the community prob-

---

15. Simon, Smithburg, and Thompson, *Public Administration*, p. 465; see also, Philip Selznick, *TVA and the Grass Roots*.
16. Selznick, *TVA and the Grass Roots*, p. 26.

lem-solving purpose of the organization may be undermined if the agency's internal functioning becomes identified with the entire meaning for its existence. The administrator of the maintenance-oriented agency, then, is constantly in danger of perceiving and acting out his role in autarchic terms, especially if he has a strong conservative inclination.

## Organizing Staff

Since the main concern of this chapter is with the goal-implementation aspects of administration and not with its executive or goal-formulation aspects, we shall direct our attention to the staff management function of the community worker's role, especially the issues and problems connected with administering the nonprofessional worker.

### Professional and Non-professional

Clearly the natural tendency for organizations dealing with interpersonal service or community action is to move in the direction of professionalization of staff, since it promises higher standards, increased efficiency to the organization, and greater responsibility for staff in the exercise of their duties. The danger, however, is that it tends also to favor "artificial inflation of training requirements, excessive specialization, and monopolization of job opportunities." [17] The non-professional and the professional differ in degree, rather than kind, in their approach to service and community action, the non-professional presumably being less committed and less competent in dealing with such factors as systematic theory, agency authority, and middle-class codes of conduct.[18] He obtains weaker agency sanction to carry out his tasks and his work orientation may not be as efficiently developed as that of the professional.

On the other hand, for organizations closely identified with the grass-roots population, the key distinction may be not the professional versus the non-professional, but rather the full-time versus

17. William Kornhauser, "Power and Participation in the Local Community," p. 498.
18. Ernest Greenwood, "The Elements of Professionalization," pp. 10–19.

the part-time or the volunteer worker. (The distinction between staff and indigenous leadership also tends to break down when both leadership and staff perform decision-making functions and organizational tasks.)

Regardless of training or background, however, the community worker needs to be as sophisticated as possible about the workings of agencies, community groups, and government. He should have the verbal ability and the know-how necessary to make appropriate use of both the mass media and of informal methods of communication. And above all, he must have an "unusual toleration for creating and maintaining a great number and variety of personal relationships." This does not mean that the community worker has to like people to an unusual degree, or even that he has an unusual need to be liked by others, but that he should have a capacity "for multiplying human relationships." [19]

Since the complexity and growing size of most community work programs requires the development of special staff leadership, however, inevitably the professional is sought to fill this role. Attention must then be directed by the administrator to an appropriate division of labor based on the nature of the job to be done, the qualifications of his staff, and his own ingenuity in the deployment of that staff. By virtue of the professional's full-time presence, his training, and discipline, he generally is given responsibility for overall direction and coordination of a variety of community-action and service efforts. His principal responsibility should be in the area of overall focus, the encouragement of general interest and concern in the community problem, the location of resources, and the basis for their application to target groups and activities. He needs also to be responsible in the area of follow-through or supervision of particular programs.

### Qualifications

The professional is someone who has been educated at least through the college degree and often beyond. He brings to his position a relatively competent grasp of administrative practice and procedure and especially a sense of job security and status that apparently only a university degree and relevant experience can

19. Robert A. Dahl, *Who Governs?*, p. 298.

confer. He is facile with concepts and can "with relative ease, both manipulate ideas and align his actions to conform with a given conceptual framework." His training has generally provided him with the "ability to anticipate problems before they arise," and he may be much more responsive to a wider range of types of interaction than the non-professional. A major strength is his acquaintance with "how to get all kinds of information and resources." [20]

The non-professional is usually someone with less than a college degree, sometimes with less than a high school diploma, and usually without extensive or formal experience as a community worker. If he is indigenous to the slum community and familiar with its problems through his own life experience, he may be particularly sensitive and naturally skillful in the use of grass-roots communication and in gaining local acceptance for new ideas and programs. His concern with his community may bring him into a high degree of identification with its members and to a high intensity of interaction with them. If he is committed to the program of the organization, he tends to give himself over totally to its implementation.

The qualifications of the professional are usually examined in terms of the extent and quality of his academic background and experience. Of special importance is his ability to work within the confines of agency purpose and structure and at the same time to maintain his professional orientation to human welfare and some degree of social change. He must demonstrate some commitment to "righting the wrongs of the world." An important criterion should be—although it often is not—his suitability to the particular community and its problems with which he must deal. He should be acceptable to the community on the basis of his particular understanding and sensitivity to the complex of problems the community faces, and he should be able not merely to tolerate, but to accept and even find satisfaction in sharing, at least partially, the life style of the community.

The professional needs also to demonstrate that although he may have "a lot to offer," he also has a "lot to learn." If he is a social worker, he should have a generalist, rather than a specialist,

20. William L. Klein, *Core Group Leader Training*, pp. 6–7.

orientation. He requires skills (especially at the grass-roots level) in working with individuals and groups on an informal as well as on a structured, formal basis. And although he may not have the competence or time to do casework or group work, he should at least be able to initiate appropriate relationships and referrals so that the more intimate problems of people are satisfactorily met. He should be able to analyze problems and plan appropriate remedies, while at the same time recognizing that flexibility of development and execution are essential if the self-worth, self-determination, and dignity of the people he is working with are to be expressed and safeguarded. The latter is the essence of the discipline of the community-work professional.

> If you see him at a meeting, you know he's a disciplined guy, because he doesn't shoot off the top of his head. He waits for his shots. He knows what he wants to say. He understands group process and individual behavior better than most people. But he doesn't try to push people around or even forward. He's patient. At the same time he can be direct, and even indignant, because he's concerned with the community, and wants to see problems solved. He can also be "militant" in subtle ways, like talking to an agency that resists program change, and getting letters and telegrams about the situation sent to the community fund or the relevant power people.

In the selection of the non-professional, the administrator needs to be guided by the notion that the non-professional performs a technical role, that he is the person who applies techniques and principles. The non-professional should be acceptable to the neighborhood groups, and especially to disadvantaged adolescents. He may be regarded as an indigenous adult who respects their norms and values, who demonstrates that he cares, is interested, and can do something to enhance their welfare and solve particular community problems which affect them. This may require that he have status and reputation in the local community. He must demonstrate that he is respected, listened to, and can influence neighborhood groups within a generally consistent framework of middle- and lower-class norms and values. He should accept and be acceptable to the representatives of the formal organizations in the community. He needs to be able to develop at least minimal understanding and acceptance of the purpose and program of such community agencies as the police, the schools, settlements, libraries, and health agencies, and he should have the capacity to develop meaningful relationships with key program or line people in these organizations.

The non-professional need not always be of the same ethnic or even class background as the community residents. Much depends on community feelings and pressures at a given time. There must, however, be clear evidence of his empathy and understanding of the needs and problems of the community's people and of their life style. The non-professional may even have a criminal background, but he must be sufficiently reformed and committed to the agency program and community problem solving so that conflict between legitimate and illegitimate values does not arise. He must be able to use his experience and background as a basis for understanding the personal and community factors which propel youngsters into delinquency and crime, and he should be skilled in their control or prevention.

## Structuring the Job of the Non-professional

There is probably more opportunity for use of non-professionals in established organizations than is currently being used. The obstacles to their employment stem generally from lack of agency and professional interest in initiating changes which will take advantage of them as a manpower resource. This lack of interest appears to be a function of several factors:

1. Failure to appreciate the growing shortage of professionally trained personnel in relation to the expanding demands in the professional field.

2. An apparent need to keep the professional and non-professional as far apart as possible. This is a result of a covert resentment by professional staff at the idea of having to deal with clients or constituents as co-workers.

3. Reluctance on the part of professional staff to consider avenues of selection and training other than those through which they themselves have gone. There is concern that the non-professional will have things made too easy for him and

will be spared the "initiation rites" through which the professional has had to struggle.

4. Lack of sufficient association with and understanding of the strengths of the disadvantaged. The professional may lack acquaintance with programs in which the non-professional functions as participant rather than recipient.

5. Larger, more complex organizations have not given sufficient priority to reworking and redefining roles to be performed and thus creating new non-professional jobs. Such a redefinition would apparently take staff time now allocated to other pressing agency projects.

6. A growing cynicism among staff about the possibility of change in agency operations. Agencies and professionals are tending to become status "in" groups, preoccupied with routines.[21]

Nor are the values of non-professional service sufficiently understood or accepted.

> The disadvantaged person can relate more easily to a client in similar circumstances. He is a privileged communicant to information not shared with the more remote middle-class professional. He can provide valuable feedback on the attitudes and needs of the poor and the delinquent which the professional does not have. His style and value system do not antagonize the client or constituent. He provides visible evidence that there is opportunity for the disadvantaged and the deviant to improve their state.[22]

In the integrated professional/non-professional staff approach, "the responsibilities of the professional are redefined so that he undertakes the direction, supervision, and highly skilled technical tasks appropriate to training and education," while the non-professional undertakes the simpler, more routine, or specific community relationship tasks.[23]

21. The New Careers Development Project, Institute for the Study of Crime and Delinquency, "Jobs and Career Development for the Poor," pp. 12–13.

22. *Ibid.*, pp. 6–7.

23. Jacob R. Fishman, William L. Klein, Beryce MacLennon, Lonnie Mitchell, Arthur Pearl, Walter Walker, *Community Apprentice Program, Training for New Careers*, p. 4.

Ideally, community work is accomplished as a team endeavor, with workers of all levels functioning together as a unit so that "staff will learn from each other and the contributions of each will result in a more effective service to the offenders" [24] and to the community. From such an integrated or team approach, new career lines can result. The tasks of professionals can be broken up and jobs restructured to "create viable functions for non-professionals." [25] Jobs can be designed to offer services not being sufficiently provided, and non-professionals can perform tasks which assist the professional, mediate the agency and the community, and constructively contribute both to community problem solving and the non-professional's own development.

More specifically the non-professional worker in his *community action* role can:

1. Transmit and interpret particular policies, procedures, and information about the organization's program to community groups and organizations.

2. Transmit and interpret community knowledge, values, attitudes, and norms relevant to the needs and problems of disadvantaged and delinquent youth to professional staff and administration of the agency.

3. Directly and indirectly ensure that the local community, especially its youth population, exercises a meaningful voice in the planning and implementation of the agency program. He can bear a special responsibility in the stimulation of local efforts to assess, plan, and carry out a variety of youth development programs, especially in the area of employment and education.

4. Assist in the gathering of data and follow-up about the effectiveness of programs.

In his *service role,* he can:

1. Direct delinquent youth to various agencies for specific relevant services.

2. Establish positive relations with such youths, individu-

24. Judith G. Benjamin, Marcia K. Freedman, and Edith Lynton, *Pros and Cons: New Roles for Non-Professionals in Corrections*, p. 108; see also Frank Reissman and Arthur Pearl, *New Careers for the Poor*, 1965.

25. Benjamin, Freedman, and Lynton, *Pros and Cons: New Roles for Non-Professionals in Corrections*, p. 105.

ally and in groups, so that effective information about community services is provided to the youth and appropriate motivation and support for their use developed.

3. Aid in the development and implementation of family life education programs.

4. Reach out to families who have terminated with agencies prematurely.

5. Act as helper-counselors, caseworkers, and group workers to existing professional staff.

6. Assist teachers with curriculum and discipline matters.

The distinctively meaningful and essential service contribution that the non-professional can play in the ghetto community is illustrated by the following:

> Mrs. L. lives her job. During the day she is a teacher's aide. At night she opens her home to adolescent boys as a clubroom, under the aegis of the local poverty action council. She has almost no formal education, is a short, dumpy woman, somewhat unkempt, her hair strewn over her face, is about thirty years old, but looks about fifty. She is a very friendly and giving person.
>
> Mrs. L. said that about fifteen boys, thirteen to eighteen years of age, come during the late afternoons and evenings to practice their musical instruments which she had been able to obtain for them through the good graces of various businesses, as well as the local boys' club.
>
> She had a sign on the wall that said, "Better Citizenzhip (sic) Club." She said the boys fool around quite a bit, but on the streets, especially, they pay a great deal of respect to her. If there is a fight on the street, or if they are angry, they usually stop fighting or quiet down, when they see her. She feels that she has been able to keep them out of trouble. She advises them a lot.
>
> She thinks the boys like what she is doing. And they have kept out of trouble.

## Staff Problems

By virtue of his training, the professional has attained prestige and authority, but to some extent he may also have sacrificed community commitment and full involvement. He is enjoined by traditional training not to be advocate or defender of people, their morals, or values. This serves to establish distance between him and the community and its problems. He tends to encourage openness and undefensiveness in others, without reciprocating. He reserves for himself the privilege of not having to admit or submit his own actions to critical review by clients or non-professionals.

> This may take the form of a kind of patronizing attitude toward the problems of others, and makes difficult any real consideration of their problems. The justification for much of this behavior can be found, if needed, in the tenets of one's own professional preparation which can be used as an effective reason for rigidity of approach. . . .[26]

Differences in class and ethnic background may further increase the professional's problem of distance; a middle-class worker may simply be unable to find anything positive in lower-class culture, and he may direct his efforts to converting lower-class adults or youths to a quasi-middle–class life style, to upward mobility. The norms and values of a particular culture to which the worker subscribes in such areas as family cohesion and commitment to education may be far removed from those of the lower-class, minority group culture.

The limitations of non-professionals also create problems. The non-professional, if he is relatively uneducated, usually lacks "an adequate conceptual framework in which to base his actions." His relations with community groups and individuals tend to be of a reactive nature "dealing with problems and crises only after they come up. . . . He finds it hard to see exactly where he and the group are going." [27]

The non-professional may know little about organized community resources available for problem solving or, indeed, how to gain access to them. He may not have command of adequate communications and social skills in interaction with other community leaders around crucial issues and may resort to emotionally charged, undisciplined outbursts which impede problem solution. He may have difficulty in using his new position of authority with fairness, or there may be a tendency to overidentify with the

26. Klein, *Core Group Leader Training*, pp. 7–8.
27. *Ibid.*, pp. 4–5.

agency and to lose his value as a communications link with the lower-class community.

A major limitation of the non-professional is his lack of understanding and skill in group process and individual client development. The non-professional often operates strictly on the basis of his own charisma or personal status, and certain relationship situations may not be exploited properly. He may not know how to pick up on ideas or suggestions at a meeting and develop them. This lack of follow-through is a special problem in the provision of service.

> Delinquents are placed on jobs by our community workers, but may not be helped in sustaining them on jobs. For example, the delinquents may get drunk on a weekend, especially after getting their first pay check, and not show up for work on Monday. The community aide does not really know what to do. He may angrily reprimand the kid or briefly advise him to go back to work.

Also, the non-professional may suffer serious psychiatric disorders or social disorientations and, unless properly guided and supported, may be highly destructive in his relationship with others. (This may occur, of course, with middle-class professionals as well.) The deficiencies of the non-professional probably must be explained on the basis of a multiplicity of factors—ethnic, class, training, and personality.

> This cute blond woman, she was almost thirty, but not married, got involved with this kid about nineteen. She was an employment counselor aide and was trying to place the kid on a job. Well, he didn't have a place to stay, so she invites him to her place. She turns around and starts having sex with him. Then she tosses him out of her apartment. He came into the office one day, threw a bucket of paint that was lying around at her, and broke three windows in the office.

Finally, there are problems which arise from the interrelationship of professional and non-professional. These are particularly critical for the non-professional. The indigenous non-professional is in a "no-man's land" [28] between the professional area and

28. Perry Levinson and Jeffry Schiller, *The Indigenous Non-Professional, Research Issues,* p. 7.

the client or constituent's territory, and he may have severe role conflicts. On the one hand, he identifies with community residents and may have difficulty accepting the notion of organizational confidentiality about cases or certain decisions. He has difficulty with the concept of supervision and may want to move ahead more militantly toward the solution of certain community problems. On the other hand, the non-professional may identify with the professional worker and seek to emulate his ways. After a time he may come to believe that he knows as much or has better skill in certain key areas, and he may begin to wonder why he cannot be given more responsibility and accorded higher status.

> Sam said the professionals in the agency were trying to maintain their superior status. But the community aides knew more about what the gangs were doing and how to reach them than the professionals. He wanted to be able to do more than he was allowed, such as making contacts in the court and with agency executives. There were things the professional should be doing better, like getting after the local alderman to support the program. Sam said he had better contacts with the alderman and could be doing a more effective job than they were.

There are problems which arise when the professional and non-professional come together in joint activity, such as the "issue of being shown up in front of an audience, of making mistakes," the difficulty of accepting criticism, actual or implied, from a colleague who performs similar tasks, yet is of different status. While the non-professional may seek public confrontations with the professional to demonstrate his equivalent or superior competence, the professional may seek to maintain his status indirectly, subtly, and through use of organizational channels of authority.[29]

Most of these problems, however, are at least partially amenable to resolution through appropriate structuring of assignments by the administrator, and especially through in-service training program and regular staff meetings.

### In-Service Training for the Non-professional

The task of developing an effective pattern of in-service training for the indigenous, non-professional community worker is ex-

29. Klein, *Core Group Leader Training*, p. 8.

tremely difficult. An indigenous person, relatively poorly educated
—at least in a formal sense—is often called upon to do a fairly
complex job, one which at times would tax the skills and resources
of a professionally trained and experienced worker. If it were not
that the life circumstances of a sensitive, bright person raised in a
slum neighborhood may well constitute the most relevant preparation for the job, hopes for the development of indigenous community workers might appear highly unrealistic.

The role of the administrator, supervisor, or trainer, therefore, is
to provide a curriculum to sharpen the understanding and skill of
relationship of the indigenous worker, to expand his knowledge
about organized community resources, and to assist him to develop
a working partnership with other staff in a new, more effective
venture of agency-community relationships.

The following is a brief list of the objectives of in-service
training for indigenous community workers. Indicated are the
kinds of training content needed and the end product competence
desired.

1. The community worker needs to become identified with
the goals and objectives of the organization. He should have
knowledge of the various programs and resources available in
and through the organization which can be made available in
relation to the needs of disadvantaged youth.

2. He should be familiar with the structure of the particular organization, especially with the roles of various staff. He
should begin to understand where and how his duties as a
community worker mesh with those of other members of the
staff.

3. He should be able to establish comfortable and purposeful relationships not only with community groups and
families, but also with social agencies. He should develop
understanding of the complex of local problems which affect
the needs and problems of disadvantaged youth.

4. He ought to have beginning skill in planning his own
schedule. He should be able to set at least short-range goals
in carrying out his job and appropriate priorities in the use of
his time. Responsibility and flexibility in scheduling are req-
uisites of the efficient community worker.

5. The community worker needs to develop a meaningful

and cohesive conception of practice relevant to the organization's present stage of development. The ideal and the reality of agency programs should be kept in mind and in appropriate balance. The worker needs to achieve a complex blend of acceptance of the authority of the agency supervisor or administrator and patience as they strive to help develop and understand his job—and make mistakes in the process.

What such training must supply are the conceptual and technical skills and knowledge that allow the non-professional to control and make effective use of his talents.[30] Attention needs to be paid by the training and administrative staff to guarding those personal traits of the non-professional which assure optimum effectiveness in community work: warmth, friendliness, flexibility, integrity, self-discipline, resourcefulness, independence, and responsibility. All this can best be accomplished by utilizing actual work experience as a major basis for the training program, intimately linking the practical with the theoretical aspects of the work.

The problems which arise in training, and later on the job, may be due to the indigenous worker himself, the structure of the organization, the philosophical differences between professionals and non-professionals, or all of these in different combinations. The means of overcoming these problems reside, in large measure, in the sensitivity, understanding, educative, and managerial skill of the administrator or supervisor. The following are brief discussions of only a few of the problems which are likely to arise and some ways to handle them.

### Role Confusion

Inevitably, professionals must serve as quasi-role models for non-professionals. The non-professional learns largely by doing, seeing, identifying, and, in part, by imitating. There are certain less complex, less sophisticated aspects of the community worker role which the professional worker will have to clearly communicate and identify for the non-professional. The non-professional will not always be sure where his role ends and the professional's begins. He will have difficulty in assessing his own performance and that of the professional. Complexities and subtleties will be

30. *Ibid.*, p. 9.

overlooked. The professional, himself, will need help in parceling out those functions and aspects of his role which should be learned (and identified with) by the non-professional. The limits of the respective roles will have to be drawn, but not in a sharp and invidious manner.

### *Fear and Blocking*

The indigenous worker may or may not have a past history of successful employment. The demands of a job which may seem and often are complex and unclear can be overwhelming. Patience, support, and limits are essential components of any helping process undertaken by the supervisor. The initial approach to a community work job is illustrated by the report of one, perhaps, atypical indigenous worker.

> I was put in charge of developing a part of a plan for recruiting delinquent kids for various employment and training programs. I had to make contacts with agencies, community groups, and kids. The first thing I did was head for the bar. For about a month I would hang around the office each morning, make a few phone calls, then right after lunch get drunk. I was stoned every afternoon and evening. I was working with another community worker. I thought he had taken care of a lot of things I hadn't. But he hadn't, and the time approached for us to hand in a design. John, the boss, was cursing me out continually. I hid from him. Finally, I came to his office and he gave me a chewing-out that lasted two hours. And you talk about a hot box, once you close that door, you just stand up there and sweat. When I came out, I had a grey shirt and a burgundy suit on, I was soaking. I hid in humiliation for about four days.
>
> Finally, we got the beginnings of a plan together. As we began to execute it, it got better and better. John spent more time with us, but that two hour chewing sure set me straight.

### *Over-Identification*

The community worker may be highly involved with his clients or constituents, over-identifying with their problems, gripes, sense of isolation and frustration. He may see agencies as standing in the way of helping disadvantaged and delinquent youths. He may become bitter and immobilized, and ultimately of little help to his client, if he cannot in some way detach himself, at least partially, from his clients' feelings. He needs assistance in developing perspective and assessing objectively the state of agency efforts, especially in terms of the limited agency resources which may exist.

The problem of over-identification with gang or delinquent norms is especially serious for certain older adolescents or young adults who become community workers. The administrator and trainer need to be aware that some ex-gang or delinquent youths may continue for a brief time with their "hustles," but that such delinquent patterns will change over time. The strength of commitment to the program must be reinforced, for example, if a youth is to be expected to give up a one hundred dollar a week part-time job as a pimp for a full-time community work at seventy or eighty dollars a week.

A reciprocal problem is the alienation of youth community workers from their peers if there is too rapid an identification with agency and legitimate norms. Former gang members who return to work in their own neighborhood may face a number of contradictory role expectations. In order to maintain the respect and authority accorded them in a previous role, they may now feel compelled to exercise agency roles more stringently than is ordinarily desirable.

> Prior to becoming a community worker, L. had been involved in an elaborate scheme of stealing shotguns and selling them, almost as soon as they had been stolen. After a discussion with his supervisor, it was decided that he would attempt to return the guns and stop the burglaries by persuasion. Both of these objectives were successfully accomplished. But a price was paid for these successes. His former friends let him know that he was now considered a member of the establishment. As a result of the incident, the worker began spending more and more time around the office, rather than face the boys in the streets.

The role shift here obviously came too abruptly. The setting of limits on delinquent behavior possibly should have occurred more gradually if long-run relationship and group-change objectives were to be achieved. The priority in the worker's efforts should have been, perhaps, reconstructing a relationship with former peers in terms of non-delinquent norms and values which he still shared with them. These should have been expanded and only later used as a base for direct sanctions against antisocial acts. This is not to deny that, depending on the nature of the criminal act, the worker may have to move sometimes more rapidly in imposing sanctions, may sometimes have to sacrifice relationships. There are risks involved either way.

### Stereotyped Effect

The community worker may be able to perform only one or a limited number of aspects of his job. He is especially prone to continue doing that which is most comfortable to him—for example, hanging around street corners and "chewing the fat" with his former peers. He may not be able to move these discussions to issues and topics related to agency objectives. He may be unable to make contacts with other members of the community. (He may be particularly fearful of contacts with agency and organized community group leadership.) In part, the supervisory solution here is to help the worker to organize his time and energies better. The non-professional needs to be motivated and supported in attempts to try new approaches and methods which at first may make him quite uncomfortable. Controls on his time may have to be firmly but gently imposed.

### Conflict with Authority

Associated with some of these other problems may be difficulty in accepting the authority implicit and explicit in the structure of staff relationships. The non-professional worker may not be able to accept the "superior" role of the administrator or supervisor. Patterns of avoidance, over-verbalization, argument, failure to keep supervisory appointments, and lack of work organization may signify the worker's difficulty in dealing with authority. The supervisory answer here again is patience and close, supportive contact with the worker. The trainer will probably need to create a careful balance of permissiveness and restraint, and much acceptance and understanding of the worker's difficulties. It is highly important that whenever possible the worker be accorded praise and gratification for work well done. His status and self-dignity must be constantly sustained.

### Frustration

Both for the professional and non-professional, the tasks of the community worker are extremely demanding on time and energy. The enormous problems of the ghetto, including those of delinquent youth, are not readily subject to simple or rapid change and solution. Feelings of frustration and the sense of being overwhelmed by the demands of the job arise. An administrator points to the extreme pressures placed on his workers.

> First, we ask the guys to work unbearable hours. In theory these people are on call twenty-four hours a day, seven days a week, three hundred and sixty-five days a year, and at times it happens that way. You'll find guys working Saturdays, Sundays, holidays. You'll find that they're called up at twelve o'clock at night, if there's a gang disturbance or race riot.
>
> Secondly, you don't see much happening fast. A person is out in the community six or eight months and sees no change occur. That's kind of frustrating, especially if he is committed. Community change is a slow process. It may take two or three years for something to really happen.
>
> Third, the job is very demanding on the personal ego, and a lot of guys can't take it. We work through the community groups and organizations, so they get the credit for the good things that happen. Our workers aren't permitted to be appointed or elected officials in any of the organizations. This is especially frustrating for certain non-professionals who want to shine, get some glory, get ahead.
>
> Fourth, our salary structure is, frankly, not adequate.

An indigenous worker, although he is familiar with the slum and understands it, at least partially, can also be overwhelmed by it, especially as he has to confront its problems in the massive doses required as part of his job.

> Mr. Jack said he felt increasingly overwhelmed by all the individual family problems he had to deal with, in addition to

the community problems. He had court cases in the morning, met with young people in the afternoon and evening, and with adult groups in the evenings too. The job kept him running from nine in the morning until eleven at night, six days a week.

There are terrific problems in the community. The housing is dilapidated. You try to get some of them to fix up their places. There are good reasons why they don't do these things. Then, there are people all over the streets. It makes you think of millions of ants, especially in the summertime. Then you wonder, "What am I doing and what can I do? Prostitution, taverns, drunkards, drug addicts."

The administrator must provide personal as well as managerial support to his workers, particularly non-professionals. He has to offer frequent opportunity to vent feelings of frustration. He must particularize and limit his workers' assignments and expectations. Interludes away from the community and scene of struggle are mandatory. Special training sessions, institutes, and courses out of the neighborhood provide opportunities not only for development of insight into coping with community problems, but also for a respite and replenishment of emotional energy.

### Rigidity of the Structure

There are times when the worker will react negatively to the roles and procedures, the practices and problems of agency operation. In part, this response may result from a desire of the trainee to be free-wheeling; in part, it may result from the rigidities of the organizational structure, itself. The non-professional may be not entirely clear about how best to channel his energies. He may be asked to do things he is not capable of or does not desire to do, for fairly good reasons. A rigid bureaucratic approach by the administrator would be a mistaken response. Flexibility of operation, movement, and scheduling must be maintained for the worker under wide limits if the purpose and character of his efforts are to be genuinely and effectively realized.

By way of summary, it might be useful to restate some of the propositions about supervisory performance which may effectively serve to develop the potentials of the indigenous community worker.

1. The administrator has to accept the present state of limited knowledge about the role of the community worker.

2. He has to permit the community worker to learn by trying approaches and techniques that have not been tried before or even seem to violate certain tenets of professional —but not moral—practice. Much of the community worker's learning will come through making mistakes.

3. The relationship of the administrator, supervisor, or trainer, with the indigenous community worker should be of a partnership variety in which the supervisor's task is to respect and protect the integrity of the community worker's experimental, or at least different-than–professional approach.

4. The supervisor has to take major responsibility for creating a climate of relationship which is both permissive and structured. There are broad guidelines within which the worker must operate, but each community worker will need to be helped to develop a uniquely integrated personal and agency style of work.

Finally, it should be noted that the traditional separation of supervision and personal counseling may have to be modified in relation to the non-professional. Ordinarily, a worker is expected to keep his personal problems clear of his job. If his work performance reflects some personality handicap, if he needs personal help or guidance, his supervisor traditionally refers him for help outside the agency. At best the supervisor usually attempts to assist the worker to limit the impact of his personality problems on work performance. But the supervisor may have to assume the position of personal counselor as well as manager of the non-professional's performance. In a sense, the community worker is perceived as part worker and part client. The worker's personal problems cannot be viewed apart from a variety of social, economic, and cultural factors. Work itself may be a crucial leverage point in solving intra- and interpersonal difficulties.

## Career Development

The first responsibility of administration is the achievement of organizational objectives in relation to community problem solving. The achievement of these objectives is largely assured through the selection of appropriate staff and the development of their skills to the highest level. The effectiveness of agency program is thus a function of staff development. Moreover, staff development may contribute directly to community problem solving. The indigenous worker is both staff member and part of the community and its problems. His social and personal development contributes directly to organizational function and community improvement. Also, by virtue of his success on the job, one more role model is provided to disadvantaged and delinquent youth as a way out of the ghetto. For these reasons, the administration needs to pay special attention to the requirements of long-range job and educational fulfillment for the non-professional. An expanded concept of staff or career development is necessary and should be limited only by the availability of agency funds and community educational resources.

Integral to career development is the idea of linkage between the different categories and levels of position in the agency. It should be possible for a worker with ability, experience, and training to progress from a less to a more advanced grade classification. It should be possible, also, for the worker to move laterally from one type of job to a related one. Most important, it ought to be ultimately possible for a worker, if he has the potential, to move from a non-professional to a professional or administrative position.

Job tasks and responsibilities should be developed or respecified so that a variety of lower- and intermediate-level, as well as upper-level, positions exist in relation to a job function such as community work. Job experiences which prepare for and qualify the employee for a next level or a different job function within the agency should be provided wherever possible. Careful supervision of these experiences is needed.

A variety of educational and training opportunities should be offered to personnel. While the primary purpose of agency training is improving the quality of service or community action, an important secondary purpose is long-term general upgrading of the qualifications of the community worker. This may require special arrangements with local educational institutions. A program of special scholarship aid should be available to enable selected and promising community workers to pursue courses, part- or full-time, towards baccalaureate and even advanced professional degrees. The beginnings of such programs are evident already in a number of agencies.

Intraorganizational work has been viewed in this chapter as largely an effort to maximize the efficiency and effectiveness of non-professional staff, mainly within the context of the maintenance-oriented organization. The non-professional is a key force for solving a community problem such as delinquency. His value is based on the assumption that people with community problems, or close to them, must and can take primary responsibility in solving them. The non-professional, as both staff member and constituent or client, is thus a focal point for effective organizing and, in the process, intraorganizing efforts.

The assumption has been that the non-professional must more or less adapt to the standards of the professional and the established agency intraorganizing. In a few present organizational contexts and especially in the future, however, the focus may be more on the accommodation of the professional to the norms and values of the grass-roots organization controlled by a constituent population. If this should prove the case, the nature of staffing problems and intraorganizing procedures might be quite different. The problems of adaptation of the professional to the organization might then constitute the primary content for discussion.

# 10

# Evaluation

Little systematic evaluation has or is being carried on in the whole field of community work practice. Many writers note the "rudimentary character, and more frequently the absence, of research studies on vital questions affecting almost every aspect of the planning and operation" of such programs.[1] "No responsible business concern would operate with as little information regarding success or failure as do nearly all of our delinquency and control programs."[2]

Strangely enough, while there have been very few rigorously devised community problem-solving programs in the area of delinquency following the model of controlled experiment, all the elements which would recommend good evaluative design are theoretically present in relation to them.

The program is something which is added to the ongoing social scene by purposive social action as opposed to events

1. Melvin Herman and Stanley Sadofsky, *Youth-Work Programs,* p. 165; see also Robert Morris, "Social Planning," pp. 185–86.

2. Stanton Wheeler and Leonard S. Cottrell, Jr., *Juvenile Delinquency: Its Prevention and Control,* p. 44; see also, Helen L. Witmer, "A Brief Guide to the Evaluation of Measures for the Prevention of Juvenile Delinquency," pp. 55–61.

which are not under the control of some individual or agency. Because an action program is under someone's control, the construction of experimental and control groups is, in principle, possible. Furthermore, the program is usually not designed to cover an entire population, but only some portion of it, so that some part of a target population would not be covered, making it possible to think in terms of control groups.[3]

In part, the absence of evaluative research results from a conflict between practice and research, between "rightness" and effectiveness. The action function has been traditionally concerned with that which is "right" within a particular framework of norms and values. Inherent in this perspective is the notion that the correctness and utility of such valued actions is not to be questioned. The research function, on the other hand, is primarily concerned with the measurement of effects in relation to stated goals and objectives—or effectiveness—and there is little commitment to the values inherent in the particular action system under investigation.

While some practitioners do not reject research in general, they often reject particular measures of effectiveness. Ultimately their claim seems to reduce to the notion that "we have the right to do good, and we reserve the right to do it in our own way, whether it is effective or not, and whether it achieves the ends we claim we wish to achieve or not." [4] This claim (and it *is* decreasingly heard) is patently absurd and unacceptable in regard to any rational problem-solving endeavor. It serves only the interests of entrenched agencies, professional groups, and supporting power structures.

## Purpose

The purpose of evaluation is to determine the degree to which goals and objectives of organizational programs are accomplished, and to assess the relative contributions of the various action com-

3. Peter H. Rossi, "Boobytraps and Pitfalls in the Evaluation of Social Action Programs," pp. 1–2.
4. Leslie T. Wilkins, *Social Deviance*, p. 9.

ponents to the measured outcomes. It must, in addition, determine the part played by program variables—as opposed to variables external to the program—in bringing about observed results.[5] Evaluation may serve, finally, to test the assumptions and theories on which a program rests, as well as to check on the efficiency of the intervention methods used.

Evaluative research should be distinguished from administrative and analytic or more basic research. (These distinctions should be regarded as emphases, rather than clear-cut differences.) Administrative research consists of descriptive and programmatic studies; for example, descriptions of the relevant characteristics of a target group (e.g., age, sex, race, occupation, delinquency record) in relation to a set of program activities. Its purpose is to enable the administrator to assess and make necessary adjustments in agency policies and program objectives. "These studies tend to be short range and often lacking in scientific exactitude." [6]

Analytic or explanatory research more often follows classic research design models. It is designed primarily to test theoretical propositions or general principles and to clarify or discover the relationship between variables.[7] Its purpose is essentially to test theory and create a more valid body of knowledge. The academic researcher is concerned only secondarily with the implications of research for development and testing devices of social intervention.

Evaluation research attempts to determine the extent to which a particular action program does what its sponsors intend it to do. It is applied, not basic, research. It tests a given hypothesis that a particular program produces certain effects. Both intended and unintended, especially "negative," effects must be assessed. It may deal with long- or short-range effects or both.[8]

The purpose of evaluation relates to the question of why the particular investigation is to occur in the first place, which is primarily a political question tending to result from the efforts of the organization to secure the support of outside groups, usually funding sources. Research is needed to demonstrate that a program has a positive effect and makes an important contribution

5. Michael P. Brooks, "The Community Action Program as a Setting for Applied Research," p. 34.

6. Herman and Sadofsky, *Youth-Work Programs,* p. 168.

7. *Ibid.,* p. 169.

8. *Ibid.,* p. 170; see also, Terence Hopkins, "Evaluation Research," pp. 59–60.

to the solution of a community problem. Funds and community support for evaluation may be solicited on the premise that such evaluation should be an important component of the particular organization's approach to resolving of the problem. The dilemma is that research might find that the effects of the program are negligible or nonexistent.

In order to undertake the evaluation of a community action program, an action-research design must be developed. It should include a description of the interrelated elements. It must specify the ways the intermediate changes are expected to be produced and provide hypotheses about the relationships between program inputs and the outcome, for example, reduction of law-violative behavior.[9] A primary consideration is testing not only action or interim objectives, but major goals of the project. If lack of employment is believed to be a factor in delinquency, then an increase in training, counseling, and employment opportunities may be legitimate interim objectives. The successful achievement of these objectives, however, would not be evidence that the end of delinquency reduction has been attained.

> Interim objectives do not provide a substitute for the general objective. If the general objective is not correctly stated, it should be amended, not replaced by a means.[10]

## Preliminary Considerations

The preliminary issues or problems which both the researcher and the community-work practitioner—the latter, particularly in his role as administrator—must be aware of include the type or model of research to be followed, the location of the research component, and some of the political consequences of evaluation.

### Research Model

There are three major areas in which evaluation of community work programs are needed: impact of the program, its process,

9. Howard E. Freeman and Clarence C. Sherwood, "Research in Large-Scale Intervention Programs," p. 15.
10. Wilkins, *Social Deviance*, p. 209.

and its organization. The study of impact is directed at assessing the effect of the program on delinquency rates, recidivism, cost of service per delinquent, client, or constituent, or some other relevant criterion. The examination of the process deals with the activities by which the effects are achieved; for example, what types of activities were initiated, the degree of people's association in the programs, the leadership patterns developed, and changes in these activities and processes over time. Changes in knowledge, attitudes, and practices of the participants in the action program also need to be assessed, and the dynamics of how a program had the desired effects need to be studied. Finally, organizational aspects of the program should be examined. To what extent were administrative procedures appropriate in relation to objectives? Did staff function effectively and what staff roles appeared most effective in the achievement of what objectives? What coordinative devices were effective in producing results?

These areas of research may be combined in different ways to form one of the several approaches to evaluative research: goal-model, systems-model, or combined model.[11] In the goal-model, we are concerned with the extent to which processes or activities and organization of the program contribute to the achievement of goals. This requires description and understanding of program variables or the set of "organized stimuli," as well as the results of the "organized stimuli"—these may be feelings, knowledge, new leadership patterns, number of jobs produced—which are conducive to achievement of the larger goal or the dependent variable.

In the systems approach, the assumption is that the various components of the program are interrelated. The evaluation problem is the weighing of the costs of one program against another. Thus, a community action program may have four major components: leadership training, housing, social services, and manpower development. The manpower component may have literacy training, work experience, vocational training, on-the-job training, and formal educational subcomponents leading in sequence to a high school diploma or junior college degree. A total amount of resources exists for expenditure on each of these components and subcomponents. An increase in the cost of one program depletes

11. See Perry Levinson, "Community Work Experience and Training Programs: A Research-Evaluation Model."

the resources available for another. Clients or constituents, further-more, can be traced through a "production" sequence in relation to needs for and participation in each of these program components and subcomponents. For example, in relation to manpower devel-opment:

> The potential market for each of the five programs must be established through an examination of the agency's case-loads, for the allocation of resources can be matched with this anticipated demand. (If 90% of the caseload is in need of literacy training, 90% of the resources should be allocated to this type of program.) The evaluation of the community work and training program would be based, not only on the extent to which the sub-programs were created to meet the differential needs of the caseload, but also on the extent to which graduates of beginning programs went on to more ad-vanced training. Thus, moving from one step of the program to another would be considered a criterion of success, not *just being employed* [or no longer committing delinquent acts].[12]

The same type of analysis of steps and determination of success criteria would be developed for the other major program compo-nents, and significant patterns of interrelationship of these larger program components would be established on the same basis.

The systems "approach involves the analysis of relationships which must exist for organizations to operate at various levels of effectiveness." Its objective is the identification of the "balance among the various component-parts which will make for higher achievement as compared to other combinations."[13]

The systems-model makes it possible to locate basic distortion in the arrangement of parts of the community action program. There may be too little or too much allocation of resources of certain types to achieve program goals.

The goal-model perspective requires that the researcher pay special attention to the determination of program and organiza-

12. *Ibid.*, pp. 4–5.
13. Amitai Etzioni and Edward W. Lehman, "Some Dangers in 'Valid' Social Measurement," pp. 7–8.

tional goals and to what extent they are attained. The systems approach thus focuses on the effectiveness of the interrelationship of program components; the goal approach on achievement of ends of particular components or the total program. The goal-model and the systems-model approaches can easily be combined if each subprogram and the total agency program is evaluated using the goal-model approach, and the significant interrelationships of the components of program or programs are comparatively evaluated using the systems-model approach. Most community-action efforts are of a "linked input-output" type and it is necessary to assess the effectiveness of each specific program and the interaction among programs. Further, the changes brought about by the subprograms in their various arrangements must be related to overall program objectives. For example, an education program and its particular pattern of component parts designed to improve reading must be assessed not only in terms of its own effectiveness, but also in relation to whether or not it reduces school dropouts. Also, the effectiveness of various programs designed to reduce dropouts has to be evaluated in terms of whether they reduce law-violative behavior. A theory of cause and effect and an intervention model are essential in the determination of the hypotheses which are to guide the analysis of the interrelationships of these various programs and their components vis-à-vis overall objectives.[14]

Whichever model (or models) of research is selected, the general elements of good research include:

1. The appropriate conceptualization of the program's goals and theories.

2. The clarity with which evaluation goals are specified and operationalized.

3. The relevance of evaluation to its intended uses.

4. The appropriateness of the instrumentation.

5. The realism of expected standards of success.

6. The securing of pre-program baseline data.

7. The communication by practitioners to the evaluators of changes or modifications in the inputs.

14. Freeman and Sherwood, "Research in Large-Scale Intervention Programs," p. 19.

8. The maintenance of design requirements.
9. Ultimately, the utilization of evaluation results.[15]

It is of course a rare evaluation program which succeeds in achieving all of these elements.

## Location

One of the first problems of an evaluation research program is the question of where it is to be lodged. If the apparatus of evaluation is lodged too close to the practice organization, research staff may be misused to satisfy expedient operational demands for administrative or accounting tasks not relevant to primary evaluational objectives. On the other hand, if the research arm is completely separated from the operational program, there is a tendency for alienative relations to develop between the two staffs. Suspicion and misconception of each other's purposes and activities may arise. For example, when evaluation is university based, the theoretical interests of the academician often may not coincide with the more "mundane" programmatic interests of the practitioners. A similar problem may develop if evaluation is conducted directly by the funding agency. The interests of the funding organization in efficiency, rather than effectiveness, may give rise to conflicts. Furthermore, the interest of the funding organization may convert or subvert research into an instrument of policy or program change in the operational agency.

The best location for research may be in a quasi-independent structure committed to study and analysis of community programs. It needs to be both dependent and independent of the agencies being evaluated. It needs to be sufficiently dependent so that the interest and needs of the practitioners are kept uppermost in mind, yet sufficiently independent so that the most relevant research designs are developed and freely implemented.

Ideally, evaluation should be developed in such a way that it contributes to the design or the framework of community action and services from the very beginning. As the action effort progresses, the research unit should evaluate its effectiveness and feed back those findings important to reinforce or correct specific action components. The final evaluation should be an aid in designing

15. Carol H. Weiss, "Planning an Action Project Evaluation," p. 19.

future programs or projects. In general, a key function of the researcher should be to provide ideas for experimentation in action programs. Such ideas are derived by the researcher through his background in social science theory and research. One of his important purposes needs to be to collect and analyze data necessary for program planning. He should provide help to the program staff in identification of those data needed for effective program planning, and he ought to be able to assist in the planning process itself by encouraging the greatest possible degree of rationality. Finally, the function of the researcher is to design and implement evaluation studies.[16]

## Political Consequences

The community-work administrator may be able to secure funds for the development of a particular program only on condition that an evaluation is performed, and there are elements of ambiguity in the context in which the research will occur which have critical implications for program—and even agency—survival. For example, the administrator may be encouraged to develop a program whose purposes are not clearly defined, or may be defined more by the nature of the funding sources than the intent of the action agency. Quite often the goals of major federal agencies (which fund the majority of community-action programs) may not be clear.[17] The consequences of all these ambiguities are felt when the program's evaluation is completed.

Furthermore, administrators of service or community-action agencies usually agree to evaluation on the assumption not only that their programs will prove effective, but that they will be significantly, or even massively, effective. But it may be that as communities come to deal more and more with hard-core social problems, the more difficult it will be to show other than minimal results, even with large inputs of resources. At a certain level of one community's development, new or increased intervention may be expected to yield marginal improvements and cost-to-benefit ratios can be expected to rise dramatically.

16. Brooks, "The Community Action Program as a Setting for Applied Research," pp. 31–34.

17. Joseph Bensman, "The Administrative Setting For Evaluation Research," p. 13.

For example, each trainee at a Job Corps camp costs some-where between five and ten thousand dollars a year as compared to considerably less than one thousand dollars per year in the usual high school. Yet, a year in Job Corps training center is not going to be five to ten times more effective than a year in a public high school.[18]

Political maneuvering by the administrator occurs when the research findings turn out negative. The administrator must protect his investment, particularly if the results fundamentally threaten the future funding of the program, and he resorts to a variety of defensive devices. The methodology of the study is attacked.[19] Questions are raised about theoretical assumptions used, sampling, questionnaire construction, design, or statistical analysis. Experts are borrowed for the occasion. Here, for example, are excerpts from a report by an agency concerning the results of a critical research evaluation:

> This report is based on faulty assumptions; it overlooks some important factors and it reflects lack of knowledge about goals and problems of working with delinquents and their families . . . [The researcher] used superficial data obtained primarily from the beginning of the program to decide to discontinue a whole program. . . . The definition of terms in the report is confusing and misleading. . . . There is a discrepancy between sessions, the statistics kept by the workers, and those used by the researcher. . . .

We shall deal with the valid basis of defensive claims by "aggrieved" agencies later. A fundamental problem here, and in many disputes between research and practitioners, may have been a lack of clear agreement initially and through ongoing communication about the complementary roles of practitioner and evaluator.

Other defensive devices by the administrator who believes his program is endangered include the call for replication, increase in sample size, or extension of time to observe more positive results. More often, the practitioner suddenly discovers that the goals of

18. Rossi, "Boobytraps and Pitfalls in the Evaluation of Social Action Programs," p. 3.
19. *Ibid.*, p. 6.

the program are not real goals, after all. (The practitioner may have established multiple goals and is not clear about their priorities or how they are related to each other.) Program planning and implementation are not highly developed arts and, consequently, a number of unintended, secondary—albeit positive—effects may be produced which the practitioner seeks to highlight. The morale of the participants in the program improves, for example:

> The results of the center's [tutorial] program present a somewhat paradoxical perspective. The students who attend are enthusiastic, the parents are enthusiastic, the faculty of the schools are enthusiastic. However, the centers have not been effective in helping children gain in their academic performance.[20]

This displacement of goals and means is clearly a failure to mesh objectives and goals. The agency may suddenly decide that "higher scores on multiple achievement tests" are not the major objective or goal, but "better attitudes to learning, a matter which the researcher neglected to evaluate." [21] Or the goals of community-work programs were not really to involve grass-roots persons in policy and program planning but to produce a stronger commitment on the part of the neighborhood residents to the programs developed by the professionals.

A frequent defensive device employed by the practitioner is the testimonial by persons of community or political importance. Important lay leaders, agency executives, grass-roots persons, and others are brought in to testify to the value and utility of the program.

> We would like to point out that during the past year the program received praise from community residents, clients, juvenile police officers, visitors from the federal government, and from experts in delinquency prevention and control. Suddenly we are confronted with a report which contradicts all other evaluation.

20. Stanley Sadofsky, "Utilization of Evaluation Results: Feedback into the Action Program," pp. 31–32.

21. Rossi, "Boobytraps and Pitfalls in the Evaluation of Social Action Programs," p. 6.

The alderman writes:

> It is well known that your program is producing a much needed service. At a time like this we certainly cannot afford to have your program terminate . . . and we want you to know that you have our wholehearted support.

The commander of the juvenile division of the police department states:

> It is our consensus that this agency is providing a much needed and extremely effective service in an area which has the highest delinquency rate in the city. . . .

Finally, it should be noted that the evaluator is not in a position to determine when the organization's program is good or bad. This is a policy decision on which his views may be solicited, but it is essentially the responsibility of the program's sponsors or funders. Further, evaluation research is not primarily explanatory research. The evaluator is not concerned with whether the agency's reasons for expecting certain effects are warranted. Evaluation takes the "program and the reasoning behind it as given. . . ." [22]

Evaluation is not some additional or secondary activity tacked onto the major program of the agency, nor is it merely an opportunity for the researcher to pursue his academic interests. The reputation and the life of the agency may be at stake, and while the researcher's position as a scientist may not be open to question, his standing in the community as a reliable program evaluator may be seriously threatened. [23]

## Technical Considerations

Program evaluation is concerned with two key concepts: effectiveness and efficiency. Effectiveness indicates the degree to which an organization realizes its goals; efficiency refers to the maximiza-

22. Terence Hopkins, "Evaluation Research," pp. 60–61.
23. Wheeler and Cottrell, Jr., *Juvenile Delinquency: Its Prevention and Control*, p. 44.

tion of net positive results to opportunity costs.[24] Efficiency is measured not only by the amount of resources expended for a unit of output, but by the change per unit cost. "What costs the most, takes the longest, and involves the greatest amount of manpower in gross terms, may have the greatest net efficiency." [25]

Efficiency and effectiveness are related but not identical. Thus, an organization may be highly efficient in its delivery of services or intervention, yet not effective in attaining a delinquency prevention or control goal. In general, we tend to incorporate, at least implicitly, the concept of efficiency in the notion of effectiveness. The assumption is that the ability of the organization to achieve its objectives and goals is at least partially related to an adequate use of available, usually scarce, resources.

The selection of meaningful criteria and measures of effectiveness is critical in determining whether organizational goals are successfully achieved. The *strength* of a community-work organization, for example, may be an extremely important criterion of effectiveness, particularly for those organizations concerned with developing the capacity of neighborhood residents to solve local community problems. Measures of strength might include the following:

1. The relative degree to which an organization can turn out membership for particular types of events or activities.

2. The relative capacity of the organization to raise funds.

3. The relative degree of autonomy of the organization.

4. Relative degree of integration of the organization of local residents into the social and power structure of the larger surrounding community.[26]

Some of these measures are, however, extremely difficult to obtain valid data for or operationalize. There is great pressure to measure those items easiest to obtain and, indeed, more acceptable

---

24. Amitai Etzioni, *Modern Organizations,* p. 8; Herbert A. Simon, Donald W. Smithburg, and Victor A. Thompson, *Public Administration,* pp. 492–93.

25. Freeman and Sherwood, "Research in Large-Scale Intervention Programs," p. 24.

26. John B. Turner, "Memo to Workshop Coordinators, NASW Project on Neighborhood Action"; Charles Shireman and Harold Finestone, *Report and Recommendations of the Illinois Youth Commission.*

from the agency and community point of view than others; for example, membership turnout and ability to raise funds. The more intangible and difficult-to-measure products, often more substantively related to goals, are ignored or underused.

> The distortion consequences of over-measuring are larger when it is impossible or impractical to quantify the more central, substantial output of an organization, and when at the same time some exterior aspects of the product, which are superficially related to its substance, are readily measurable.[27]

The use of soft data—impressions and observations on intergroup or political processes—highly relevant to the key criteria studied may be preferred to the use of seemingly hard data—attendance figures on the numbers of activities launched, for example. Journalistic and anthropological styles of data collecting and measurement may be highly useful—and possibly the only valid means at this stage of research technology—in testing certain community-organization notions.

The goal of decreasing delinquency rate is peculiarly apt to distortion and faulty measurement. Is the goal reduction of illegal acts by youths, or the reduction of those conditions conducive to delinquent behavior, or both? Focus on the former goal would emphasize the development of relevant control and rehabilitative programs for individual youths. Focus on the latter goal, for example, might lead to modification of discriminatory practices in the legal process or of changing employer discriminatory practices against youths with arrest records. It may be simpler programmatically and from a research point of view to concentrate on the control or rehabilitation aspects, even though the environment and social action implications are more substantive and originally preferred. The measures of effectiveness selected by agencies may more accurately reveal their strategic orientation (and that also of their research operations) than their stated goals.

The effectiveness and efficiency of a program are also directly related to the clarity and degree of commitment to goals of the various echelons of action staff in the organization.

27. Etzioni, *Modern Organizations*, pp. 9–10.

We found a divergency where the executive was thinking one thing, the people who were immediately supervising the program another, and the people in the field still another in relation to a particular goal.

Measures of effectiveness may also presume a certain level or quality of performance by the worker which may not consistently exist.

The notion of effectiveness makes most sense for practice mainly on a comparative program basis.[28] That is, the results of one community action approach need to be compared with the results of another of similar intent, using similar measures. A feature of such comparative evaluation lies in the control exercised by the researcher over the processes by which subjects are allocated to one program rather than to another, or to an experimental rather than a control group. But there are many ways in which this kind of comparative research can go wrong, particularly in relation to the development of placebo experiences as control devices. Practitioners are extremely reluctant to allow researchers to deny certain clients treatment intervention or service opportunities which are deemed diagnostically appropriate by the criteria of a particular action approach. Effective placebo or alternate intervention, however, can be devised—where there is sufficient imagination.

> For example, a placebo treatment [or comparative experience] for a job retraining program may be conceived of as some treatment designed to help men get jobs, but which does not involve retraining, and over which the training program should demonstrate some advantage. Perhaps testing and intensive counseling might be an acceptable placebo for a control group in an experimental evaluation of job training.[29]

There is special difficulty when the researcher attempts to carry out rigorously controlled experimentation, since the program may not generate enough clients or constituents to fill up both the experimental and control groups. Additionally, other programs

28. Weiss, "Planning an Action Project in Evaluation," p. 16.
29. Rossi, "Boobytraps and Pitfalls in the Evaluation of Social Action Programs," p. 9.

tend to contaminate the control group experience. Furthermore, "There is the risk in long-range experimental designs that the world may provide experiences to control, which would duplicate in some essential fashion, the experimental treatment." [30] Thus, a comparison of the effectiveness of a program seeking to provide youths with jobs (or adults with a variety of community-action participatory experiences) against a program which provides youths only with counseling and training (or adults with limited or no participatory experiences) may break down when there are a variety of opportunities for jobs (or participatory experiences) available in the community at large.

The researcher must, nevertheless, attempt to identify—if not rule out—extraneous influences which contaminate intervention activities with measured outcomes. He must thus pay systematic attention to ruling out alternative explanations of observed effects, and he must be able to estimate the magnitude of the errors he was unable to eliminate in these observations. [31]

We should note, finally, that an important measure of efficiency is cost. Cost analysis may, however, be related both to effectiveness and efficiency of programs. An advantage of the cost method of program evaluation is that it provides a composite rather than a single measure. Arrest, court petition, or institutionalization rates are generally used to measure delinquency levels and to evaluate program effects in relation to cost of program inputs and outputs. There are, however, many valid and practical problems with use of these measures, including differential application of police enforcement and legal procedures. For example, it may be important to distinguish between the severity of offenses as well as incidence and differential control or rehabilitative consequences which have cost implications.

> A juvenile may be arrested several times for minor offenses and released with warnings, with supervision, or with brief detentions. On the other hand, he may be arrested once for a serious offense and placed in a major rehabilitative center, such as a forestry camp or a state training school. The difference between these two cases is not adequately de-

---

30. *Ibid.*
31. Hopkins, "Evaluation Research," p. 60; Herman and Sadofsky, *Youth-Work Programs*, pp. 172–73.

scribed by the use of arrest rates, nor even by the frequency of police, court, or correctional actions.[32]

A more satisfactory and useful device, especially from the view of policymaking and community acceptability, may well be the measure of dollar costs of correctional action in relation to delinquent acts. "Thus the cost of a number of relatively minor actions for lesser offenses is low, compared to the cost of one serious action taken in connection with one major offense." [33] For example, if the independent-stimulus program variable is street gang work, before and after correctional costs can be computed, then average correctional costs per gang member can be ascertained by cumulating all expenditures for arrests, court appearances, periods of detention, incarceration, and supervision, divided by the number of gang members. The monetary values used in the accounting procedure can be actual or estimated figures provided by county or state officials. The average costs can be compared for gangs across the before and after periods. The served and the unserved group can also be compared with each other, both in the before and after periods. "Finally, trends in average costs for each gang between the before and after periods can be compared to whether costs change at different rates under different circumstances." [34]

If data are available, costs to the victims and his family, as well as costs to the taxpayer, can be computed. In essence, this type of analysis presupposes that efforts to minimize the "total cost of the whole system over time would be a reasonable objective," [35] especially on the part of the planning and funding structure.

# Limitations of Evaluation

The practitioner tends to be expedient in his orientation.[36] He must survive and deal with organizational problems from day to

32. Stuart Adams, Roger E. Rice, and Borden Olive, "A Cost Analysis of the Effectiveness of the Group Guidance Program," p. 4; see also, Thorsten Sellin and Marvin E. Wolfgang, *The Measurement of Delinquency*, 1964.
33. Adams, Rice, and Olive, "A Cost Analysis of the Effectiveness of the Group Guidance Program," p. 4.
34. *Ibid.,* p. 8.
35. Emory F. Hodges, "New Lights on Delinquency through Operations Research," pp. 5–6.
36. June L. Shmelzer, editor, *Learning in Action,* p. 2.

day. The demands of starting a new program, for example, may be too compelling to allow time for the systematization of procedures, record keeping, or analysis essential for collaboration with the researcher. He is keenly aware of the tremendous unmet needs of disadvantaged people and may press for the expansion of services and more intervention at the expense of evaluation activities.

For his part, the researcher is confronted with enormous problems when the simplest kinds of data are not forthcoming from the agency—for example, "who is eligible for each program, who gets into it, how many sessions each participant attends, and with whom he attends these sessions." [37] In general, it may be anticipated that with new, complex community-action programs, staffed by relatively few professionals, the researcher will encounter even greater difficulty in obtaining the kinds of data he needs. Consequently, the more likely are the data obtained to contain "unknown amounts of error, and the more costly the analysis phase is to be." [38] Under such circumstances it behooves the researcher to obtain as much of the basic data as he can through his own accounting and instrumentation procedures. While this entails a considerable initial expenditure of resources, it may be cheaper in the long run, and it certainly provides for more adequate research.

It may also be argued that evaluation is of questionable value, particularly for programs in a state of beginning or flux, "with no describable theoretical orientation, in which the nature of the input shifts from day to day." [39] The staff may not be able to reach consensus on the acts and behavior it intends to produce. The counter-argument here is that the problem is not so much whether research or evaluation is appropriate, but, indeed, whether the program should be mounted at all. We are discussing a nonprogram if goals, objectives, and patterns of intervention have not been developed. The rebuttal of the actionist is that intervention objectives have to be defined broadly, and that he modifies "his methods and organization as he perceives the need for adjustment." [40]

37. Bensman, "The Administrative Setting For Evaluation Research," p. 15.
38. Hopkins, "Evaluation Research," p. 64.
39. Weiss, "Planning an Action Project in Evaluation," p. 6.
40. Herman and Sadofsky, *Youth-Work Programs,* pp. 177–78.

There is, nevertheless, little question that the beginning stages of a program are not a valid time to test its effectiveness. (It should be noted, however, that the time perspectives in relation to the effects of intervention tend to be shorter for the researcher than for the practitioner. The researcher generally believes he should be able to observe changes much earlier than does the practitioner.)

Of key importance in evaluation research is the construction of a satisfactory working relationship between the practitioner and the researcher. Each must understand what the other is trying to do, accept, and cooperate fully in the partnership enterprise. One agency executive states the nature of the agreement between researcher and practitioner as follows:

> There has to be a philosophy of research agreed upon by all parties. There have to be ground rules as to powers and procedures of all concerned. We have to give evidence of the competence of ourselves as practitioners. The researcher has to meet minimum standards of research competence. Finally, the researcher must be relatively independent of vested interest in the success or failure of the program.

The researcher bears a special responsibility in "reaching out" to the program staff. He needs to involve administrators and practitioners in determination of evaluation goals design. He should provide early feedback of preliminary information, and attend even to whimsical program requests for information. He needs to complete study results promptly and report them, spelling out program implications and alternatives. His reporting of major conclusions should be "attractive and simple." [41]

Some writers have also spoken of the "miscast role" of research, especially in relation to demonstration-project evaluation. Rein and Miller [42] claim that research scope may be so ambitious as to interfere with effective research, and state that the

> demands for rigor in social science technology have led researchers to favor the more traditional and tested ap-

41. Virginia M. Burns and Leonard W. Stern, "The Prevention of Juvenile Delinquency," p. 406.
42. Martin Rein and S. M. Miller, "The Demonstration Project as a Strategy of Change," pp. 25–27; see also, Peter Marris and Martin Rein, *Dilemmas of Social Reform.*

proaches, such as surveys of individual attitudes, self-perceptions, role models, etc. They have avoided base line inquiries which would examine how organizational behavior bars low-income youth from achievement. They have neglected institutional analysis in favor of a more individualistic approach.[43]

They conclude their discussion with the following:

> Present-day research methodology is inadequate for measuring the impact of programs. An image of weight-machine research prevails in which inputs are fed in a machine, outputs are precisely calculated by the machine and then stamped out and neatly packaged into a research report to be fed to funding sources. We lack good output measures; we generally lack adequate control groups; we cannot ascertain which element of a bushel of programs is having any impact.[44]

These criticisms of evaluative research seem somewhat over-generalized and inaccurate, however. It may indeed be impossible with present-day evaluation technology to achieve net impact research of complex action programs on a large community, but more limited program impact and community process studies are feasible and have been made. Many researchers are highly creative and not bound by traditional technology. The use of base-line inquiries, moreover, is traditionally a part of good community analysis and research. Rein and Miller are unduly pessimistic in their appraisal.

## Conclusion

Evaluative research must operate under the limiting conditions of the real world. "The best of all possible research designs can be employed in a compromised world, full of evil as it is."[45] It is

43. Rein and Miller, "The Demonstration Project as a Strategy of Change," p. 26.
44. *Ibid.*, p. 27.
45. Rossi, "Boobytraps and Pitfalls in the Evaluation of Social Action Programs," p. 10.

necessary to make do with what is possible, within the limits of time and resources. What is essential is for the practitioner and the researcher, collaboratively, to set up those conditions most appropriate and relevant for doing the job of evaluation.

A working agreement between the researcher and the practice staff must be founded on the notion that "in most cases the effects of action programs are slight, and that there is an off chance possibility that evaluation will produce non-positive results." [46] The policy implications of such findings must be clearly worked out and acceptable to the community work agency.

Special attention must be paid to the development of comparative or controlled research. Obstacles especially need to be worked out with practitioners to gain acceptance of differential service or action designs.[47] The researchers need to be far more creative in assisting in the design of comparable programs for control purposes. Research efforts should, whenever possible, evaluate several types of service or intervention approaches simultaneously "so that the outcomes will be more useful to the setting of [future] program policy." [48]

Also, a strategy for the use of different techniques of evaluation by the researcher should be worked out. Rigorous, controlled research may not be essential under all conditions and must be used appropriately. When, for example, massive effects are expected, soft techniques (use of ex post facto, correlational designs, or absence of control groups) may be preferred to hard techniques (use of control groups, precise and adequate sampling procedures). If it is desired that all delinquents who are served find jobs and cease delinquent activity after exposure to a program, then it is hardly necessary to have a control group. Furthermore, it may be worthwhile

> to consider soft methods as the first stage in evaluation research, discarding treatment which shows no effects and retaining those with opposite characteristics to be tested at a later time with more powerful designs of the controlled experimental kind.[49]

46. *Ibid.*     47. *Ibid.*, pp. 10–11.     48. *Ibid.*, p. 11.
49. *Ibid.*, p. 12.

Evaluation is integral to any effort at rational problem solving. While the theory and methodology of evaluative research leave much to be desired at the present time, a poor or half-developed evaluative instrument is better than none. The practitioner as a professional, non-professional, or volunteer cannot afford to reject measurement and avoid the testing of his beliefs, hunches, or actions if his concern for people and commitment to problem solving are indeed genuine.

Both practitioner and researcher need to attend to problems of the use of research findings. Measurement of impact and redesign of particular agency and community programs may be only one of the important objectives. It may be that the "most important use for evaluation is at a more distant location. The people with the motivation and capability to implement the findings are likely to be legislators, funding bodies, directors of State agencies, voluntary agency executives, and similar policymakers." [50]

Unfortunately, the methods for effectively disseminating the results of evaluative research have not been developed. What is needed is a central mechanism for translating and transmitting evaluation results to key audiences as widely as possible. A unit in the federal government appears to be the appropriate means for disseminating such knowledge. [51] Such an agency does not now exist.

Finally, researchers, community workers, community leaders, and citizens, need to ponder and cope with the great hidden issue of the *"unused and apparently unwanted results of evaluation."* [52] To what extent are cherished practices, "knowledge," and beliefs deflated by evaluation research? To what extent do research findings pose a threat to vested agency and professional interests? How much community work and agency service, therefore, are honest problem solving?

50. Burns and Stern, "The Prevention of Juvenile Delinquency," p. 407.
51. *Ibid.,* p. 406.    52. Richard Cloward, "Concepts," p. 25.

# 11

# Conclusion

We have attempted in the previous chapters to analyze various kinds of organizational strategies and tactics of intervention in relation to the problem of delinquency. We have described selected community characteristics and processes which, we believe, determine the course of delinquency. We have also discussed a variety of methods and techniques for modifying or influencing organizational behavior in relation to it. Essentially our inquiry has been guided by the assumption that two major purposeful approaches to community problem solving exist—social stability and social change. Both are generally necessary for the positive development of community life and the continued viability of a democratic society, and both contribute to the solution of the problem of delinquency.

Serious difficulties, however, may arise in a time of great technological and social change and sharply rising cultural aspirations. If the fruits of technological change and economic development are adequately apportioned and distributed to the members of the community, if established institutions are sufficiently flexible and provide widespread opportunities for the achievement of culturally approved status by all, and if conditions conducive to personal dignity and self-worth are generated and safeguarded, only rela-

303

tively minor transitional problems result. Under these circumstances the need for distinctive social change organizations is minimized. Their function has already been incorporated by existing groups.

When, however, the fruits of the affluent society are not vouchsafed to all, or equitably distributed, when significant classes of people, whether Negroes, Puerto Ricans, Appalachian whites, youths, delinquents, the aged—or even women—are denied adequate access to the means for dignified and meaningful existence, serious social problems may ensue. It is at such times that social-change organizations may play a vital, reequilibrating role. Communities are enabled more effectively to solve their problems, social progress is assured, and the ultimate stability of the democratic society itself is guaranteed.

But should change-oriented organizations fail to mitigate or remove problems, or fail to aid in the redistribution of the rewards of the socioeconomic system, a severely deprived and highly sensitized people may riot and revolt. It is possible that our communities are now entering just such a time. We have for too long supported an outdated system of organizations and institutions which no longer adequately serves the needs of people. The basic social wants and cultural aspirations of large sections of our society are not being fulfilled. The American consensus—whether myth or reality, founded on equal social and political opportunity—no longer exists. Only a vigorous development of change-oriented approaches by both new and old organizations can assure that critical social problems are resolved and moral integration in our cities reconstituted.

It is apparent that the resources of our communities are, at the present time, over-committed to social-stability purposes. The continued effectiveness of the democratic society, therefore, demands far greater support for change-oriented organizations and groups than they now have. It is obvious, also, that community problem solving is not amenable to strictly local efforts. The complexity and interdependency of the units of society require commitment-to–change goals at all levels of community—the neighborhood, the city, the state, the region, and the nation. A special responsibility for problem solving, however, resides at the national level—particularly with the congress and the President—where key decisions are made and resources allocated. Public policies which support radical changes in the conditions creating slum housing, poverty, mental illness, delinquency, racism, ignorance, and unemployment must be established and vigorously carried out.

Institutional changes relevant to the problem of juvenile delinquency must be regarded as only one set of a larger constellation of social goals to deal with the variety of interrelated social ills which afflict our cities, but we should like to discuss such changes briefly here. (We will not, however, address essential policies for direct control of deviant behavior, and the further development of maintenance strategies, since these have received consideration elsewhere.[1]) Four major policies will be delineated.

### First

*We must "target in" on those youths, defined as delinquents, who most need the community's concern and help.*[2] A basic premise of this book is that both the delinquent and the community system which have produced him are elements of the social problem to be solved. We have attempted, however, to address those factors of community and organization which contribute to the problem. There are two types of errors which policy makers often make. First, they may continue to stigmatize delinquents through the punitive character and the inferior quality of opportunities and services they provide them. For example, correctional institutions, and even some of the so-called "treatment" institutions, have become established as schools for crime rather than as remedial centers. Alternatively, policy makers may emphasize programs for *all* low-income youths, generally avoiding stigmatic processes. In recent years, well-meaning, large-scale programs of education, retraining, counseling and job placement have, however, only "skimmed" the surface of the delinquency problem. The delin-

1. For example, chapter X, "Control of Fire Arms," pp. 239–44 and chapter XI, "Science and Technology," pp. 245–72, in President's Commission on Law Enforcement and Administration of Justice, *The Challenge of Crime in a Free Society;* see also, President's Commission on Law Enforcement and Administration of Justice, *et al., National Symposium on Science and Criminal Justice;* Irving Spergel, *Street Gang Work: Theory and Practice.*

2. Adapted in part from Irving Spergel, "Politics, Policies, and the Delinquency Problem."

quent has been ignored or has received only limited attention, because of attempts to provide broad coverage. He has been "sieved" out of many programs.

The appropriate guide to policy development is full recognition of the complexities of the problem of delinquency, avoiding both stigmatizing and "skimming" pitfalls. We should give high priority to programs for adolescent delinquents who engage in serious antisocial acts, as well as to other children. We must become positively concerned with youths who are repeatedly arrested and who most frequently appear in juvenile, family, youth, or criminal courts. We have concentrated on programs for preschool and early-school age children, without sufficient or meaningful attention to older youth groups. What good is it to expend resources on younger children, without follow-up and application of resources to their problems in later years? It is important to recognize that there are distinctive social and cultural forces acting on adolescents to cause problematic behavior. Regardless of what is done in the early years, given age-specific pressures for adolescent status and role integrity—especially in the slums—problems may arise anyway.

Most of the established youth-serving agencies and the newer manpower retraining programs have not adequately reached and served adolescent delinquents. The established agencies tend to concentrate on the younger, more conforming youths in the slums; the newer programs, mainly supported through funds from the Labor Department, Office of Economic Opportunity, and the Health, Education, and Welfare Department, do not *effectively engage* the majority of serious delinquents. Our antipoverty programs have wittingly and unwittingly selected the promising and eliminated the unpromising youths. Local community-action and militant grass-roots organizations, no less than national programs (such as Job Corps), have been guilty of this same screening and "weeding out" process.

Policies and programs must be devised, consequently, which zero in on the community's youths *most* in need of the services and opportunities required for the development of their personal, social, educational, and vocational skills. Social agencies, schools, special projects, and the employment market must provide the fullest and most qualitative support to these youths.

### Second

*An effective attack on delinquency requires the expansion of target-relevant programs and the creation of new ones.* The insufficiency of resources to provide basic opportunities for low-income delinquent youths has contributed more than any other factor to the severity of the problem. The paucity of opportunities available to delinquents, even with the antipoverty program, has produced a condition which encourages stability-oriented agencies to continue "business as usual." A subeconomy of scarcity remains which prevents organizations from expanding and trying to innovate programs. Only a few additional delinquents have been afforded the means to find their way back into the mainstream of conforming society. The waste of teenage potential grows at a pace faster than the growth of the youth population itself.

At the same time, a basis for program expansion exists. While youth agencies—and in particular the antipoverty programs—have avoided a full and direct assault on the problem of delinquency, they do, nevertheless, provide a partial foundation for meaningful action. They need to be expanded and restructured so that they can more adequately target in on the delinquent population. And new types of massive programs must be added.

It does little good to make education, training, jobs, and other opportunities available, unless they are efficiently used by delinquents. The character or style of delivery, as well as the quantity of social opportunities, is a crucial consideration. In this regard, we need to depend on classic as well as newer social-work and human-relations approaches. The connecting points between delinquents and opportunities must be people who are knowledgeable, skilled, and experienced—whether professionals or non-professionals—in the use of great patience, sensitivity, human understanding, and respect for the dignity and worth of each individual. The opportunity and service delivery systems, even with their inevitable bureaucratic structures and mechanisms, must nevertheless be made to operate through individual human connectors who can maximize chances for self-determination, development of self-discipline, and personal integrity by each delinquent. Staffing these expanded and new programs will require the availability of a great many additional professionals and non-professionals. And as we

have shown, many of the non-professionals can be drawn from the
ranks of the delinquent population itself.

At the present time, Neighborhood Youth Corps, Manpower
Development and Training, Job Corps, VISTA, Peace Corps,
either systematically exclude delinquents or deal with them in such
a manner that they are haphazardly or peripherally engaged. In
order to increase the relevant coverage of these programs, a quota
system may be required by which a sustained number or proportion of those who are recruited and selected must be so-called
hard-core or delinquent youths.

In regard specifically to reconstructing and improving the quality of programs such as Neighborhood Youth Corps and Manpower Development and Training—particularly as they are oper-
ated by a variety of local agencies—greater articulation with
schools and industry is required. A much higher proportion of
delinquents needs to be selected for jobs in which a training
component is supplied. Delinquents, furthermore, should be able
to move directly from various training programs to full-time positions. Special remedial or rehabilitative arrangements should be
available, if needed, for certain delinquents in their initial adjustment both to training and especially during initial exposure to
full-time work experience. Furthermore, the emphasis in the
Neighborhood Youth Corps needs to be on career line development and not just the provision of temporary or seasonal jobs.

Neighborhood Youth Corps may constitute the basis for a more
inclusive Domestic Youth Corps which will emphasize the provisions of meaningful jobs particularly related to the rehabilitation of
the slums. Delinquents and youths of the ghetto could be organized
as part of an urban army to physically and socially change the face
of the slum—and in the process learn the vocational skills which
provide access to long-term jobs which promise adequate income
and social meaning. It should be possible for youths to move
progressively from part-time and base-line jobs to full-time and
senior positions, depending on training, skill, and experience acquired. This assumes manpower development to be a key principle
of all training and employment programs. Further, it assumes a
condition of flexibility which makes possible repeated cycles of
training and retraining and movement from one type of job experi-

ence to another, depending on the needs of youths as well as the task of ghetto rehabilitation to be done.

Drastic changes are required in the Job Corps. Hard-core delinquents should not be excluded. The evidence available does not indicate that the delinquents who are accepted make a poorer adjustment than trainees with no records. Indeed, the disturbances and riots which have occasionally arisen in the camps were not apparently precipitated by "official" delinquents. Rather, problems seem to arise from herding large numbers of youths with diversely deprived backgrounds together. Highly bureaucratic control and isolation from the mainstream of urban activity tend to create intense dissatisfaction and frustration, if not actual attitudes of rebellion and riot.

Smaller, more personalized camp sites and activities are probably required if education, training, and retraining efforts are to be successful. Most Job Corps sites should be located directly in, or on the fringes of urban areas. Large-scale experimentation with day or night residential programs should be undertaken. Many delinquents may need to work or undergo training at camp during the day and return home at night, or conversely work and study during the day and return to the camp site in the evening for further study and "home life." Opportunities for joint programming with state youth correctional authorities should be developed. Job Corps programs might be fashioned so that a youth can move from one type of training or work experience and a certain type of living experience progressively to another, ending up in a relatively small "half-way house" experience in his home or "discharge" community before he fully graduates. The positive value of Job Corps could be enhanced by making it a highly desirable academy for the training of youth in appropriate and advanced social and vocational skills useful for urban existence.

VISTA and Peace Corps programs at the present time do not recruit significant numbers of lower-class youths and young adults, especially delinquents, and they do not afford them opportunities for significant community service at home and abroad. Development of non-professional job categories, relevant training programs, and in-service opportunities for promotion should occur. Collaborative living and working side by side with middle-class college youths would provide an invaluable democratic learning experience for all concerned. Furthermore, the life experience of the delinquent may fit him particularly well for work with people from other lower-class cultures and deprived environments. The delinquent—or now, the ex-delinquent—may be extraordinarily useful in efforts to rehabilitate delinquents both in this country and abroad.

Perhaps, more than any other experience, military life—especially in time of war—has provided opportunities for hard-core delinquents to overcome social and educational handicaps, resulting ultimately in successful reintegration into civilian life. The U. S. Army during World War II succeeded remarkably well in rehabilitating delinquents and young adult criminals. Since then, however, the military has developed a more selective intake process and effectively excluded hard-core delinquents. In recent years, when delinquents have on occasion been admitted to military service, they have generally not done well. The problem of adaptation of delinquents to a peace-time military service and to the more technical and specialized requirements of modern warfare, however, can be solved. Again, the answer lies in large measure through the provision of more resources for specialized remedial education and job training within a rehabilitation framework. The mission of the military services should be not only to protect the society from external enemies, but also to train youths to fully undertake their responsibilities in order to prevent social disorder from within.

These various programs need to be integrated. Choices should be available to delinquents and ghetto youths to participate in any, or a meaningful succession, of these programs. Opportunities for structural integration of Job Corps and military experiences should be especially investigated. The military might take responsibility for the extensive resocialization programs, the Job Corps for the short-term, transitional or reintegration phases of the delinquent's return to the community.

Inasmuch as decent jobs with good advancement possibilities is a major objective of this policy, business and industry need to be a focal point for the expansion of opportunities for delinquent adolescents. Specially tailored training and job development programs should be initiated. The preparation of these youths for the world of work by industry should be encouraged through federal subsidy and tax incentives.

Finally, the extension of a Career Public Health Service concept to combat delinquency might be explored. A special unit of professional and non-professional officers dedicated to service and experimentation on the problem of delinquency could be established under federal auspices. The scope of demonstrations, research, training, and specialized service programs would be very broad. These federal delinquency prevention officers could collaborate or work out of existing correctional and social agencies, schools, industry, churches, urban renewal authorities, mental health agencies, antipoverty programs, etc. They could spearhead the public commitment to develop new forms of approaches to solving the problems of delinquency. Long-term career opportunities should be made available for the highly trained and specialized professional—and for the non-professional, who might be a school dropout and a former delinquent. Opportunities for additional formal training might be provided. The creation and development of such an elite corps of delinquency prevention officers would be based on the recruitment of the most promising candidates from the entire nation.

### Third

*New youth community organizations must be facilitated.* We assume that existing institutions, including the more recent antipoverty programs, have failed to adequately reach and assist the delinquent youths in the ghettos. Education, training, and manpower programs—imposed generally from outside on youth and gang structures—have been insufficient and often irrelevant. The delinquent subcultures themselves must be penetrated and used as a major lever for the rehabilitation of delinquents and the slum. Under appropriate supervision, delinquents must be accorded the resources and power to develop their own organizations committed to positive personal and social change. This approach assumes that delinquents have the capacity and potential and, therefore, can be given significant responsibility for solution of their own problems and those of the community. Youth community organizations must be established which can mediate the world of the alienated delinquent and the middle-class or stable working-class culture. This approach assumes further that the youth organization would be a key agent in recruiting and selecting youths for the new and expanded programs described above, and even for shaping some of them.

Recent experience in New York City, Washington, D. C., Columbus, Ohio, Los Angeles, Chicago, and elsewhere suggests that hard-core delinquents have considerable interest and skill in the organization and implementation of positive community programs. They are deeply concerned with the problems of the ghetto and no longer alienated from its dominant life style. They can act out its central fears, anxieties, and hostilities. Either they will serve as the destructive shock troops of the bloody revolts that have and may again occur, or they will perform as the vital agents for the human and physical rehabilitation of ghetto communities.

New types of youth organizational structures can be developed. Delinquents already are serving as members of boards of directors or policymaking groups of youth and other kinds of local organizations. In a few instances they have been given the power to hire administrative and professional staffs, and to critically influence programs of recreation, training, and job development. They are engaging in serious efforts to remedy problems of slum housing, education, public assistance, sanitation, unemployment—and delinquency. While it is too early to fully evaluate their efforts, there is evidence of preliminary success. To date, new, paid, and meaningful community roles have been established for them. They have proved self-disciplined and effective in leading demonstrations, negotiating with political and bureaucratic leaders, and in providing referral, limited counseling, gang control, and recreational services.

Youth organizations may have immense potential for the significant involvement of delinquents in legitimate social change, community development, and individual socialization. The federal government and the major private foundations should set high priority for stimulating and funding these projects on a wide scale. Links between youth organizations and the various training and employment programs must be carefully worked out. The youth organization may constitute a radically new institutional device for solving an age-old problem in our industrialized civilization—the gap between adolescent lack of responsibility and adult career development. To the extent that it is a new device, we must anticipate opposition—if not fierce antagonism—from certain agencies whose established roles may thereby be threatened.

### Fourth

*Programs of youth rehabilitation and delinquency prevention must be integrated into a larger scheme for the creation of authentic community life.* The prevention of delinquency is only a part of a massive, interrelated effort required to rid our society of its destructive communities. The vision of the positive or authentic community which serves the needs of its inhabitants for personal dignity, self-respect, and human realization must be achieved in the very near future. The slum community—its homes, schools, businesses, jobs—must be reconstructed for the benefit of its people. In this process, the affluent members of the society must more equitably share their wealth to provide needed opportunities for those who do not presently have them. Appropriate tax and income redistribution policies are essential.

The massive resistance to such benefactions may well be mitigated by the human instinct for self-preservation. Fear for personal well-being and protection of property may yet make good Samaritans of us all, or at least a majority of us. The good community can no longer be separated from the bad community. Each human being in our complexly interrelated society, whether black or white, rich or poor, competent or incompetent, is inexorably linked. Hatred, terror, and violence cannot be walled in. The desperation of the dispossessed, unless it is mitigated, will engulf and destroy not only bricks and mortar, livelihood and life, but the democratic society as well.

A new basis for human rights must evolve in which the emphasis is on the rational use of resources to meet the unequal social needs of people in our presently defective communities.

# Bibliography

Adams, D. W., and Havens, A. E. "The Use of Socio-Economic Research in Developing a Strategy of Change for Rural Communities: A Colombian Example." *Economic Development and Cultural Change* 14 (1966): 204–16.

Adams, Stuart. "A Cost Approach to the Assessment of Gang Rehabilitation Techniques," *Journal of Research in Crime and Delinquency* 4 (1967): 166–82.

Adams, Stuart; Rice, Roger E.; and Borden, Olive. "A Cost Analysis of the Effectiveness of the Group Guidance Program." Mimeographed. Research Memorandum, 63–65, Los Angeles County Probation Department, Research Office, January, 1965.

Alinsky, Saul D. "Citizen Participation and Community Organization in Planning and Urban Renewal." Mimeographed. Chicago: Industrial Areas Foundation, January, 1962.

———. "Community Analysis and Organization," *American Journal of Sociology* 46 (1941): 797–808.

———. *Reveille for Radicals.* Chicago: University of Chicago Press, 1945.

Angell, Robert C. "The Sociology of Human Conflict." In *The Nature of Human Conflict,* ed. Elton B. McNeil. Englewood Cliffs, N. J.: Prentice-Hall, 1965.

Asbury, Herbert. *The Gangs of New York: An Informal History of the Underworld.* New York: Alfred A. Knopf, 1927.

315

Banfield, Edward C. *Political Influence*. New York: Free Press of Glencoe, 1961.

Benjamin, Judith G.; Freedman, Marcia K.; and Lynton, Edith. *Pros and Cons: New Roles for Non-Professionals in Corrections*. U. S. Department of Health, Education, and Welfare, Office of Juvenile Delinquency. Washington, D. C.: Government Printing Office, 1966.

Bennis, Warren G., and Peter, Hollis W. "Applying Behavioral Science for Organizational Change." In *Comparative Theories of Social Change,* ed. Hollis W. Peter. Ann Arbor, Michigan: Foundation for Research on Human Behavior, 1966.

Bennis, Warren G.; Benne, Kenneth D.; and Chin, Robert, eds. *The Planning of Change*. New York: Holt, Rinehart & Winston, 1962.

Bensman, Joseph. "The Administrative Setting for Evaluation Research." In Research Department, Community Council of Greater New York, *Issues in Community Action Research*. New York: Community Council of Greater N. Y., 1967.

Bernstein, Saul. *Alternatives to Violence*. New York: Association Press, 1967.

Blake, Robert R., and Morton, Jane S. "The Intergroup Dynamics of Win-Lose Conflict." In *Intergroup Relations and Leadership,* ed. Muzafer Sherif. New York: John Wiley and Sons, 1962.

Blau, Peter M., and Scott, W. Richard. *Formal Organizations: A Comparative Approach*. San Francisco: Chandler Publishing Co., 1962.

Bogardus, Edward S. "A Social Distance Scale." *Sociology and Social Research,* 17 (1933): 265–71.

Bondurant, Joan V. *Conquest of Violence,* rev. ed. Berkeley and Los Angeles: University of California Press, 1965.

Boulding, Kenneth E. "The Economics of Human Conflict." In *The Nature of Human Conflict,* ed. Elton B. McNeil. Englewood Cliffs, N. J.: Prentice-Hall, 1965.

Boulding, Kenneth E. "Social Justice in Social Dynamics." In *Social Justice,* ed. Richard B. Brandt. Englewood Cliffs, N. J.: Prentice-Hall, 1962.

Brager, George. "The Indigenous Worker: A New Approach to the Social Work Technician." *Social Work* 10 (1965): 33–40.

Brandt, Richard B. *Social Justice.* Englewood Cliffs, N. J.: Prentice-Hall, 1962.

Brooks, Michael P. "The Community Action Program as a Setting for Applied Research." *Journal of Social Issues* 21 (1965): 29–40.

Buell, Bradley, and Associates. *Community Planning for Human Services.* New York: Columbia University Press, 1952.

Burnham, David, "Crime Research is Found Lagging." *The New York Times.* April 14, 1968.

Burns, Virginia M., and Stern, Leonard W. "The Prevention of Juvenile Delinquency." In the President's Commission on Law Enforcement and Administration of Justice, *Task Force Report: Juvenile Delinquency and Youth Crime.* Washington, D. C.: Government Printing Office, 1967.

Cahill, Thomas J. "The Police and Community Tensions." *Police Community Relations* (1966): 3.

Caplow, Theodore. *Principles of Organization.* New York: Harcourt, Brace and World, 1964.

Carter, Genevieve W. "Social Work Community Organization Methods and Processes." In *Concepts and Methods of Social Work,* ed. Walter A. Friedlander. Englewood Cliffs, N. J.: Prentice-Hall, 1958.

Catholic Welfare Bureau. *Imperial Courts Community Development Project.* Mimeographed. Los Angeles: Catholic Welfare Bureau of the Archdiocese, n.d.

Chamberlain, Neil W. *Private and Public Planning.* New York: McGraw-Hill, 1965.

Clark, John P., and Haurek, Edward W. "A Preliminary Investigation of the Integration of the Social Control System." Mimeographed. Urbana, Ill.: Department of Sociology, University of Illinois, Urbana, n.d.

Clinard, Marshall B. *Slums and Community Development.* New York: Free Press of Glencoe, 1966.

Cloward, Richard A. *The Administration of Services to Children and Youth.* New York: Institute for Public Administration, 1963.

———. "Concepts." In Research Department, Community Council of Greater New York, *Issues in Community Action Research.* New York: Community Council of Greater N. Y., 1967.

Cloward, Richard A., and Ohlin, Lloyd E. *Delinquency and Opportunity.* Glencoe, Ill.: Free Press, 1960.

Cohen, Albert K. *Delinquent Boys: The Culture of the Gang.* Glencoe, Ill.: Free Press, 1955.

——. *Deviance and Control.* Englewood Cliffs, N. J.: Prentice-Hall, 1966.

Coleman, James S. *Community Conflict.* New York: Free Press of Glencoe, 1957.

Community Chest and Council of the Cincinnati Area. "Aid for Troubled Children under Twelve Years of Age." In National Clearinghouse for Mental Health Information, National Institute of Mental Health, *International Bibliography on Crime and Delinquency* 3 (1965): 263–64.

Coser, Lewis A. *Continuities in the Study of Social Conflict.* New York: Free Press of Glencoe, 1967.

——. *The Functions of Social Conflict.* Glencoe, Ill.: Free Press, 1956.

——. "Some Social Functions of Violence." *The Annals of the American Academy of Political and Social Science* 364 (1966): 8–18.

Cottrell, Leonard S., Jr. "Social Planning, The Competent Community and Mental Health." In Group for the Advancement of Psychiatry, *Urban America and the Planning of Mental Health Services* 5 (1964): 397.

Cumming, Elaine. "Allocation of Care to the Mentally Ill." In *Organizing for Community Welfare,* ed. Mayer N. Zald. Chicago: Quadrangle Books, 1967.

Dahl, Robert A. *Who Governs?* New Haven: Yale University Press, 1961.

Dahl, Robert A., and Lindbloom, Charles E. *Politics, Economics, and Welfare.* New York: Harper and Bros., 1953.

Daniels, Lincoln. *A Look at Community Planning and Juvenile Delinquency.* Mimeographed. Community Services Branch, Division of Juvenile Delinquency Service, Children's Bureau, Department of Health Education, and Welfare, April, 1962.

Davies, J. Clarence, III. *Neighborhood Groups and Urban Renewal*. New York: Columbia University Press, 1966.

De Reuck, Anthony V., and Knight, Julie, eds. *Conflict in Society*. London: J. and A. Churchill, 1966.

Dodge, Donald. "Community Planning and Fact Vacuum." In Employment Security Institute on the Management and Operation of Youth Opportunity Programs, An Inter-Agency and Community Approach to Youth Problems. Boulder, Colo.: University of Colorado, 1964.

Duhl, Leonard J., ed. *The Urban Condition*. New York: Basic Books, 1963.

Durkheim, Emile. *The Rules of Sociological Method*. Chicago, 1938.

Easton, David, ed. *Varieties of Political Theory*. Englewood Cliffs, N. J.: Prentice-Hall, 1966.

Etzioni, Amitai. *Modern Organizations*. Englewood Cliffs, N. J.: Prentice-Hall, 1964.

Etzioni, Amitai, and Lehman, Edward W. "Some Dangers in 'Valid' Social Measurement." *Annals of the American Academy of Political and Social Science* 373 (1967): 1–15.

Fanon, Frantz. *The Wretched of the Earth*. Trans. Constance Farrington. New York: Grove Press, 1963.

Fellin, Philip, and Litwak, Eugene. "The Neighborhood in Urban American Society." *Social Work* 13 (1968): 72–80.

Finestone, Harold. "A Report on the Operations of the Division of Community Services." In Illinois Youth Commission *Report and Recommendations on the Illinois Youth Commission,* September, 1962.

Fishman, Jacob R.; Klein, William L.; MacLennon, Beryce; Mitchell, Lonnie; Pearl, Arthur; and Walker, Walter. *Community Apprentice Program, Training for New Careers*. Washington, D. C.: Government Printing Office, 1965.

Fitch, Lyle C. "Social Planning in the Urban Cosmos." In *Urban Research and Policy Planning,* ed. Leo F. Schnore and Henry Fagin. Beverly Hills, California: Sage Publications, 1967.

Fleischer, Belton M. *The Economics of Delinquency*. Chicago: Quadrangle Books, 1966.

Freeman, Howard E., and Sherwood, Clarence C. "Research in Large-Scale Intervention Programs." *Journal of Social Issues* 21 (1968): 11–28.

Fried, Marc. "Social Problems and Psychopathology." In Group For the Advancement of Psychiatry, *Urban America and the Planning of Mental Health Services* 10 (1966): 286.

Friedlander, Walter A. *Introduction to Social Welfare,* 2d ed. Englewood Cliffs, New Jersey: Prentice-Hall, 1961.

Glaser, Daniel. "National Goals and Indicators for the Reduction of Crime and Delinquency." *Annals of the American Academy of Political and Social Science* 371 (1967): 104–26.

Glueck, Sheldon and Eleanor T. "Paths to Prevention." In *The Problem of Delinquency,* edited by Sheldon Glueck. Boston: Houghton Mifflin, 1959.

Goodenough, Ward Hunt. *Cooperation in Change.* New York: Russell Sage Foundation, 1963.

Gottlieb, David; Reeves, Jon; and Ten Houten, Warren D. *The Emergence of Youth Societies.* New York: Free Press of Glencoe, 1966.

Greenwood, Ernest. "The Elements of Professionalization." In *Professionalization,* ed. Howard M. Vollmer and Donald L. Mills. Englewood Cliffs, N. J.: Prentice-Hall, 1966.

Greer, Scott. *The Emerging City.* New York: Free Press of Glencoe, 1962.

Group for the Advancement of Psychiatry. *Urban America and the Planning of Mental Health Services* 5 (November, 1964).

Harper, Ernest B., and Dunham, Arthur. *Community Organization in Action.* New York: Association Press, 1959.

Herman, Melvin, and Sadofsky, Stanley. *Youth-Work Programs.* New York: Center for the Study of Unemployed Youth, Graduate School of Social Work, New York University, 1966.

Himes, Jerome S. "The Functions of Racial Conflict." *Social Forces* 45 (1966): 1–10.

Hodges, Emory F. "New Lights on Delinquency through Operations Research." Paper given at joint meeting of the Sociedad Mexicana de Neurologia y Psiquiatria and The American Psychiatric Association. Mexico City, Mexico, May 10, 1964.

Hopkins, Terence. "Evaluation Research." In Research Department, Community Council of Greater New York, *Issues in Community Action Research.* New York: Community Council of Greater New York, 1967.

Houle, Cyril O. *The Effective Board.* New York: Association Press, 1960.

Joint Commission on Correctional Manpower Training. *Offenders as a Correctional Manpower Resource.* Washington, D. C.: Joint Commission on Correctional Manpower and Training, June, 1968.

Jones, Howard. "Punishment and Social Values." In *Criminology in Transition,* ed. Tadeusz Grygier, Howard Jones, and John C. Spencer. London: Tavistock Publications, 1965.

Kahn, Alfred J. *Planning Community Services for Children in Trouble.* New York: Columbia University Press, 1963.

Kershaw, Joseph A. "The Need for Better Planning and Coordination in Manpower." Mimeographed. Office of Economic Opportunity, n.d.

Klein, William L. *Core Group Leader Training,* Training Report no. 11. Washington, D. C.: Howard University, Center for Youth and Community Studies, April, 1965.

Kornhauser, William. "Power and Participation in the Local Community." In *Perspectives on the American Community,* ed. Roland Warren. Chicago: Rand-McNally, 1966.

Kruse, Arthur H. "The Management Function in Planning Human Care Services." Lecture delivered at the School of Social Work of Ohio State University, Columbus, Ohio. New York: United Community Funds and Councils of America, 1967.

Laumann, Edward O. *Prestige and Association in an Urban Community.* Indianapolis: Bobbs-Merrill, 1966.

Lemert, Edwin M. *Human Deviance, Social Problems, and Social Control.* Englewood Cliffs, N. J.: Prentice-Hall, 1967.

Levinson, Perry. "Community Work Experience and Training Programs: A Research-Evaluation Model." Mimeographed. Department of Health, Education, and Welfare, n.d.

Levinson, Perry, and Schiller, Jeffry. *The Indigenous Non-Professional, Research Issues.* Research Working Paper no. 6, U. S.

Department of Health, Education, and Welfare, Welfare Administration, Division of Research, March, 1965.

Lichtman, Richard. *Toward Community: A Criticism of Contemporary Capitalism.* Santa Barbara, Calif.: Center for the Study of Democratic Institutions of the Fund of the Republic, 1966.

Lindblom, Charles E. *The Intelligence of Democracy.* New York: Free Press of Glencoe, 1965.

Lippitt, Ronald; Watson, Jeanne; and Westley, Bruce. *The Dynamics of Planned Change.* New York: Harcourt, Brace & World, 1958.

Lipset, Seymour Martin. *Political Man.* New York: Doubleday & Camp (Anchor Books), 1963.

Litwak, Eugene, and Meyer, Henry J. "A Balance Theory of Coordination Between Bureaucratic Organization and Primary Groups." *Administrative Science Quarterly* 11 (1966): 35–58.

Lohman, Joseph D., and Carey, James T. "Rehabilitation Programs for Deviant Youth." In *Social Democracy Among Youth,* the Sixty-fifth Yearbook of the National Society for the Study of Education.

Long, Norton E. "The Local Community as an Ecology of Games." *American Journal of Sociology* 64 (1958): 251–61.

McNeil, Elton B., ed. *The Nature of Human Conflict.* Englewood Cliffs, N. J.: Prentice-Hall, 1965.

MacRae, Robert H. "Social Work and Social Action." *Social Service Review* 40 (1966): 1–7.

Madison, James. "The Inevitability of Faction." *In The Nature of Politics,* ed. Michael Curtis. New York: Avon Books, 1963.

Mannheim, Karl. *Ideology and Utopia.* New York: Harcourt, Brace & World (Harvest Book), 1964.

March, James G. "The Power of Power." In *Varieties of Political Theory,* ed. David Easton. Englewood Cliffs, N. J.: Prentice-Hall, 1966.

Marris, Peter, and Rein, Martin. *Dilemmas of Social Reform.* New York: Atherton Press, 1967.

Matza, David. *Delinquency and Drift.* New York: John Wiley & Sons, 1964.

Meyerson, Martin, and Banfield, Edward C. *Policies, Planning and the Public Interest.* (Paper ed.) New York: Free Press of Glencoe, 1964.

Miller, Walter B. "The Impact of a 'Total Community' Delinquency Controls Project." *Social Problems* 10 (1962): 168–91.

Miller, Walter B.; Baum, Rainer C.; and McNeil, Rosetta. "Delinquency Prevention and Organizational Relations." In *Controlling Delinquents,* ed. Stanton Wheeler. New York: John Wiley and Sons, 1968.

Moles, Oliver; Lippitt, Ronald; and Withey, Stephen A. *Selective Review of Research and Theory on Delinquency.* Ann Arbor: Institute for Social Research, University of Michigan, September, 1959.

Morris, Albert, ed. "What's New in the Prevention of Youthful Offending?" *Correctional Research* 4 (1964): 54–55.

Morris, Robert. "Social Planning." In *Five Fields of Social Service: Reviews of Research,* ed. Henry S. Maas. New York: National Association of Social Workers, January, 1966.

Morris, Robert, and Binstock, Robert H. *Feasible Planning for Social Change.* New York: Columbia University Press, 1966.

National Association of Social Workers. *Defining Community Organization Practice.* New York: The Association, December, 1962.

The New Careers Development Project, Institute for the Study of Crime and Delinquency. "Jobs and Career Development for the Poor." Mimeographed. California Office of Economic Opportunity, October, 1965.

Park, Robert E., and Burgess, Ernest W. *Introduction to the Science of Sociology.* Chicago: University of Chicago Press, 1921.

Parsons, Talcott. "The Political Aspect of Social Structure and Process." In *Varieties of Political Theory,* ed. David Easton. Englewood Cliffs, N. J.: Prentice-Hall, 1966.

Perlman, Robert, and Jones, David. *Neighborhood Service Centers.* U. S. Department of Health, Education, and Welfare. Washington, D. C.: Government Printing Office, 1967.

Peter, Hollis W., ed. *Comparative Theories of Social Change.* Ann

Arbor: Foundation for Research on Human Behavior, November, 1966.

Piliavin, Irving, and Briar, Scott. "Police Encounters with Juveniles." *American Journal of Sociology* 70 (1964): 205–14.

Powers, Edwin, and Witmer, Helen. *An Experiment in the Prevention of Delinquency: The Cambridge-Somerville Youth Study.* New York: Columbia University Press, 1951.

President's Commission on Law Enforcement and Administration of Justice. *The Challenge of Crime in a Free Society.* Washington, D. C.: Government Printing Office, 1967.

President's Commission on Law Enforcement and Administration of Justice *et al. National Symposium on Science and Criminal, June 22–23, 1966.* Washington, D. C.: Government Printing Office, 1967.

Pumphrey, Muriel W. "The Teaching of Values and Ethics" *Curriculum Study,* XIII. New York: Council on Social Work Education, 1959.

Raymond, Ray. "The Role of the Community Worker." Mimeographed. Illinois Youth Commission, Division of Community Service, Cook County Unit, n.d.

Rein, Martin, and Miller, S. M. "The Demonstration Project as a Strategy of Change." Paper presented at the Columbia University Mobilization for Youth Training Institute Workshop, April 30, 1964.

Rein, Martin, and Morris, Robert. "Goals, Structures, and Strategies for Community Change." In *Social Work Practice, 1962, Selected Papers, 89th Annual Forum, National Conference on Social Welfare.* New York: Columbia University Press, 1962.

Reissman, Frank. "The 'Helper' Therapy Principle." *Social Work* 10 (1965): 27–32.

Reissman, Frank, and Pearl, Arthur. *New Careers for the Poor.* New York: Free Press of Glencoe, 1965.

Research Department, Community Council of Greater New York. *Issues in Community Action Research.* New York: The Council, 1967.

Robison, Sophia M. *Juvenile Delinquency.* New York: Holt, Rinehart & Winston, 1960.

Ross, Murray G. *Community Organization: Theory and Principles,* 2d ed. New York: Harper & Row, 1967.

Rossi, Peter H. "Boobytraps and Pitfalls in the Evaluation of Social Action Programs." Mimeographed. Paper Presented at the Annual Meeting of the American Statistical Association in Los Angeles, California, August 16, 1966. Chicago: National Opinion Research Center, University of Chicago.

Rothman, Jack. "An Analysis of Goals and Roles in Community Organization." *Social Work* 11 (1964): 24–31.

Sadofsky, Stanley. "Utilization of Evaluation Results: Feedback into the Action Program." In *Learning in Action,* ed. June L. Shmelzer. U. S. Department of Health, Education, and Welfare. Washington, D. C.: Government Printing Office, 1966.

Schelling, Thomas C. *The Strategy of Conflict.* New York: Oxford University Press, 1963.

Schnore, Leo, and Fagin, Henry, eds. *Urban Research and Policy Planning.* Beverly Hills, Calif.: Sage Publications, 1967.

Schwartz, Meyer. "Community Organization." In *Encyclopedia of Social Work,* ed. Henry L. Lurie. New York: National Association of Social Workers, 1965.

Scott, W. Richard. "Theory of Organizations." In *Handbook of Modern Sociology,* ed. Robert E. L. Faris. Chicago: Rand, McNally, 1964.

Sellin, Thorsten, and Wolfgang, Marvin E. *The Measurement of Delinquency.* New York: John Wiley & Sons, 1964.

Selznick, Philip. *TVA and the Grass Roots.* Berkeley and Los Angeles: University of California Press, 1949.

Sherif, Muzafer, and Sherif, Carolyn W. *Reference Groups.* New York: Harper & Row, 1964.

Shireman, Charles, and Finestone, Harold. *Report and Recommendations of the Illinois Youth Commission.* Springfield, Illinois: Illinois Youth Commission, September, 1962.

Shmelzer, June L., ed. *Learning in Action.* U. S. Department of Health, Education, and Welfare. Washington, D. C.: Government Printing Office, 1966.

Shulman, Harry M. *Juvenile Delinquency in American Society.* New York: Harper & Bros., 1961.

Sieder, Violet M. *An Exploratory Study of State Level Planning for Prevention and Control of Juvenile Delinquency.* Waltham, Mass.: Florence Heller Graduate School of Advanced Studies in Social Welfare, Brandeis University, May 25, 1965.

————. *The Rehabilitation Agency and Community Work: A Source Book of Professional Training.* Washington, D. C.: U. S. Department of Health, Education, and Welfare, 1966.

————. "The Tasks of the Community Organization Worker." In *The Community Organization Method in Social Work Education,* no. 4 of *The Curriculum Study,* edited by Harry M. Lurie. New York: Council on Social Work Education, 1959.

Sigurdson, Herbert. "The Community—The Locus for Delinquency Prevention." Employment Security Institute on the Management and Operation of Youth Opportunity Programs, *An Inter-Agency and Community Approach to Youth Problems.* Boulder, Colo.: University of Colorado, October 5–23, 1964.

Silberman, Charles E. *Crisis in Black and White.* New York: Random House, 1964.

Simmel, Georg. *Conflict.* Trans. Kurt H. Wolff. Glencoe, Ill.: Free Press, 1955.

Simon, Herbert A. *Administative Behavior.* New York: Macmillan, 1961.

Simon, Herbert A.; Smithburg, Donald W.; and Thompson, Victor A. *Public Administration.* New York: Alfred A. Knopf, 1964.

Slavson, S. R. *Reclaiming The Delinquent.* New York: Free Press of Glencoe, 1965.

Solomon, Frederic, M.D.; Walker, W. L.; O'Connor, G. J.; and Fishman, J. R. "Civil Rights Activity and Reduction in Crime Among Negroes." *Archives of General Psychiatry* 12 (1965): 227–36.

Sorenson, Roy. *The Art of Board Membership.* New York: Association Press, 1950.

Spergel, Irving. "Politics, Policies, and the Delinquency Problem." Mimeographed. President's Committee on Juvenile Delinquency and Youth Development, September, 1966.

————. *Racketville, Slumtown, Haulburg.* Chicago: University of Chicago Press, 1964.

————. "Role Behavior and Supervision of the Untrained Group Worker." *Social Work* 7 (1962): 69–76.

————. *Street Gang Work: Theory and Practice.* Reading, Mass.: Addison-Wesley, 1966.

Stagner, Ross. "The Psychology of Human Conflict." In *The Nature of Human Conflict,* ed. Elton B. McNeil. Englewood Cliffs, N. J.: Prentice-Hall, 1965.

Street, David; Vinter, Robert D.; and Perrow, Charles. *Organization for Treatment.* New York: Free Press of Glencoe, 1966.

Sutherland, Edwin H. *White Collar Crime.* New York: Dryden Press, 1949.

Sykes, Gresham M., and Matzah, David. "Techniques of Neutralization: A Theory of Delinquency." *American Sociological Review* 22 (1957): 664–70.

Thompson, James D., and McEwen, William J. "Organizational Goals and Environment: Goal-Setting as an Interaction Process." In *Social Welfare Institutions,* ed. Mayer N. Zald. New York: John Wiley & Sons, 1965.

Thrasher, Frederic M. *The Gang.* Chicago: University of Chicago Press, 1927.

Tocqueville, Alexis de. *Democracy in America,* vol. 1. New York: Vintage Books, 1954.

Trecker, Audrey R., and Harleigh B. *Committee Common Sense.* New York: Whiteside, 1954.

Turk, Austin T. "Conflict and Criminality." *American Sociological Review* 31 (1966): 338–52.

Turner, John B. "Memo to Workshop Coordinators, NASW Project on Neighborhood Action." Mimeographed. Cleveland, Ohio: Western Reserve University, November 11, 1966.

U. S. Department of Health, Education, and Welfare, Children's Bureau. *Juvenile Delinquency in the United States.* Washington, D. C.: Government Printing Office, 1965.

U. S. Riot Commission Report. *Report of National Advisory Commission on Civil Disorders.* New York: Bantam Books, March, 1968.

Van Dorn, J. A. A. "Conflict in Forward Organizations." In *Conflict in Society,* ed. Anthony de Reuck and Julie Knight. London: J. and A. Churchill, 1966.

Von Hoffman, Nicholas. "Finding and Making Leaders." Mimeographed. Students for a Democratic Society, 1964.

————. "Reorganization in the Casbah." *Social Progress* 52 (1962): 33–44.

Warren, Roland L. *The Community in America.* Chicago: Rand, McNally, 1963.

————. "The Impact of New Designs of Community Organization." *Child Welfare* 44 (1961): 494–500.

————. "Types of Purposive Social Change at the Community Level." No. 11, papers in social welfare. Waltham, Mass.: The Florence Heller Graduate School for Advanced Studies in Social Welfare, Brandeis University, 1965.

————, ed. *Perspectives on the American Community.* Chicago: Rand, McNally, 1966.

Weiss, Carol H. "Planning an Action Project Evaluation." In *Learning in Action,* ed. June L. Shmelzer. U. S. Department of Health, Education, and Welfare. Washington, D. C.: Government Printing Office, 1966.

Werthman, Carl. "The Function of Social Definitions in the Development of Delinquent Careers." *Task Force Report: Juvenile Delinquency and Youth Crime.* The President's Commission on Law Enforcement and Administration of Justice, 1967.

Wheeler, Stanton, and Cottrell, Leonard S., Jr. *Juvenile Delinquency: Its Prevention and Control.* New York: Russell Sage Foundation, 1966.

Wilkins, Leslie T. *Social Deviance.* Englewood Cliffs, N. J.: Prentice-Hall, 1965.

Wilson, James Q. "The Police and the Delinquency in Two Cities." In *Controlling Delinquents,* ed. Stanton Wheeler. New York: John Wiley and Sons, 1968.

Witmer, Helen L. "A Brief Guide to the Evaluation of Measures for the Prevention of Juvenile Delinquency." *International Review of Criminal Policy* 21 (1963): 55–61.

Witmer, Helen L., and Tufts, Edith. *The Effectiveness of Delinquency Prevention Programs.* Children's Bureau. Washington, D. C.: Government Printing Office, 1954.

Wooten, Barbara. *Crime and the Criminal Law.* London: Stevens and Sons, 1963.

Zald, Mayer N., and Ash, Roberta. "Social Movement Organizations: Growth, Decay, and Change." *Social Forces* 44 (1966): 327–41.

# Index

**331**

"The good community can no longer be separated from the bad community. Each human being in our complexly interrelated society, whether black or white, rich or poor, competent or incompetent, is inexorably linked. Hatred, terror, and violence cannot be walled in. The desperation of the dispossessed, unless it is mitigated, will engulf and destroy not only bricks and mortar, livelihood and life, but democratic society as well."

This, Professor Spergel maintains, is the situation we face in America's urban communities. Asserting that delinquency and other critical problems of our inner cities must be confronted consciously and systematically rather than intuitively, he explores the variety of approaches available for both the professional social worker and the concerned layman. Of particular value is the scope of the book. Spergel carefully brings together classic social-work methods with newer strategies and tactics which have evolved in recent years as a result of anti-poverty programs, the civil rights movement, black-power struggles, new types of grass-roots organizing, and large-scale social planning.